Trending Islam

The **ISEAS – Yusof Ishak Institute** (formerly Institute of Southeast Asian Studies) is an autonomous organization established in 1968. It is a regional centre dedicated to the study of socio-political, security, and economic trends and developments in Southeast Asia and its wider geostrategic and economic environment. The Institute's research programmes are grouped under Regional Economic Studies (RES), Regional Strategic and Political Studies (RSPS), and Regional Social and Cultural Studies (RSCS). The Institute is also home to the ASEAN Studies Centre (ASC), the Singapore APEC Study Centre, and the Temasek History Research Centre (THRC).

ISEAS Publishing, an established academic press, has issued more than 2,000 books and journals. It is the largest scholarly publisher of research about Southeast Asia from within the region. ISEAS Publishing works with many other academic and trade publishers and distributors to disseminate important research and analyses from and about Southeast Asia to the rest of the world.

Edited By Norshahril Saat,
A'an Suryana and Mohd Faizal Musa

Trending Islam

Cases from Southeast Asia

YUSOF ISHAK INSTITUTE

First published in Singapore in 2023 by
ISEAS Publishing
30 Heng Mui Keng Terrace
Singapore 119614

E-mail: publish@iseas.edu.sg
Website: <http://bookshop.iseas.edu.sg>

All rights reserved. No part of this publication may be reproduced, stored in a retrieval system, or transmitted in any form or by any means, electronic, mechanical, photocopying, recording or otherwise, without the prior permission of the ISEAS – Yusof Ishak Institute.

© 2023 ISEAS – Yusof Ishak Institute, Singapore

The responsibility for facts and opinions in this publication rests exclusively with the authors and their interpretations do not necessarily reflect the views or the policy of the publisher or its supporters.

ISEAS Library Cataloguing-in-Publication Data

Name(s): Norshahril Saat, editor. | A'an Suryana, editor. | Mohd Faizal Musa, editor.
Title: Trending Islam : cases from Southeast Asia / edited by Norshahril Saat, A'an Suryana and Mohd Faizal Musa.
Description: Singapore : ISEAS-Yusof Ishak Institute, 2023. | Includes bibliographical references and index.
Identifiers: ISBN 978-981-5104-33-2 (soft cover) | ISBN 978-981-5104-34-9 (e-book PDF) | ISBN 978-981-5104-35-6 (epub)
Subjects: LCSH: Islam—Southeast Asia—21st century. | Islam and politics—Southeast Asia. | Islam and civil society—Southeast Asia.
Classification: LCC BP63 A9T79

Cover design by Refine Define Pte Ltd
Index compiled by DiacriTech Technologies Private Limited
Typesetting by International Typesetters Pte Ltd
Printed in Singapore by Mainland Press Pte Ltd

CONTENTS

Foreword		vii
Tunku Zain Al-'Abidin ibni Tuanku Muhriz		
About the Contributors		xviii
1.	Introduction	1
	Norshahril Saat, A'an Suryana, and Mohd Faizal Musa	

Part I: Continuing and Emerging Trends

2.	The Trendsetters of Islam throughout Indonesian History	15
	Komaruddin Hidayat	
3.	The Salafi-Jihadi Identity and Malaysia's Battle with Islamist Extremism	34
	Ahmad Fauzi Abdul Hamid	

Part II: States and Organizations Driving Trends

4.	Extremism in Malaysia: Civil Servants as Trendsetters and Conduits of Trends	65
	Mohd Faizal Musa	
5.	Digital Anti-Islamist Activism at the Forefront of Political Polarization in Indonesia	87
	Yuji Mizuno	

6.	Surveillance Capitalism and Dataization among Religious Organizations in Singapore	109
	Faris Ridzuan and Afra Alatas	
7.	Being Funny is Trendy: *NU Garis Lurus* vs *NU Garis Lucu*	129
	A'an Suryana	

Part III: Influencers Driving Trends

8.	*Amar Makruf dan Nahi Mungkar*: Moral Policing of Female Muslim Celebrities and Influencers in Brunei, Malaysia, and Indonesia	155
	Sharifah Nurul Huda Alkaff	
9.	YouTube Islamic Web Series and the Mediatized Piety among Urban Muslims in Indonesia	183
	Andina Dwifatma	
10.	Being Spiritual and Trendy: Singapore's Islamic Authority in the Age of Capitalism and Populism	198
	Norshahril Saat	

Index	221

FOREWORD

Tunku Zain Al-'Abidin ibni Tuanku Muhriz

Introduction

To appreciate contemporary trends, one must appreciate historical origins, for they continue to define and influence the evolution of religious observance. Thus, there is a need to understand the ways in which Islam initially came into what is now Southeast Asia, especially the power of trade and proselytization in precolonial times, the impact of European colonial competition and imperial administration, followed by the impact of postcolonial nation-building.

Although only three countries in Southeast Asia have Muslim-majority populations, the narratives of Muslim-minority communities form a vital part of Southeast Asian Islam. For example, there are the Rohingya in Myanmar, the Chams of Cambodia, the Muslims in the former Sultanates of Pattani or Maguindanao, and the Malays in Singapore.

Proper treatment of this topic also demands a thorough grounding of regional geopolitics and an intimate knowledge of the domestic politics within specific countries. The nexus between religion and politics has grown in intensity all around the world, even in nominally secular countries such as the United States or India. Whether one is referring to evangelical Christianity, resurgent Hindutva, or Islamism allied with ethnic supremacy, we can see how almost every area of public policy has become infused with religious rhetoric: in justifying national budgets, tax policy, education policy, international relations, trade rules, housing and neighbourhood regulations, abortion rights, regulation of Islamic Finance which now includes fintech, and the administration of justice itself.

This edited volume showcases some of the emerging trends in Southeast Asian Islam. There are many ways of reading this book: one may choose to read the chapters to have a deeper understanding of the trends surrounding Islam in specific countries in the region—mainly Indonesia, Malaysia, Singapore and Brunei—or one can compare cases across state boundaries given that all these societies are now confronted with a new mode of religious transmission in the form of social media. The faithful are no longer studying religion solely from the mosque or *madrasah*, but they are doing so through the Internet and social media platforms such as YouTube, Facebook, Twitter, Instagram, and Tik Tok.

Malaysia

I am rather inspired by Professor Komaruddin Hidayat's incredibly insightful piece on Indonesia (Chapter 2), so this Foreword will focus on Malaysia.

Malaysia was known for a long time as a tolerant Muslim country, and there were many affirmations of this. Many Muslim countries marvelled at Malaysia's physical infrastructure, obviously burgeoning middle class, apparent political stability, and multicultural, multi-faith harmony. I genuinely do recall a time when there was a feel-good zeitgeist about being Malay, Muslim, and Malaysian at the same time.

Of course, today I know that my experience was not necessarily representative of others' experiences, and more importantly, to the extent that there was a shared experience, there has since been much movement in how Malaysians think of themselves. If ever there was a halcyon period of consensus about "Bangsa Malaysia", that has now been distorted by social, economic, and political pressures as a result of explicit government initiatives from Vision 2020 to Islam Hadhari to 1 Malaysia to Keluarga Malaysia, and of course its antecedents in the form of the National Culture Policy, Rukun Negara, and of course the Federal Constitution itself. All of these things had their own inputs into the shaping of Malaysian identity, and naturally triggered responses from other actors in society as well, sustaining into the twenty-first century the pre-Malayan Kaum Tua and Kaum Muda dichotomy of a century before (Roff 1994).

Added to the mix of course were two other important phenomena. First, the sociological aspect, as the rapid urbanization of a developing economy brought traditionally rural communities into cities. Second, the rise of political Islam often symbolized by the Iranian Revolution of 1979 and its repercussions, both in terms of new oil money being invested in Muslim institutions across the Sunni world, and domestic political shifts as parties felt the need to compete on the grounds of religiosity, in Malaysia encapsulated by the hitherto secular United Malays National Organisation (UMNO) increasingly adopting Islamic vocabulary to keep Parti Islam Se-Malaysia (PAS) at bay (Norani Othman, Puthucheary and Kessler 2008). It is important to note that PAS was not static either; both parties dabbled with different formulations in defining their desired electorates.

Political competition, accompanied by ever increasing concentration of power in the Executive, the centralization of power from the states to the federal government, and the curtailment of check and balance institutions meant that the project of politically motivated Islamization could flourish with the Prime Ministers' approval, with new institutions being created or vastly expanded—Jabatan Kemajuan Islam Malaysia (Department of Islamic Development Malaysia, JAKIM) being the obvious example—in order to pursue it (Liow 2009). And today, its actors are equally invested in the patronage structures that surround the Malaysian state, from appointments in Government-Linked Companies (GLCs) to its associated perks including titles and overseas trips.

The intellectual justifications seemed alluring and able to be invoked by politicians even without the important academic caveats. Seeing Al-Attas' "Islamization of Knowledge" as a philosophical *tour de force* for the long-term advancement of Muslims and others is a world away from politicians superimposing their own supposedly "Islamic" bent on nation-building. The same can be said about the habit of politicians seizing upon anything with perceived scholarly value in order to defend government policy. The opposition to International Convention on Elimination of All Forms of Racial Discrimination (ICERD) and the Rome Statute is one relatively recent example. Furthermore, some professors may end up being seen as complicit in political objectives, further eroding faith in academic independence.

This politically motivated Islamization project was increasingly conflated with Malay identity, to the extent that our history curriculum equates the beginning of Malay civilization with Islam (Barr and Govindasamy 2010). In this regard we have much to learn from our Egyptian, Indonesian, and Jordanian friends who celebrate the Pyramids of Giza, Borobudur, and Petra respectively without any diminishing of their Islamic credentials.

However, the cues for this social change were evident for many years. The increased use of the hijab through the 1980s and 1990s, and the charge of "Arabization" began to be made when the ubiquity of *baju Melayu* and *baju kurung* was challenged by *jubbahs*. Of course, there are now very famous (and less famous) brands of hijabster fashion houses that first established themselves on social media through influencers and eventually made their way to trendy malls. All sorts of products are now marketed as particularly Muslim-friendly, well beyond the halal certification that was once deemed sufficient. And again, social media plays a big part in marketing and reviewing products, and also creating communities of customers.

Speaking of social media, the most successful preachers in Malaysia— well, indeed the world—now use YouTube, Instagram and TikTok to disseminate their *fatwa* and commentaries, being orders of magnitude more popular than the official videos of *tazkirahs* (short speeches) in mosques. Indeed, these preachers represent the "2.0" of the Islamization project started decades earlier, acquiring a life of their own that now supersedes the influence of the original advocates of the project.

And certainly, the commentary and tone of this community—which really boils down to the few very successful, very popular preachers given the nature of the algorithms that govern social media feeds —sets the atmosphere whenever controversial debates arise in public.

The perceived "insults towards Islam" trigger the most vociferous reactions from self-appointed defenders of the faith, and each incident is an opportunity to advocate for more punishment through existing or new laws.

Indeed, the existence of punitive legislation is sometimes seen as a benchmark of how "Islamic" a society is, as we can see in the discourse surrounding RUU 355, the bill to amend the Syariah Courts (Criminal Jurisdiction) Act 1965. Over time, these calls have an incremental effect that normalizes such reactions and makes it more difficult for those who disagree to air their disagreements publicly for fear of being ostracized or labelled as a *munafik* (hypocrite), Muslim liberal, and so on. Ideas of compassion and mercy are absent from the discourse, as Sharifah Nurul Huda Alkaff discusses in her assessment of Instagram comments on the accounts of celebrities and social media influencers (Chapter 8).

Another casualty of this wider phenomenon is in our popular culture. It is only thanks to the legendary status of P Ramlee that we are still sometimes able to see Malays drinking gin and tonic (or *iblis* and tonic in the clip from *Labu Labi*), or the summoning of "mambang tanah, mambang air, mambang api, mambang angin" (spirits of the land, water, fire, and wind) and so on in *Pendekar Bujang Lapok*. Of course, there are still some very good Malay films both in terms of story and production values—but references to alcohol and the supernatural are now tightly regulated. The same goes for our music, art and batik, where abstract forms have completely replaced mythical creature designs, although Indonesian batik retains such iconography. And even in the palaces, *keris* (daggers) with animal hilts have been eschewed in favour of simpler designs, and carved bird heads atop even humble fishing boats in Terengganu are no more.

And as much as one thinks that Hari Raya has been celebrated in the same way since time immemorial, the official terminology used by the Keeper of the Rulers' Seal remains Hari Raya Puasa and Hari Raya Korban respectively, not Aidilfitri and Aidiladha. Even more absent in the public consciousness is the ritual of *mandi safar*. The practice has several origin stories, among them commemorating the last time the Prophet Muhammad was able to bathe, but video evidence suggests it primarily consisted of Muslims going to the beach for the day; FINAS has uploaded a retrospective on YouTube which is worth watching. After just one generation, *mandi safar* is now totally erased from the public consciousness.

Some inexplicable contradictions exist in Malaysian society, such as the love for horror films and sightings of *pontianak* and *toyol*, a continued belief and use of black magic (famously practised even by senior politicians), or the routine contradictions of celebrities expressing their supposed piety while flogging luxury designer goods. The survival of these quirks indicates that there is hope yet for Malaysia, in that they show that divergence even of a religious kind can be tolerated.

The contradictions in Malaysia's foreign policy are unfortunately more jarring. Malaysia's political leaders go on at length about defending their Palestinian brothers and sisters, and similarly much has been said about ongoing persecution of the Rohingya. But even low-hanging fruits like signing the 1951 United Nations (UN) Refugee Convention—that would actually help people from those countries already in Malaysia—remains elusive. While it is unlikely that Israel's recent rapprochement with more of its Arab neighbours will change Malaysia's official attitude towards that country, Wisma Putra's recent engagement with Myanmar's National Unity Government, the first by an ASEAN country, was impressive. Perhaps the best example of Malaysia actually acting on Muslim solidarity was with the Bosnians in the 1990s, resulting in an entire cohort of Bosnian alumni from the International Islamic University Malaysia (IIUM) who are leaders in politics, business, diplomacy, and civil society in that country. Yet, compared to the Palestinians, Rohingya and Bosnians, outrage about the persecution of Uighurs remains comparatively silent. Whether this is due to acceptance of official explanations of the situation, or because of trade concerns, remains to be addressed.

Civil Society

There are two ingredients which I think will contribute greatly to Islam in Malaysia. The first is the ever-increasing permanence and influence of civil society organizations (CSOs), particularly those that emerged in the last two decades or so, espousing progressive and democratic positions (Lee 2010). Of course, new conservative ones also sprouted, but arguably their added value to the landscape was minimal because in truth they already existed in some form prior, including within the establishment itself.

The Institute for Democracy and Economic Affairs (IDEAS) is one of the earliest independent think tanks in Malaysia, in the sense that it is not affiliated to any political party and took no government money. It is allied to what it sees as the vision of liberty and justice espoused by Tunku Abdul Rahman in 1957 and again in 1963—when Singapore too established Malaysia. There is virtually no area of public policy in which it has not been active through research and advocacy—from education, housing, transport, agriculture, tax, budget transparency, parliamentary reform, open government and the like—and although it is clearly not a religious-based think tank, there have been many areas where it has cooperated with organizations that are religious-based, especially in the areas of children's and women's rights and refugee issues.

Indeed, if one of the consequences of Malaysia's religious transformation is the pervasiveness of conservative Islamic vocabulary in the formulation of public policy, then one logical consequence of the growth of civil society is the injection of progressive Islamic vocabulary in its critique. Although Malaysian democracy since 2018 has seen pendulum swings, one long-term change for the better is the permanence of civil society. Not only are there now so many organizations around, but their boards and advisors are stuffed full of distinguished people—or members of the elite—that would make it difficult for the government to quickly shut everyone down. Selected persecutions may still exist, but not against civil society in general.

Indeed, after the Sheraton Move in February 2020, newly empowered politicians have been very keen to engage with civil society. They recognized their lack of electoral legitimacy and sought to acquire it by showing their engagement with civil society instead. Indeed, on numerous occasions the government will test a policy by citing the work of think tanks, de facto normalizing the process of debate, research and advocacy that has enabled a proposal to get that far in the first place. In 2018, many such ideas made it into party manifestoes and some of those even became law, perhaps most famously Undi18 and automatic voter registration. Increasingly, universities, including publicly-funded ones, have become natural partners in this process too.

In tandem with other reforms, civil society will certainly grow as a trendsetter in Malaysian Islam. For instance, unjustified party-hopping was one of the scourges of Malaysian democracy, and legislative efforts to prevent changes of government through leaders bribing opposition legislators to their side were enacted. This has only been made possible because finally, the politicians see that the practice is undermining all of them. Individual Members of Parliament (MPs) do not want to continually hedge their bets as to who will be in power, and to be ready to change parties, and then be eternally condemned for doing so. Thus there is an opportunity now to stop the practice while politicians feel it is more valuable to remain loyal than possibly jump ship.

Alongside this is political financing reform, so that donations to campaigns and candidates are fairer and more transparent. IDEAS is secretariat to the All Party Parliamentary Group (APPG) on Political Financing, which would have been inconceivable several years ago. This has only been made possible by the introduction of Parliamentary Select Committees—which was a manifesto commitment that IDEAS had long championed—and efforts such as the Speakers' Lectures Series which set a precedent for CSOs to be involved in parliament.

The reason for this example is to suggest that increasingly, politicians may conclude that trying to out-Islamize each other in the political space will be a race to the bottom, too. Indeed, it is somewhat of a paradox that the more Malay politicians talk about Malay unity, the more Malay division results, and today we have UMNO, PAS, Parti Pribumi Bersatu (Bersatu) and Pejuang—and of course we can ask whether the ostensibly multi-racial parties really are multi-racial in composition and attitude.

Already civil society engagements with politicians, including from Malay-Muslim parties, have succeeded in achieving progressive policy stances in certain cases, such as the introduction of the Anti-Sexual Harassment Bill. Perhaps one day this evolving dynamic between civil society, parliament, political parties and civil servants will enable an important new trend in the administration of Malaysian Islam.

Monarchy

To be sure, in Malaysia's constitutional setup, there is an existing mechanism that can prevent any further slides towards exclusion and extremism. That institution is the monarchy. The Federal Constitution makes clear that the Rulers are Heads of Islam in their states, or the Yang di-Pertuan Agong in respect of the four gubernatorial states (Abdul Aziz Bari 2013).

As mentioned earlier, it is still the case that it is the Keeper of the Rulers' Seal, not a political figure, who announces the most important dates of the Islamic calendar. Indeed, this was particularly relevant when in 2022, Hari Raya Aidilfitri was celebrated a day earlier in Malaysia compared to Singapore. One might think this is mere symbolism, yet the power of symbolism and ceremony in Malay culture has endured.

However, not every incident in Malaysia happened with the endorsement of the Rulers. In reality, the concentration of power in the Executive in the 1980s and 1990s, coinciding with the Islamization as conceived by politicians, made this a technicality. It is only now, with the emergence of greater political competition, that the constitutional intent is being restored.

For example, when in April 2022 JAKIM wanted to ban the Tarekat Naqsyabandiah al-Aliyyah Syeikh Nazim al-Haqqani, a Sufi order that has been officially recognized in Negeri Sembilan since 2018, it was a statement from the Sultan of Selangor in his capacity as Chairman of the National Council of Islamic Religious Affairs that confirmed the *tarekat*'s (Sufi religious order) continued acceptance. The Sultan of Selangor was also in the news more recently for his defence of the Bon Odori festival in contrast to PAS politicians who wanted to prevent Muslim attendance. There are numerous past instances in different states which have illustrated royal progressiveness. For example, when the Sultan of Johor lambasted a Muslim-only laundry, the many speeches on national unity by the Sultan of Perak and Yang di-Pertuan Besar of Negeri Sembilan, and Negeri Sembilan's initiative to address the issue of unilateral conversion of children to Islam, by requiring the marriage to be dissolved in the civil courts before any recognition of conversion is allowed.

In addition, there are many initiatives to increase multicultural interaction away from the eyes of the media. Royal patronage and participation in sports is one area of unsung success, for it is on sports fields and courts that multiracial, multi-religious respect for rules is nurtured.

Finally, traditions and ceremonies that happen at the state level that in fact celebrate the diversity of Islam continue to hold some degree of significance. Interestingly, the Negeri Sembilan State Constitution defines the religion of the state as "Islam as heretofore practiced in the state", a formulation that implies a nod not only to unique Minangkabau elements such as matrilineality, but also the presence of different Muslim traditions in the state. Mosques within a state usually use *khutbah* (sermons) written in that state—a point that was highlighted some years ago when *khutbah* in the Federal Territories were criticized as being provocative. During the *Maulidur Rasul* (commemoration of Prophet Muhammad's birthday), the Yang di-Pertuan Besar and *Undangs* (Ruling Chiefs elected within their clans within the state's culture of Adat Perpateh) still lead the procession and sing the *selawat* (prayers for the Prophet), unlike in some states where it is now eschewed. *Ya Hanana* continues to be sung by thousands who assemble in fields. Additionally, many mosques still revere the teachings of local *ulama* (religious scholars), such as Tuan Tulis who apparently treated my great-great-grandfather Tuanku Muhammad's illness when he was in London in 1925, despite Tuan Tulis having died in Seri Menanti three years prior!

Although these rituals, practices and stories might seem far removed from the contentious points of policy, their continued existence is in truth vital in demonstrating that diversity can and does exist within Islam in Malaysia. These can still serve as the roots for expanding that diversity once again.

International

By way of conclusion, it is worthwhile to draw attention to international efforts introduced in the name of Islam and diversity. For example, we should remember the 2004 Amman Message which expanded recognition of Muslims by other Muslims. Malaysia has eight signatories. We should read the 2012 Al-Azhar Declaration that spoke of the modern democratic nation-state, freedom of belief, and freedom of expression. We should learn from Morocco's women preachers, the *morchidat*, who advance women's rights there. We should embody the 2016 Marrakesh Declaration that champions the "just treatment of religious minorities in Muslim countries and to raise awareness as to their rights" (2016) and the 2019 Abu Dhabi Declaration between Pope Francis and Sheikh Al-Azhar which called on rediscovering "the values of peace, justice, goodness, beauty, human fraternity and coexistence" (2019). These things speak to the universality of our religion, and yet, will not threaten the traditions of Malaysian and Southeast Asian Islam that the exclusivists would rather see.

In conclusion, there are exciting opportunities for trendsetting in Malaysian Islam. To some extent, Malaysia still tolerates religious divergence. This is a form of social capital that can be utilized to promote a more inclusive and cosmopolitan society. With an appreciation of the history of Malaysian Islam, the combination of increased political competition, the growth of civil society, and the re-empowerment of traditional institutions together can elevate the Malaysian *umma*. More importantly, there are many lessons that can be drawn from the Malaysian experience which applies to other parts of Southeast Asia. While I have discussed the case of Malaysia—a country that I am familiar with—I hope readers will adopt a critical lens when reading the other chapters which cover Malaysia's neighbouring countries. I wish to congratulate the editors of this timely volume and hope for more publications of such nature in the future.

REFERENCES

Abdul Aziz Bari. 2013. *The Monarchy and the Constitution in Malaysia*. Kuala Lumpur: Institute for Democracy and Economic Affairs.

"Apostolic Journey to the United Arab Emirates (3–5 February 2019): Document on Human Fraternity for World Peace and Living Together". 2019. Signed by His Holiness Pope Francis and the Grand Imam of Al-Azhar Ahamad al-Tayyib.

Barr, Michael D. and Anantha Raman Govindasamy. 2010. "The Islamisation of Malaysia: Religious Nationalism in the Service of Ethnonationalism". *Australian Journal of International Affairs* 64, no. 3: 293–311.

"Executive Summary of the Marrakesh Declaration on the Rights of Religious Minorities in Predominantly Muslim Majority Communities". 2016.

Lee, Julian. 2010. *Islamization and Activism in Malaysia*. Singapore: Institute of Southeast Asian Studies.

Liow, Joseph Chinyong. 2009. *Piety and Politics: Islamism in Contemporary Malaysia*. Oxford; New York: Oxford University Press.

Norani Othman, Mavis C. Puthucheary, and Clive Kessler. 2008. *Sharing the Nation: Faith, Difference, Power and the State 50 Years After Merdeka*. Petaling Jaya, Selangor: SIRD.

Roff, William. 1994 *The Origins of Malay Nationalism*. Kuala Lumpur: Oxford University Press.

ABOUT THE CONTRIBUTORS

A'an Suryana (PhD) is Visiting Fellow at the ISEAS – Yusof Ishak Institute. He is also a Lecturer in Political Science at the Faculty of Social Sciences, Universitas Islam Internasional Indonesia (UIII).

Afra Alatas is Research Officer in the Regional Social and Cultural Studies Programme, ISEAS – Yusof Ishak Institute.

Ahmad Fauzi Abdul Hamid is Professor of Political Science at the School of Distance Education, Universiti Sains Malaysia (USM).

Andina Dwifatma is a PhD candidate and researcher at the Herb Feith Indonesia Engagement Centre. She is also Lecturer at the School of Communication, Atma Jaya Catholic University of Indonesia.

Faris Ridzuan is a Master's candidate in the Department of Malay Studies, National University of Singapore (NUS).

Komaruddin Hidayat is Professor and Rector of the Universitas Islam Internasional Indonesia (UIII).

Mohd Faizal Musa (PhD) is Visiting Fellow at the ISEAS – Yusof Ishak Institute. He is also a Research Fellow at the Institute of the Malay World and Civilization (ATMA), National University of Malaysia (UKM).

Norshahril Saat (PhD) is Senior Fellow at the ISEAS – Yusof Ishak Institute. He is Coordinator of the Regional Social and Cultural Studies Programme.

Sharifah Nurul Huda Alkaff is Senior Assistant Professor and Programme Leader in the English Studies Programme of the Faculty of Arts and Social Sciences, Universiti Brunei Darussalam (UBD).

Tunku Zain Al-'Abidin ibni Tuanku Muhriz is the Founding President of the Institute for Democracy and Economic Affairs (IDEAS), Malaysia.

Yuji Mizuno is a researcher at the Institute of Developing Economies (IDE-JETRO), Tokyo.

1

INTRODUCTION

Norshahril Saat, A'an Suryana, and Mohd Faizal Musa

Due to its strategic location, maritime Southeast Asia serves as an economic hub that connects the East and the West, with the Straits of Malacca serving as an important route for business access. Maritime Southeast Asia remains essential today, if not more significant, as the economies within the region continue to grow faster than many other regions in the world. Its strategic location and the advancement of its combined economy make the region a premiere meeting point, offline and online, for many people worldwide as more people look for investment opportunities and leisure activities in more prosperous Southeast Asia.

Apart from its economic and strategic positioning, maritime Southeast Asia is a significant area for analysis as the region also serves as a hub for the cross-pollination of ideas. During the Cold war period (1945–91), Southeast Asia became the battleground for the forces of neo-liberal capitalism and communism. But an equally interesting scope of scholarly interest is the development and exchange of religious ideas, particularly concerning Islam. Azra's (2004) study

The Origins of Islamic Reformism in Southeast Asia, among others, remain one of the most important contributions capturing the network of Malay-Indonesian and Middle Eastern ideas in the seventeenth and eighteenth centuries.

Maritime Southeast Asia is home to the largest Muslim society in the world, namely Indonesia. Eighty-nine per cent of its 281 million people are Muslims. However, the community is not homogenous, depending on where they live, and the extent to which they immerse cultural and ethnic influences into their religious life. Some would reckon that the country is also changing, from one that was referred to as the smiling face of Islam to one that is currently experiencing a conservative turn (Van Bruinessen 2013; Feillard and Madinier 2011); or a hotbed of political Islam and radicalism (Ayoob 2008).

Maritime Southeast Asia is also home to the relatively homogenous and traditional Islamic polity of Brunei Darussalam, which ties the concept of the monarchy to Islam and Malay culture. Based on its 2021 census, Brunei has a population of 333,600 citizens, 89 per cent of which are Malays (Department of Economic Planning and Statistics, Brunei 2023).

Though less homogenous due to its multicultural demography, modern-day Malaysia also combines Malay royalty and Islamic identity, and has a Muslim-majority population. 61.3 per cent of its 28 million population are Muslims, spreading across West and East Malaysia, though the majority reside in the former. Three states in maritime Southeast Asia—Singapore, Thailand, and the Philippines—host sizeable Muslim minorities. Singapore, where 15 per cent of its 5.4 million population profess Islam, upholds secularism and multiculturalism as non-negotiable in the social contract, and the government's relationship with Muslims is generally peaceful.

Still, in Thailand and the Philippines, Muslims are well-concentrated in specific locations, often termed as the Deep South, far from the capital cities. There have been occasional occurrences of tension and some that witnessed violence between Muslims and the respective governments. Covering maritime Southeast Asia does not negate the fact that Muslims live as minorities in other Southeast Asian states too; there is a sizeable Muslim community in Vietnam, Cambodia, and Myanmar. While some are at peace with the government, others, such as in Myanmar, are not (i.e. the Rohingya crisis).

The Transmission of Islam: Emerging and Old Ideas

In the past, Islam was transmitted to Southeast Asia through, first, Middle Eastern *ulama* (religious scholars), preachers and missionaries; and second, Southeast Asian *ulama* who went to study in the Middle East and then disseminated either puritanical or reformist ideas of Islam to their students and people in their respective countries of origin (Burhanudin 2012, pp. 31–37). Nowadays, due to the advancement of Internet technology, the transmission of Islamic ideas in Southeast Asia is faster and more widespread as people in this increasingly prosperous region can quickly get access to the Internet due to the increase of their purchasing power. World Bank data shows that more and more people across the world—including in Southeast Asia—have been gaining increasing access to the Internet in the last few decades (World Bank 2021). For example, in Singapore, 71 per cent of the population used the Internet (through their computers and mobile phones) in 2011, and this number increased to 92 per cent in 2020. Malaysia experienced a similar increase in the same time period, from 61 per cent in 2011 to 97 per cent in 2020. In contrast, in Indonesia, the figure rose by five times from 12 per cent in 2011 to 62 per cent in 2021. This data thus underlines the crucial role that the Internet can play in the transmission of ideas.

The Internet has democratized the way Muslims interpret the tenets of Islam. To be sure, the *ulama* class no longer hold exclusive access to interpreting and disseminating Islamic ideas (Norshahril and Ahmad Najib 2021). In the past, religious transmission happened in classrooms, madrasahs, mosques, through the pulpits; in written form, through books, columns in newspapers, and newsletters. Today, even radio and television are considered anachronistic. Slowly, the televangelist era is making way for social media *imam* and *ustaz*. Even rituals commonly practised in Southeast Asia—such as communal prayers and recitation of the Qur'an—that once required face-to-face contact, are now conducted online. The lockdowns during the COVID-19 pandemic accelerated the digitization of Islamic rituals.

The democratization of the public sphere is fruitful for human civilization because it offers societies, including Muslims, access to a variety of ideas in Islam. Muslims can therefore make their own choices about which ideas suit them. At the same time, greater access to the Internet or social media also means that these platforms can be used to promote religious moderation and tolerance for alternative ideas.

However, social media serves as a double-edged sword; it can either be beneficial or detrimental to social relations. On the other hand, the lack of surveillance and unmitigated use of Internet technology can bring harm to society. Many people, including Muslims, are trapped in social media algorithms and filter bubbles promoting dangerous ideas such as violent jihad, which are no longer spread only in physical religious classes or in remote battlefields in the Middle East. Social media is also being used to propagate hatred against particular religious groups, including religious minorities. It is also the culprit behind deep social polarization in Indonesia which is especially fanned by fake news. For example, the country suffered from deep social polarization ahead of the 2014 and 2019 presidential elections that pit Joko Widodo's supporters against his rival candidate, Prabowo Subianto. Additionally, Denny Januar Ali and Eriyanto (2021) found that the use (read: abuse) of Twitter hashtags on topics related to Joko Widodo's policy in handling the spread of COVID-19 divided the public into pro- and anti-Joko Widodo camps. In Malaysia, elections are no longer fought only on campaign trails and through grassroots machinery, but also on social media. Politicians continuously utilize online campaigns to respond to questions regarding policy positions. Furthermore, the online battle is no longer targeted only at the urban electorate, but rural voters too are increasingly integrated into politicking via social media. This was clearly the case in the last three General Elections (GE) in 2013, 2018, and 2022. For example, during GE15, the last election held in November 2022, some quarters used Tik Tok to promote exclusive ideas and used race and religion to fan fear among the electorate. The outcome was that parties that relied on religious ideas performed well.

This book thus dedicates a considerable amount of space to discuss the role of the Internet in the dissemination of ideas. Several chapters in this book highlight the critical role of the Internet in the dissemination of Islamic ideas, in particular the use of social media to either advance interpretations of Islamic ideas or to gain influence in the public sphere. These chapters cover topics on digital anti-Islamist activism, the online policing of the personal morality of celebrities, the use of social media to enhance piety among urban Muslims, and its significance as a battleground for competing traditionalist ideas among Muslims.

When posed with the topic on the transmission of ideas in the contemporary world, it is natural to deal with social media, digitization, and the Internet. These issues are certainly relevant and trendy. However, a book on trends and trendsetters cannot escape discussing old ideas such as extremism and terrorism which may be deemed less fashionable to scholars. Although this is not the main focus of the book, some chapters will deal with such problems as terrorism and violence, and how and why some of them persist and take new forms. Nonetheless, the book will give more weightage to analysing extremism of the non-violent type and how progressive groups respond to it. The latter are usually ignored in contemporary scholarly work.

This book is a reflection of the authors' years of doing fieldwork and engaging with informants, activists, and ordinary people on the ground. Rather than relegating maritime Southeast Asia to the view that it is becoming a bastion of Salafism, Wahhabism, and terrorism, and is becoming more volatile and conservative, this book takes a more balanced approach. At the outset, the book argues that Southeast Asian Islamic discourse is not turning towards conservatism even though they are elements of this in some societies, like in other diverse regions. Instead, what is happening on the ground is that there is greater contestation of ideas and orientations between groups (Muslims and non-Muslims) and within groups (intra-Muslim). In the case of the latter, social, generational, and digital divides are pivotal elements driving the debates.

To extend the argument and to further showcase the complexity of Southeast Asia, chapters in this book illustrate how there are even clashes within organizations, and not just between them. This is to say that dominant organizations such as Nahdlatul Ulama (NU) and Muhammadiyah in Indonesia are not as homogenous as we might think. Equally so, the so-called Islamists of neighbouring Malaysia, Singapore, and Brunei also manifest in different shades. Thus, one can no longer argue that competition in Southeast Asia is easily characterized as *between* progressives and conservatives, liberals and traditionalists, Wahhabis and Sufis, to name a few. Competition also exists *within* these categories. The Internet and social media provide platforms that accentuate and amplify these contestations, as groups and individuals compete for foothold in the already saturated religious market.

Objectives of this Book

This edited volume examines the evolution and transmission of emerging ideas on Islam in maritime Southeast Asia, particularly in Indonesia, Malaysia, Singapore, and Brunei. Chapters in this book broadly ask the following questions: What are the forces/trends driving extremism in Southeast Asia? How does the rapidly changing political situation in these countries affect social cohesion? To what extent are Muslim extremist and segregationist ideologies becoming more mainstream? How are certain groups/individuals using social media to transmit their ideas, and what impact does this have on Islamic discourse? Are there competing discourses to counter extremism? If these discourses do exist, how are they transmitted?

In addressing these questions, this book has two objectives: (1) To map out emerging ideas from these countries; to know how these ideas are acquired and then transmitted, and to analyse which ones dominate and in which spheres; (2) to examine the transmitters of new trends, which include key personalities, groups or institutions to watch. Hence, when referring to trends or trendsetters, we refer to personalities and groups, discourse, and medium.

In their attempt to meet these objectives, the chapters are organized into three parts: Part I looks at continuing and emerging trends. It focuses on two countries with the largest Muslim populations in Southeast Asia—Indonesia and Malaysia. Komaruddin Hidayat (Chapter 2) covers the development and evolution of trends and actors in Indonesian Islam from the Dutch colonial period to the New Order period under President Suharto, and the contemporary period. Unlike many discussions of contemporary Indonesian Islam, Komaruddin examines the contestations between the conservatives and liberals and why the latter's influence in shaping the community must not be ignored. Chapter 3 by Ahmad Fauzi Abdul Hamid covers another dimension of Malaysian Islam. While it looks at how Salafi-Jihadi ideology is critical to terrorist networks such as the Islamic State in Iraq and Syria (ISIS) which did have an impact in attracting Malaysians, he shows how physical violence has not taken root even though Salafi ideas might be dominant. In all, the two chapters in this introductory part of the volume consistently present the role of ideas and how they are transmitted, the institutions they have sustained over the years, and how certain trends began, continued, and declined over the years as social, political, and economic circumstances changed. Although the ideologies discussed in the two countries are on the extreme poles if placed on a spectrum—progressives in Indonesia and radicals in Malaysia—this is not to give the impression that all is well in the former but in trouble in the latter. To be sure, the scholarship studying radicalism through the security lens in Indonesia is more developed compared to other parts of Southeast Asia.

Part II serves as a bridge between ideas and the complex world wide web (www) domain, before crossing into an in-depth discussion on digital and social media. It covers the role of state and organizations. Southeast Asia has always been characterized by strong and dominant states that shaped its miraculous economic progress in the post-colonial world. Singapore, Malaysia, Indonesia, and Thailand, for example, were characterized as Tiger economies during the authoritarian phase of the 1980s and 1990s. Islam in these countries revolved around competition between state (governments) and civil society. There were periods in which states could dictate what type of Islam defined governance, but as authoritarian rule weakened, civil society began to assert its role again, though competition between state and organizations continues. The chapters in this part look at several aspects, though the list and issues are not exhaustive. In Chapter 4, Mohd Faizal Musa looks at the role of the Malaysian civil service as both a supplier and receiver of trends. With globalization, Malaysia is not shielded from exclusivist discourse, and the state is not as homogeneous in promoting progressive and secular ideas, since Malaysia is multi-religious and multicultural. Yet, when implementing government policies, the civil servants can take matters into their own hands based on their Islamic worldview. This part also reckons that organizations are not static, and they ride on new mediums to assert their ideology and gain followership. In a way, Chapters 3 and 4 complement each other in demonstrating that while extremism is prevalent in Malaysia, the focus of analysis for Islam in the region must go beyond terrorism and non-violent extremism.

Rather than focusing on grassroots activism and institutions, other chapters in this part look at the online participation of state and organizations. Yuji Mizuno (Chapter 5) examines liberal Muslim actors and how they utilize social media to counter the Islamists. He discusses some of the opportunities and challenges facing liberal Muslims under the Joko Widodo government in their battle with their conservative counterparts amidst political polarization in the country. Still, on social media and digital platforms, Faris Ridzuan and Afra Alatas (Chapter 6) examine the role of key institutions in Singapore in utilizing data as part of surveillance capitalism. The chapter focuses on the Islamic Religious Council of Singapore (MUIS), a state institution, and the Singapore Islamic Scholars and Religious Teachers Association (PERGAS), a non-governmental organization (NGO). As two key institutions that oversee and wield significant influence on the community's religious life, the use of data does not really solve social problems or alleviate regressive orientations, but reinforces traditionalism and a neo-liberal ideology. In Chapter 7, A'an Suryana further deconstructs the perception that organizations are homogenous entities, and illustrates how within one organization, there are forces which have usurped external trends and propagated them to their respective camps and supporters. A'an divides the contestation in NU between the progressives and conservatives. The conservatives, which are represented by NU Garis Lurus camp, have already established a firm grip online, but to challenge the group, the progressives, in the form of NU Garis Lucu camp, use humour to appeal to their younger followers and are deemed as promoting "cool" Islam.

Part III covers a new dimension of trendsetters, namely individuals. Online and digital platforms have challenged the role of states and NGOs but allow individuals to act on their own accord. Individual behaviour accounts for prevailing social responses and religious orientations in society. Sharifah Nurul Huda Alkaff (Chapter 8) examines how netizens are heavily involved in moral policing online. She compares how female celebrities and influencers in Brunei, Malaysia, and Indonesia are subject to constant moral policing, and individuals are prepared to shame celebrities publicly, demonstrating conservative and exclusivist viewpoints. Interestingly, she shows how the Qur'anic verse *"amar maaruf nahi mungkar"* (promoting good and preventing evil) is used to legitimize actions that are against the basic principles of human rights, privacy, and freedom of expression. In Chapter 9, Andina Dwifatma provides another angle of prevalent Indonesian netizen behaviour. She discusses web-based series on YouTube and how they are popular among Indonesians, appealing to topics that cover matchmaking, family life, and career. Analysing the *Cinta Subuh* (Love at Dawn) series, she shares new forms of mediatized piety that surface the themes of self-development, ritualism, and halal lifestyle. In Chapter 10, Norshahril Saat examines new trends of individual religious preachers in Singapore. Legitimized by the state through licensing as "official preachers", which originally was intended to tackle radicalism and terrorism, these influential preachers promote religiosity that does not contribute to critical thinking and progressive Islam. Rather, there is a constant harping on issues related to spirituality and self-help. There are also instances where these state-endorsed religious elites promote anti-intellectual ideas in the form of irrationalism and magic, which are not in sync with modern scientific inquiry.

Book's Limitations

Examining emerging and old ideas about Islam in this region is a complex endeavour. With this complexity in mind, the editors of this volume declare at the outset the limitations of compiling a book on Southeast Asian Islam and Muslim such as this one. Even though this book focuses on maritime Southeast Asia, there are countries or cases that have not been excluded. The best way to read this book is to regard the chapters as snapshots of key episodes and incidences that can provide a gateway for further introspection and study. The chapters included in this volume do not necessarily regard these issues as the most pressing in Southeast Asia, and the editors do not discount the urgency of other issues. To be sure, studying Islam in Southeast Asia in totality requires multiple volumes, as the ISEAS – Yusof Ishak Institute has previously compiled.

Critics of this volume can easily point out the gaps and countries that have not been included in this volume. For example, Thailand, the Philippines, Cambodia, Myanmar, and Laos are excluded. This is not to deny developments in these countries which are related to Islam and politics, and the use of the Internet to promote piety and religiosity. While these are important, space constraints do not permit inclusion of these perspectives. Moreover, the findings and analysis of this volume can draw comparisons with other cases in the region.

Even for the countries included in this book, not all angles have been explored, such as the role of Islamic education in influencing religious behaviour; external influencers from the Middle East, United States, Asia Pacific; and cross-state interactions in the region. These are issues that the editors plan to expand on going forward, as the topic on trendsetters is not only a developing area, but is continuously evolving. We recommend that readers read this edited volume in tandem with previous publications to reflect on continuity and changes in the region.

This volume would not have been possible without the support and help of the following individuals. The editors wish to express our gratitude to Mr Choi Shing Kwok, Director and Chief Executive Officer of ISEAS – Yusof Ishak Institute, and Dr Terence Chong, Director, Research Division and Deputy Chief Executive Officer, for their continuous support in the study of Islamic societies in Southeast Asia. We would also like to thank Mr Ng Kok Kiong, Director, Publishing Division and Sheryl Sin Bing Peng for all the hard work in stringing this volume together, as in the past ISEAS publications on similar themes. We also wish to thank ISEAS research officers and assistants for their hard work: Afra Alatas, Faris Ridzuan, Nur Syafiqah Taufek, Nadirah Norruddin, Siti Suhaila Mohd Harith, Irna Nurlina Masron, Chin Hong Jie, and Muhammad Danial Sazali.

Norshahril Saat, A'an Suryana, and Mohd Faizal Musa
June 2023

REFERENCES

Ayoob, Mohammed. 2008. *The Many Faces of Political Islam: Religion and Politics in the Muslim World*. Singapore: NUS Press.

Azhar Ibrahim. 2014. *Contemporary Islamic Discourse in the Malay-Indonesian World: Critical Perspectives*. Selangor: Strategic Information and Research Development Centre.

Azyumardi Azra. 2004. *The Origins of Islamic Reformism in Southeast Asia: Network of Malay-Indonesian And Middle Eastern 'Ulama' in The Seventeenth and Eighteenth-Centuries*. Crows Nest, N.S.W: Allen & Unwin; Honolulu, Hawaii: University of Hawai'i Press.

Burhanudin, Jajat. 2012. *Ulama dan Kekuasaan: Pergumulan Elite Muslim dalam Sejarah Indonesia*. Jakarta: PT Mizan Publika.

Denny Januar Ali and Eriyanto. 2021. "Political Polarization and Selective Exposure of Social Media Users in Indonesia". *Jurnal Ilmu Sosial dan Ilmu Politik* 24, no. 3: 268–83.

Department of Economic Planning and Statistics, Brunei. 2023. "Population". https://deps.mofe.gov.bn/SitePages/Population.aspx (accessed 17 February 2023).

Feillard, Andrée and Rémy Madinier. 2011. *The End of Innocence? Indonesian Islam and the Temptations of Radicalism*, translated by Wong Wee. Singapore: NUS Press.

Norshahril Saat and Ahmad Najib Burhani, eds. 2021. *The New Santri: Challenges to Traditional Religious Authority in Indonesia*. Singapore: ISEAS – Yusof Ishak Institute.

Van Bruinessen, Martin, ed. 2013. *Contemporary Developments in Indonesian Islam: Explaining the "Conservative Turn"*. Singapore: ISEAS – Yusof Ishak Institute.

World Bank. 2021. "Individuals Using the Internet (% of Population)". https://data.worldbank.org/indicator/IT.NET.USER.ZS?end=2021&most_recent_value_desc=true&start=2007 (accessed 18 February 2023).

PART I

Continuing and Emerging Trends

2

THE TRENDSETTERS OF ISLAM THROUGHOUT INDONESIAN HISTORY

Komaruddin Hidayat

Over the years, two broad groups have shaped Islam in Indonesia: (1) the pluralists and (2) the conservative Islamists. Contestations between the two groups have coloured Islam throughout the country's history. Scholars normally associate the pluralists with the leaders of secular nationalist parties, Muslim intellectuals in the New Order regime, and members of the two largest Muslim mass organizations, Nahdlatul Ulama (NU) and Muhammadiyah. These actors imagine Indonesia to be an inclusive nation embracing ethnic and religious diversity, and promoting equal standing among Indonesian citizens. By contrast, the Islamists include leaders of Muslim mass organizations or parties influenced by transnational Islamic movements aiming to Islamize the state and Indonesian society.

I argue that in Indonesia, the pluralists have been the more dominant actors in the public sphere, though their Islamist rivals somewhat challenge their authority in this digital age. The pluralists have made Indonesia a religiously neutral state and an inclusive society.

Scholars argue that the pluralists' dominance results not only from their intellectual capacity to harmonize Islam and civic pluralism, but they are also well-funded and receive support from the state. Robert Hefner's (2000) study on *Civil Islam* is correct. During the New Order period, the role of Muslim intellectuals such as Nurcholish Madjid (Cak Nur) and Abdurrahman Wahid (Gus Dur) in promoting moderate Islam was crucial in the pluralists' triumph.

This trend continues during the post-New Order era. Here, I refer to the people's moral opposition towards religious intolerance and sectarianism. This component, I believe, has been more visible in recent years, and it is a positive development in Indonesian Islam. It has helped Indonesia's civic pluralism thrive amidst heated religious tension in Indonesia's recent political history.

The thoughts of Abdurrahman Wahid, Nurcholish Madjid, and Syafi'i Maarif (Buya Syafii) remain essential and relevant to the current state of Indonesian Islam, defying some arguments that Indonesia is experiencing a "conservative turn". Many have admitted that there was not much difference in the three figures' thoughts despite coming from different cultural and organizational backgrounds. They grew up and emerged out of three mainstream Muslim communities in the country.

Like a locomotive, the three pulled the large traditional Muslim carriage into the modern era that cherishes inclusivity and diversity, and thus placed Islam as an important source in building modern Indonesia. They prioritized Islam in substance rather than form, especially in the context of building the nation and state.

In retrospect, the thoughts of Nurcholish Madjid and Syafi'i Maarif nicely blended Eastern and Western thinking. They studied religion in *pesantren* (Islamic boarding schools) and applied modern methods from prestigious universities following the Western tradition in a broad social context. Similarly, Abdurrahman Wahid's ideas reflected traditional Islamic thought but remained advanced and open.

Therefore, it is safe to say that building the pluralist Indonesian Islamic school of thought is akin to synthesizing three icons: Nurcholish Madjid, Abdurrahman Wahid, and Syafi'i Maarif. All three agree that Pancasila, democracy, and social justice come together to form the final mantra of the Indonesian nation. Their legacy remains fundamental despite being challenged by the Islamists in the contemporary setting, which this chapter will discuss shortly.

The Dutch Colonial Period and the Old Order Era

This section traces the historical evolution of the pluralist-Islamist contestation from the colonial period. One Islamist organization that became influential during the Dutch colonial era was *Persatuan Islam* (Islam United) or Persis. Established in 1923 by Muslim merchants in West Java, Persis' leading figure was Ahmad Hassan, a textile businessman. He was succeeded by his student, Muhammad Natsir. Later during the New Order period, Natsir played a prominent role in strengthening the link between Islam in Indonesia and the Middle East, propagating a more orthodox variant of Islam (Hasan 2006). His adherence to orthodox Islam had been visible since the creation of Persis. The organization was often involved in debates, either in private or public, with traditionalist Muslims or Christians to teach them puritan Islam as practised during the Prophet's era (Federspiel 2001). Furthermore, Persis also adeptly utilized print media to propagate its orthodox Islam and Islamism to a wider audience. The organization managed various media including a journal called *Pembela Islam* (Defenders of Islam), and several periodicals. These media found their readership in modernist Muslims in Java and outer islands such as Sumatra, Kalimantan and Sulawesi (ibid.). Persis also used these media to express its criticism of the pluralist groups that promoted civic pluralism and the idea of a secular state.

Following the birth of one of the most important Islamist groups, pluralist-nationalist groups also began to emerge. They were the direct product of the western education promoted by the Dutch through their Ethical Policy. The main figure from this group was Sukarno, a Javanese *priyayi* who was educated in Dutch schools. He established Partai Nasional Indonesia (Indonesia National Party, PNI) in 1927 that was secular in nature and rejected Islamism. He believed that the unity of Indonesia was essential in the struggle for independence from the Dutch and that Indonesia must not be divided along religious or ethnic lines (Ricklefs 2001).

The inclusive view of PNI thus became its strength in mobilizing mass support from people of wide-ranging backgrounds, particularly those worried by the growth of the Islamist groups. PNI supporters included the so-called *abangan* Muslims, non-Muslims, and minority groups such as Chinese and Arabs (Ricklefs 2001). PNI's inclusivity was reflected in the Youth Congress initiated by PNI's youth wing,

Indonesia Muda (Indonesian Youth) in 1928 (Foulcher 2000). This congress produced *Sumpah Pemuda* (Youth Pledge) which expressed the commitment of youth organizations—either Muslim or non-Muslim—from various areas of Indonesia to uphold the vision of one motherland, Indonesia, one nation, Indonesia, with one language, Indonesian. While Islamist youth wings also participated in the congress, they did not endorse the Youth Pledge that acknowledged unity in Indonesia's diversity (Suryadinata 1978).

The pluralist-Islamist contestation during this period often took place through mass media and mail correspondence. It was mainly between Sukarno of the PNI and Hassan and Natsir from Persis. Should independent Indonesia be a secular or Islamic state? Although it was agreed that Pancasila would be Indonesia's founding ideology, in the 1955 election, the nationalist and Islamist parties were equally matched in terms of strength. In 1957, President Sukarno through the implementation of "guided democracy" sought to weaken the Islamist power significantly by jailing the figures of Masyumi (the political vehicle of the Islamists) (Feillard and Madinier 2011). Thus, Pancasila thrived as the national ideology of Indonesia which legitimized civic pluralism in the country.

The New Order Era

Pancasila continued under the New Order regime and was strengthened by civil Islam. Throughout the New Order period, Pancasila was heavily manipulated by the government, under Suharto, an *abangan* of military background. The ideology became a tool to preserve his political power and control (Hefner 2000; Pringle 2010). Under his regime, the Islamist groups were suppressed as they were deemed to be anti-Pancasila. On the other hand, cultural expressions of Islam that were infused with pluralist teachings promoted by Muslim intellectuals were endorsed. Thus, most Muslim organizations shifted to socio-cultural activities. For instance, NU decided to return to its original socio-religious objective (*"Kembali ke Khittah 1926"*) while in 1967, Masyumi leaders created a new organization called Dewan Dakwah Islam Indonesia (Indonesian Islamic Propagation Council, DDII). With no political challenge posed by the Islamists, the pluralist groups, particularly Muslim intellectuals, were relatively dominant in influencing public discourse during the New Order period.

The emergence of Muslim intellectuals from a more educated cohort during the New Order era saw some key individuals rise to prominence and shape public discourse on Islam and civic pluralism. Their activities initially started as a limited group discussion among Muslim intellectuals at Institut Agama Islam Negeri (State Institute of Islamic Studies, IAIN) Yogyakarta under the patronage of Mukti Ali. Ali once held a position as the Vice Rector of IAIN and later the Minister of Religious Affairs from 1973 to 1978 (Munhanif 1996). Established in 1963, IAIN (later State Islamic University or Universitas Islam Negeri, UIN) is a network of state institutes of Islamic studies which were initially located in Jakarta and Yogyakarta. The network produced Muslim intellectuals who brought pluralist and liberal Islam to the fore (Saeed 1999; van Bruinessen 2009). A critical development in IAIN's history was when Mukti Ali returned to the institute after graduating from McGill University. Ali brought back with him knowledge of comparative religion which he learnt from Wilfred Cantwell Smith, the founder and director of the Institute of Islamic Studies at McGill University (Munhanif 1996). While at IAIN Yogyakarta, he reformed the curriculum and sent his best students to western universities to learn about Islam.

Inspired by the development of the social sciences in western education, the young Muslim intellectuals criticized orthodox Islam and popularized hermeneutic analysis that enabled them to contextualize Islam with modern development. The most prominent figure of these intellectuals was none other than Nurcholish Madjid. He was initially a member of Himpunan Mahasiswa Islam (Muslim Students' Association, HMI), a youth organization ideologically close to Masyumi. Madjid was highly regarded as a "young Natsir" due to his intellect and leadership. Nevertheless, instead of inheriting Natsir's Islamist ideas, he propagated the separation of religion and practical politics. After graduating from IAIN Jakarta, he continued his studies at The University of Chicago as a PhD student under the supervision of Fazlur Rahman, a neo-modernist Muslim from Pakistan (Barton 1997). He brought Rahman's liberal ideas on Islam to Indonesia and shocked the senior members of Masyumi with his popular phrase, "Islam Yes, Islamic Party No" in 1970. For Madjid, Islam was a source of moral teachings, not legal prescriptions (Mujiburrahman 2006). Therefore, he rejected the idea of establishing an Islamic state. Regarding civic pluralism, he also promoted an "inclusive Islamic theology" that viewed all religions, despite having distinctive characteristics, as aiming for similar salvation (ibid.). Hence, Muslims should treat non-Muslims as brothers and sisters, recognizing that they are under a "common platform" (*kalimatun sawa*) of One Truth (Husein 2004). From 1986, these religious interpretations were propagated by Paramadina, an education institute that was later turned into a university.

Another prominent figure of this so-called renewal movement was Abdurrahman Wahid from NU. He was the grandson of Hasyim Asy'ari, the founder of NU. He occupied a prominent position in the organization which he led from 1984 to 1999. While Wahid did not have the chance to pursue formal education in the West, he had been well-equipped with western knowledge during his studies on social theory and European philosophy in Baghdad from 1964 to 1970 (Barton 1996). Thus, when he returned to Indonesia, he actively participated in academic forums and study groups on Islam and civic pluralism which were initiated by Nurcholish Madjid and other Muslim intellectuals (ibid.). Given his traditionalist and NU background, he spread his ideas on civic pluralism to NU and to the *pesantren*. NU withdrew from formal politics during his chairmanship and returned to its original objectives centred around social and educational activities. Only by being outside government circles, Wahid believed, could NU play a more significant role in promoting democracy and religious tolerance outside the state's monopoly over the interpretation of Pancasila (ibid.).

Overall, Wahid did not contest the state's pluralist interpretation of Pancasila. He believed Pancasila to be a "living political compromise which allows all Indonesians to live together in a national, unitary, non-Islamic state" (Ramage 1996). Nevertheless, he denounced religious orthodoxy and defended various minority sects of Islam in Indonesia, such as the Shi'as and Ahmadiyyas by promoting "Islamic universalism" (Mujiburrahman 1999; van Bruinessen 2009). Wahid was also a proponent of democracy and rejected Suharto's abuse of Pancasila to legitimize his authoritarian style (Ramage 1996, p. 229). He was aware of the threat from Islamists who continued to contest Pancasila and sought to establish a religiously segregated Indonesian society (ibid.). Therefore, under his leadership, he gradually transformed NU to defend Indonesia against the Islamist groups and protect Pancasila and civic pluralism (Ramage 1996). He supported the creation of non-governmental organizations (NGOs) by NU's Muslim intellectuals including his own NGO, Wahid Foundation, established in 2004, which promotes human rights, democracy, and civic pluralism in Indonesia (Barton 1996; van Bruinessen 2009).

These intellectuals played important roles in the dissemination of civic pluralism during the New Order era. Nurcholis Madjid and Abdurrahman Wahid were able to promote civic pluralism in Islam and contributed to civil Islam's emergence in Indonesia. Despite the popularity of civil Islam in the New Order period, Islamist activism did not cease. The Islamists remained active, propagating their teachings underground and preparing to resurface once the regime became more supportive. This threat materialized when Suharto shifted his stance from Islamophobic to seeking courtship of the Muslim community in the late 1980s (Liddle 1996). This Islamic turn, as scholars have observed, opened the opportunity for the Islamist groups to seek the state's patronage and grow their influence in the public sphere.

The Post-New Order Era

The momentum for the Islamist groups arrived in the post-New Order period (post-1998) after Indonesia experienced greater democratization. The implication for a democratizing Indonesia is that the state no longer suppresses the Islamists; thus, they have more freedom to spread their ideas in the public sphere. Mass support has become an essential means of gaining general influence, in addition to the state's support which was absent during the New Order period. In other words, Muslims' moral opposition towards religious intolerance and sectarianism has become key to maintaining civic pluralism in Indonesia, but this changed during the post-New Order.

However, surveys on the Indonesian Muslim population in general show that they are moderate in religious orientation. Contrary to what is reported in the media, those who have joined the Islamists to strive for an Islamic state or engage radical activities are the minority. However, moderate Indonesian Muslims tend to be passive when responding to inter-faith issues or Islamist threats in Indonesia. Scholars call them the "silent majority" (Abuza 2007; Hefner 2003). Given the government's neoliberal policies, Indonesian citizens generally focus more on self-development and consumerist culture rather than sociopolitical issues such as inter-faith relations.

The aspiration for upward mobility is what the Islamists successfully captured to gradually mobilize more Muslims towards their conservative and sectarian teachings. For instance, in the early *reformasi* period, new preachers emerged (Hoesterey 2015; Howell 2008; Watson 2005; Rudnyckyj 2011; Sakai 2012). These preachers lacked formal Islamic studies backgrounds. However, the public regarded them as religious authorities. They appeared frequently on national media, attracting audiences ranging in the thousands. The new Muslim preachers shared an interest in business and halal consumption that resonated with the everyday issues of Muslims in neoliberal times. These new preachers endorsed work as a form of worship and emphasized the importance of Muslims gaining wealth. They created management consultant firms to provide public and private companies with training and workshops. They were also concerned with the broader Muslim community's economic issues, promoting entrepreneurship, Islamic philanthropy and halal consumption (Hasyim 2021). They also used popular media channels such as novels, movies, and social media to spread their Islamic teachings (Hasan 2013; Sakai 2012).

These practices of *dakwah bil hal* or *dakwah* through *amal* (sharing knowledge of Islam through socio-economic practices) and halal consumption thus came to represent the interests of Indonesian Muslims in the neoliberal post-New Order Indonesia that shifted away from formal politics (Kailani and Slama 2019; Meuleman 2011; Sakai and Fauzia 2014). The shift of Islamism from politics to becoming more oriented towards socio-cultural issues has been observed by scholars in the Muslim world. Roy (1994), for instance, argues that political Islam has "failed" in the Middle East. He observes that this failure has resulted in "the advancement of Islam as a social phenomenon", whereby "Islamic symbols are penetrating the society and the political discourse of the Muslim world more than ever" (ibid., p. 78). This *dakwah*, however, has led to increasing sectarianism, whereby Muslim social engagements have become more narrowly directed towards the Muslim community (Hasyim 2022; Sakai and Isbah 2014).

Besides their ability to attract Muslims to their conservative and sectarian teachings, some Islamist groups have also received support from Indonesia's political elites to pursue these agendas. With the enactment of the relatively freer and more transparent elections in post-New Order Indonesia, political elites have to compete among themselves (Fealy and Aspinall 2003). Some played the Islamic card by seeking courtship from the Islamist groups. For instance, there have been attempts to implement Islam through formal politics using the adoption of *perda syariah* (Islamic law) in several local areas of Indonesia such as Aceh and Banten. The *reformasi* era of Indonesia was followed by a decentralization process that granted greater power to localities up to the regency level. Thus, several localities adopted Islamic law to govern their people, whether Muslim or non-Muslim. For instance, the law obliges Muslim women to wear *hijab* in the public sphere, while non-Muslims are asked to wear appropriate clothing as suggested by Muslims (Bush 2008). The implementation of Islamic law in these localities was supported by Islamist parties and secular parties that used Islam to attract Muslim voters (ibid.; Mujiburrahman 2013).

Besides formal politics, Islamist groups have also resorted to violence. In general, the violent Islamist groups in Indonesia can be classified into two categories: Muslim terrorists and Muslim vigilante groups. Muslim terrorists are influenced by Salafism, a puritanical teaching that aims to cleanse society from heresy *bid'ah* (heresy) and *syirik* (idolatry). These groups were mostly formed by former *mujahidin* (Muslim jihad fighters) in the anti-Soviet war in Afghanistan (Fealy 2004). They believe that the violent route to establish a society and state free from *bid'ah* and *syirik* is required, given that the United States also uses power to suppress Islam (ibid.). Therefore, in the context of Indonesia, a radical Muslim group, Laskar Jihad, waged war against Christians in Maluku in 2000. Likewise, another terrorist group, Jamaah Islamiyah, was involved in the bombing of 35 churches on Christmas Eve in 2000, two cafes in Bali in 2002, and the Marriot Hotel in Jakarta in 2003. Thousands of deaths resulted from the violence of these groups. Besides ex-combatants of the anti-Soviet war in Afghanistan, these groups also mobilized unemployed university students to support their *jihadi* activities as an extension of the campus Islam phenomenon during the New Order era (Hasan 2010). During the *reformasi* era, the activism of these groups remained mostly underground to maintain the secrecy of their strategies in conducting radical activities in Indonesia.

On the other hand, the military initially created the Muslim vigilante groups to thwart student demonstrations against Suharto in 1998 (Wilson 2008). One of Indonesia's most high-profile vigilante groups is Fron Pembela Islam (Islamic Defenders Front, FPI), established by Habib Rizieq Shihab in 1998. Shihab is a graduate of Lembaga Ilmu Pengetahuan Islam and Arab (Islamic and Arabic College of Indonesia, LIPIA) and later continued his studies in Saudi Arabia. Thus, there is also the influence of Salafism in FPI. During the current *reformasi* era, unlike the less visible activism of the terrorist Islamist groups, FPI has been active in conducting "sweeps" in public. Dozens of FPI members often target activities or places deemed un-Islamic such as cafés, discotheques, or non-Muslims prayer areas, violently forcing staff and participants to end their activities (ibid.).

While Islamism has found more freedom in post-New Order Indonesia, Muslim intellectuals and moderate Muslim mass organizations have gradually been squeezed out of the public sphere. This is not to say that they have become inactive in promoting civic pluralism. Islamic intellectualism continues to thrive during this period. For instance, besides NU, another large Muslim mass organization in Indonesia, Muhammadiyah, has also been perceived as the defender of civic pluralism, particularly under the leadership of Amin Abdullah and Syafii Maarif (Akmaliah et al. 2022; Burhani 2013). Furthermore, other scholars with liberal interpretations of Islam have also established a network of pluralist Muslim intellectuals called *Jaringan Islam Liberal* (Liberal Islam Network, JIL) in 2001 (Ali 2005; Nurdin 2005). The emergence of these actors demonstrate that the intellectual tradition of pluralist Muslims in Indonesia has continued in post-New Order Indonesia. Nevertheless, the pluralists are no longer the dominant actors in the public sphere, as they face strong contestation from the Islamist groups.

One organization that has proven to be an obstacle to the development of a liberal interpretation of Islam in post-New Order Indonesia is Majelis Ulama Indonesia (Indonesian Council of Islamic Scholars, MUI). MUI was initially a semi-state organization established by the New Order regime in 1975. Suharto aimed to position MUI as the representative body for Islamic authorities in Indonesia, which would protect Islamic orthodoxy while simultaneously providing a bridge between the president and the Indonesian Muslim community (Hasyim 2015). The membership of MUI comprises representatives of

Muslim organizations in Indonesia. Due to the dominance of pluralist Islam during the New Order era as promoted by Muslim intellectuals, MUI found that its relevance in representing and guarding the Muslim community against heterodox practices was contested (Gillespie 2007). Thus, following the *reformasi* era and social turmoil due to the 1998 financial crisis, MUI transformed into a civil society organization and positioned itself as the defender of the nation's morality (ibid.). At the same time, MUI opened its membership to Islamist groups such as Hizbut Tahrir Indonesia (HTI) and jihadist Muslims (ibid.; Ichwan 2013). Thus, the intrusion of Islamism to the organization has led to a more orthodox interpretation of Islam as reflected in its *fatwa*.

The clearest *fatwa* that reflects MUI's increasing orthodoxy is *fatwa* no. 7 issued in 2005 which declares secularism, pluralism, and liberal Islamic movements as *haram* or forbidden in Islam. The terms pluralism, secularism, and liberalism are not fully defined by MUI. Thus, this *fatwa* is open to various interpretations by Muslims. According to Gillespie (2007, p. 222), the implication of this *fatwa* is the rejection of "equality between different religions". Ichwan (2013, p. 82) argues that this *fatwa* "was also bound to impinge on inter-religious relations in such a religiously plural society". Thus, this *fatwa* undermines the notions of civic pluralism and inclusive citizenship among people from different religious backgrounds that Indonesia theoretically upholds through Pancasila.

In practice, while the *fatwa* is not legally binding, it has posed a clear challenge to the liberal interpretation of Islam by Muslim intellectuals (Hasyim 2020a). It has been difficult for the latter to legitimize their pluralist teachings in accordance with Islam, as through this *fatwa* pluralist Islam has been labelled un-Islamic or deviant.

Recent Trends in Indonesian Islam

In recent years, following the growth of socio-cultural Islamism in contemporary Indonesia, more concerted efforts to counter Islamist growth have been visible. These efforts have come from not only the government and moderate Muslim mass organizations such as NU and Muhammadiyah, but also broader ordinary Indonesian Muslims. These wide responses, I argue, resulted from the massive exploitation of religious identity and the use of social media in political mobilizations in the last decade.

Following the popularity of social media in the late 2010s, the 2012 Jakarta gubernatorial election witnessed the beginning of the utilization of social media in Indonesia's elections. The strategic use of social media played a prominent role in Jokowi's victory at the 2012 Jakarta gubernatorial election. His victory was a surprise for many observers, given that he was not originally from the circle of oligarchs that traditionally dominated Indonesian politics due to their ownership of mainstream media (Tapsell 2017). Tapsell (2015) describes Jokowi's career as the "Jokowi Phenomenon" and points to the use of social media as the main factor contributing to his success.

The use of social media in broader politics was reflected when Jokowi tried to boost his political career in the 2014 presidential election. In this election, Jokowi applied the same strategy of utilizing social media for his campaign. However, he became a victim of an intense black campaign led by the fundamentalist Muslim groups that supported Prabowo Subianto, his rival in the 2014 and later the 2019 presidential elections (Tyson and Purnomo 2017).

To be sure, since his involvement in the 2012 Jakarta gubernatorial election, Jokowi had already been the victim of a black campaign. This campaign claimed that the Christians and Jews would rule over Jakarta if Jokowi won, as he was partnering with Basuki Tjahaja Purnama (Ahok), a Chinese Christian. His status as a double minority meant that he easily became the target of ethno-religious provocations by fundamentalist Muslim groups. This provocation was spread among the grassroots using printed flyers and repeated during the 2014 presidential election. Again, in the 2014 election, the campaign used ethno-religious sentiment based on hoaxes, mainly questioning Jokowi's religion by accusing him of being the son of a Singaporean Christian (Tyson and Purnomo 2017). Jokowi was also accused of being a member of an Indonesian communist party that had been banned by the New Order regime (ibid.). One of the notable sources of these rumours was *Obor Rakyat*, a printed newspaper that spread rumours about Jokowi's religion (ibid.).

Despite this black campaign occurring in print media, in 2014, the content had also begun to spread through social media. For instance, the 2014 presidential election witnessed the rise of social media provocateurs like Jonru who propagated similar hoaxes like *Obor Rakyat*. With thousands of followers on Twitter and Facebook, the black campaign had a wider reach than print media. Therefore, some observers described the 2014 presidential election as "the most negative and hostile election witnessed since the fall of Suharto's authoritarian regime in 1998" (Tyson and Purnomo 2017, p. 117).

However, the black campaign did not stop after the 2014 presidential election. After Jokowi won the election by a slight margin, the black campaign became even fiercer as Ahok, the former vice-governor of Jakarta, replaced Jokowi as governor. Provocations against Ahok reached its peak after a video showing Ahok giving a speech to people in Kepulauan Seribu (a regency in Jakarta) in 2016 went viral on social media. The video was trimmed to give the impression that Ahok had accused the Qur'an of deceiving Muslims not to vote for non-Muslims during elections. The video thus went viral and triggered the outrage of fundamentalist Muslims in Indonesia. Rallies of mass demonstrations were initiated to demand the imprisonment of Ahok due to his alleged blasphemy against the Qur'an and Islam (Hasyim 2020). Hundreds of thousands of Muslims attended these demonstrations, the most notable one being Aksi Bela Islam (Action to Defend Islam) in 2016 (Lim 2017, p. 412). Lim described this demonstration as "the largest mass demonstration in the history of Indonesia". As a result, in the next 2017 Jakarta gubernatorial election, Ahok lost and was later imprisoned because of his blasphemy case.

The massive Islamic populist campaigns in those years forced the government and the broader segment of moderate Muslims in Indonesia to act, as Islamist campaigns could potentially disrupt the nation's unity. Unlike his predecessor Susilo Bambang Yudhoyono, Jokowi took decisive steps to weaken intolerant groups (Aspinall and Mietzner 2019). For instance, in 2017, he dissolved HTI which had been legally established since 2006. In addition, the government did not extend the legal permit of FPI after it expired in 2019.

Jokowi has also attempted to strengthen the nationalist and pluralist character of Indonesian citizens through several initiatives. First, in 2014, he introduced a national programme of *Revolusi Mental* (Mental Revolution) that promotes three core values of integrity, work ethos, and *gotong-royong*. *Gotong-royong* here invokes a sense of Indonesian unity regardless of ethnic and religious background as promoted by Sukarno when he introduced Pancasila in 1945 (Bowen 1986). Second, in 2018 Jokowi established Badan Pembinaan Ideologi Pancasila (Agency for Pancasila Ideology Education) which focuses on formulating the roadmap of Pancasila education for all Indonesian citizens. Third, Jokowi has endorsed *wasathiyah Islam* (Middle Way Islam) as the character of Indonesian Islam that values moderation, tolerance, and inclusivity (Hoesterey 2018). Included in the third point was the creation of the Universitas Islam Internasional Indonesia (UIII) to promote Indonesia as a centre of Islamic studies which is based on the moderate teachings of Indonesian Islam (Hidayat and Darmadi 2019).

In addition to Jokowi's support for Indonesian Islam, NU officially introduced *Islam Nusantara* (Archipelagic Islam) as its brand of Islam during its 33rd congress in 2015. On the other hand, in the same year, Muhammadiyah during its 47th congress came up with its own Islamic formulation called *Islam Berkemajuan* (Progressive Islam). Beyond these two organizations, ordinary Muslims have also sporadically initiated online campaigns to promote moderate Islam and religious toleration that have been more visible with the proliferation of social media. Here, I agree with Hefner who said: "These efforts [of the Islamists] have in turn catalysed a significant counter-mobilisation... dedicated to a more inclusive understanding of Islam and Indonesian citizenship" (2019, p. 376).

Conclusion

Indonesia underwent an Islamic turn at the end of the New Order period (Liddle 1996) and a conservative turn during the early phases of the *reformasi* era (Sebastian et al. 2020; van Bruinessen 2013). Most recently, as a response towards massive Islamist political campaigns, Indonesia has been experiencing a traditionalist turn whereby moderate Muslim mass organizations, particularly NU, have restored their influence in shaping public discourse (Jati 2022). What is notable in Indonesia today is that Indonesian citizens' sense of moral opposition towards the Islamists is now more apparent in contrast to the past when they were often seen as the silent majority. Indonesia is currently enjoying a demographic bonus with a relatively young and productive population. This momentum should be used to preserve the commitment of Indonesian Muslims towards moderate Islam. To make it sustainable, education is the key to promoting and developing an Indonesian Islam that is not only known for its inclusivity, but also plays a broader role in all aspects of life in Indonesia and beyond.

The current government under Jokowi has also adopted both hard-handed and soft-handed approaches in balancing the influence of the pluralists and Islamists. The former comes in the form of banning problematic groups, while the latter in the form of moderate ideology. But are these efforts enough, considering new trends in social media, especially when influencers are also shaping the religious discourse more than the *ulama* and intellectuals? Where is Indonesian Islam heading? As the largest Muslim country in the world, neighbouring Southeast Asian countries must continue to observe events in Indonesia for happenings there may also shape trends in its neighbouring countries.

REFERENCES

Abuza, Zachary. 2007. *Political Islam and Violence in Indonesia*. Abingdon and New York: Routledge.

Ahmad Najib Burhani. 2013. "Transmission of Islamic Reform from the United States to Indonesia: Studying Fazlur Rahman's Legacy through the Works of Ahmad Syafii Maarif". *Indonesia and the Malay World* 41, no. 119: 29–47.

Akmaliah, Wahyudi, Priyambudi Sulistiyanto, and Sukendar. 2022. "Making Moderate Islam in Indonesia". *Studies in Conflict & Terrorism*: 1–15.

Ali, Muhammad Ali. 2005. "The Rise of the Liberal Islam Network (JIL) in Contemporary Indonesia". *American Journal of Islamic Social Sciences* 22, no. 1: 1–27.

Aspinall, Edward and Marcus Mietzner. 2019. "Southeast Asia's Troubling Elections: Nondemocratic Pluralism in Indonesia". *Journal of Democracy* 30, no. 4: 104–18.

Aspinall, Edward, Marcus Mietzner, and Dirk Tomsa, eds. 2015. *The Yudhoyono Presidency: Indonesia's Decade of Stability and Stagnation*. Singapore: ISEAS – Yusof Ishak Institute.

Barton, Greg. 1996. "The Liberal, Progressive Roots of Abdurrahman Wahid's Thought". In *Nadhlatul Ulama, Traditional Islam and Modernity in Indonesia*, edited by Greg Fealy and Greg Barton, pp. 190–226. Clayton: Monash Asia Institute.

──────. 1997. "Indonesia's Nurcholish Madjid and Abdurrahman Wahid as Intellectual Ulama: The Meeting of Islamic Traditionalism and Modernism in Neo-modernist Thought". *Islam and Christian-Muslim Relations* 8, no. 3: 323–50.

Bowen, John R. 1986. "On the Political Construction of Tradition: Gotong Royong in Indonesia". *The Journal of Asian Studies* 45, no. 3: 545–61.

Bush, Robin. 2008. "Regional Sharia Regulations in Indonesia: Anomaly or Symptom?" In *Expressing Islam: Religious Life and Politics in Indonesia*, edited by Greg Fealy and Sally White, pp. 174–91. Singapore: ISEAS – Yusof Ishak Institute.

Fealy, Greg. 2004. "Islamic Radicalism in Indonesia: The Faltering Revival?" *Southeast Asian Affairs*, no. 1: 104–21.

Fealy, Greg and Edward Aspinall. 2003. *Local Power and Politics in Indonesia: Decentralisation and Democratisation*. Singapore: ISEAS – Yusof Ishak Institute.

Federspiel, Howard M. 2001. *Islam and Ideology in the Emerging Indonesian State: The Persatuan Islam (PERSIS), 1923 to 1957*. Leiden: Brill.

Feillard, Andrée and Rémy Madinier. 2011. *The End of Innocence? Indonesian Islam and the Temptations of Radicalism*, translated by Wong Wee. Singapore: NUS Press.

Foulcher, Keith. 2000. "Sumpah Pemuda: The Making and Meaning of a Symbol of Indonesian Nationhood". *Asian Studies Review* 24, no. 3: 377–410.

Geertz, Clifford. 1964. *The Religion of Java*. New York: Free Press.

Gillespie, Piers. 2007. "Current Issues in Indonesian Islam: Analysing the 2005 Council of Indonesian Ulama Fatwa No. 7 Opposing Pluralism, Liberalism and Secularism". *Journal of Islamic Studies* 18, no. 2: 202–40.

Hasan, Noorhaidi. 2006. *Laskar Jihad: Islam, Militancy, and the Quest for Identity in Post-New Order Indonesia*. Ithaca: SEAP Publications, Cornell University.

——. 2010. "The Drama of Jihad: The Emergence of Salafi Youth in Indonesia". In *Being Young and Muslim: New Cultural Politics in the Global South and North*, edited by Linda Herrera and Asef Bayat, pp. 49–62. Oxford: Oxford University Press.

——. 2013. *The Making of Public Islam Piety, Democracy and Youth in Indonesian Politics*. Carlsbad: Suka Press.

Hasyim, Syafiq. 2015. "Majelis Ulama Indonesia and Pluralism in Indonesia". *Philosophy & Social Criticism* 41, nos. 4–5: 487–95.

——. 2020a. "Fatwas and Democracy: Majelis Ulama Indonesia (MUI, Indonesian Ulema Council) and Rising Conservatism in Indonesian Islam". *TRaNS: Trans-Regional and-National Studies of Southeast Asia* 8, no. 1: 21–35.

——. 2020b. "MUI and its Discursive Relevance for 'Aksi Bela Islam': A Growing Trend of Islamic Conservatism in Indonesia". In *Rising Islamic Conservatism in Indonesia*, pp. 116–32. London; New York: Routledge.

——. 2021. "Halal Issues, Ijtihād, and Fatwa-making in Indonesia and Malaysia". In *Rethinking Halal: Genealogy, Current Trends, and New Interpretations*, pp. 80–107. Brill.

——. 2022. "The Politics of 'Halal': From Cultural to Structural Shariatisation in Indonesia". *Australian Journal of Asian Law* 22, no. 1: 81–97.

Hefner, Robert W. 2000. *Civil Islam: Muslims and Democratization in Indonesia*. Princeton: Princeton University Press.

———. 2003. "Civic Pluralism Denied? The New Media and Jihadi Violence in Indonesia". In *New Media in the Muslim World: The Emerging Public Sphere*, edited by Dale F. Eickelman and Jon W. Anderson, pp. 158–79. Bloomington: Indiana University Press.

———. 2019. "Whatever Happened to Civil Islam? Islam and Democratisation in Indonesia, 20 Years On". *Asian Studies Review* 43, no. 3: 375–96.

Hidayat, Komaruddin and Dadi Darmadi. 2019. "Indonesia and Two Great Narratives on Islamic Studies". *Studia Islamika* 26, no. 1: 201–5.

Hoesterey, James Bourk. 2015. *Rebranding Islam: Piety, Prosperity, and a Self-help Guru*. Palo Alto: Stanford University Press.

———. 2018. "Public Diplomacy and the Global Dissemination of 'Moderate Islam'". In *Routledge Handbook of Contemporary Indonesia*, edited by Robert Hefner, pp. 406–16. Abingdon and New York: Routledge.

Howell, Julia Day. 2008. "Modulations of Active Piety: Professors and Televangelists as Promoters of Indonesian Sufism". In *Expressing Islam: Religious Life and Politics in Indonesia*, edited by Greg Fealy and Sally White, pp. 40–62. Singapore: ISEAS – Yusof Ishak Institute.

Husein, Fatimah. 2004. *Muslim-Christian Relations in the New Order Indonesia: The Exclusivist and Inclusivist Muslims' Perspectives*. Jakarta: PT Mizan Publika.

Ichwan, Moch Nur. 2013. "Towards a Puritanical Moderate Islam: The Majelis Ulama Indonesia and the Politics of Religious Orthodoxy". In *Contemporary Developments in Indonesian Islam: Explaining the 'Conservative Turn'*, edited by Martin van Bruinessen, pp. 60–104. Singapore: ISEAS – Yusof Ishak Institute.

Kailani, Najib and Martin Slama. 2019. "Accelerating Islamic Charities in Indonesia: *Zakat, Sedekah* and the Immediacy of Social Media". *South East Asia Research* 28, no. 1: 70–86.

Liddle, R. William. 1996. "The Islamic Turn in Indonesia: A Political Explanation". *The Journal of Asian Studies* 55, no. 3: 613–34.

Lim, Merlyna. 2017. "Freedom to Hate: Social Media, Algorithmic Enclaves, and the Rise of Tribal Nationalism in Indonesia". *Critical Asian Studies* 49, no. 3: 411–27.

Meuleman, Johan. 2011. "*Dakwah*, Competition for Authority, and Development". *Bijdragen tot de taal-, land-en volkenkunde/Journal of the Humanities and Social Sciences of Southeast Asia* 167, nos. 2–3: 236–69.

Mujiburrahman. 1999. "Islam and Politics in Indonesia: The Political Thought of Abdurrahman Wahid". *Islam and Christian-Muslim Relations* 10, no. 3: 339–52.

———. 2006. *Feeling Threatened: Muslim-Christian Relations in Indonesia's New Order*. Leiden: Amsterdam University Press.

———. 2013. "The Politics of Shariah: The Struggle of the KPPSI in South Sulawesi". In *Contemporary Developments in Indonesian Islam: Explaining the 'Conservative Turn'*, edited by Martin van Bruinessen, pp. 145–89. Singapore: ISEAS – Yusof Ishak Institute.

Munhanif, Ahmad. 1996. "Islam and the Struggle for Religious Pluralism in Indonesia: A Political Reading of the Religious Thought of Mukti Ali". *Studia Islamika* 3, no. 1: 79–126.

Nurdin, Ahmad Ali. 2005. "Islam and State: A Study of the Liberal Islamic Network in Indonesia, 1999–2004". *New Zealand Journal of Asian Studies* 7, no. 2: 20–39.

Pringle, Robert. 2010. *Understanding Islam in Indonesia: Politics and Diversity*. Honolulu: University of Hawaii Press.

Ramage, Douglas. 1996. "Democratization, Religious Tolerance and Pancasila: The Political Thought of Abdurrahman Wahid". In *Nahdlatul Ulama, Traditional Islam and Modernity in Indonesia*, edited by Greg Barton and Greg Fealy. Clayton: Monash Asia Institute.

Ricklefs, Merle C. 2001. *A History of Modern Indonesia since c. 1200*. London: Macmillan International Higher Education.

Roy, Olivier. 1994. *The Failure of Political Islam*. Cambridge: Harvard University Press.

Rudnyckyj, Daromir. 2011. *Spiritual Economies: Islam, Globalization, and the Afterlife of Development*. Ithaca: Cornell University Press.

Saeed, Abdullah. 1999. "Towards Religious Tolerance through Reform in Islamic Education: The Case of the State Institute of Islamic Studies of Indonesia". *Indonesia and the Malay World* 27, no. 79: 177–91.

Sakai, Minako. 2012. "Preaching to Muslim Youth in Indonesia: The 'Dakwah' Activities of Habiburrahman El Shirazy". *RIMA: Review of Indonesian and Malaysian Affairs* 46, no. 1: 9–31.

Sakai, Minako and Amelia Fauzia. 2014. "Islamic Orientations in Contemporary Indonesia: Islamism on the Rise?" *Asian Ethnicity* 15, no. 1: 41–61.

Sakai, Minako and M. Falikul Isbah. 2014. "Limits to Religious Diversity Practice in Indonesia: Case Studies from Religious Philanthropic Institutions and Traditional Islamic Schools". *Asian Journal of Social Science* 42, no. 6: 722–46.

Sebastian, Leonard, Syafiq Hasyim, and Alexander Arifianto, eds. 2020. *Rising Islamic Conservatism in Indonesia: Islamic Groups and Identity Politics*. London; New York: Routledge.

Suryadinata, Leo. 1978. "Indonesian Nationalism and the Pre-war Youth Movement: A Reexamination". *Journal of Southeast Asian Studies* 9, no. 1: 99–114.

Tapsell, Ross. 2015. "Indonesia's Media Oligarchy and the 'Jokowi Phenomenon'". *Indonesia* 99: 29–50.

———. 2017. *Media Power in Indonesia: Oligarchs, Citizens and the Digital Revolution*. Lanham: Rowman & Littlefield.

Tyson, Adam and Budi Purnomo. 2017. "President Jokowi and the 2014 Obor Rakyat Controversy in Indonesia". *Critical Asian Studies* 49, no. 1: 117–36.

van Bruinessen, Martin. 2009. "Modernism and Anti-Modernism in Indonesian Muslim Responses to Globalisation". Paper presented at the Workshop "Islam and Development in Southeast Asia: Southeast Asian Muslim Responses to Globalization", organized by JICA (Japan International Cooperation Agency) Research Institute, Singapore, 21–22 November 2009.

———, ed. 2013. *Contemporary Developments in Indonesian Islam: Explaining the "Conservative Turn"*. Singapore: ISEAS – Yusof Ishak Institute.

Wasisto Raharjo Jati. 2022. "Nahdlatul Ulama's Traditionalist Campaign Shaping Mainstream Indonesian Islamic Discourse". *Fulcrum*, 25 April 2022. https://fulcrum.sg/nahdlatul-ulamas-traditionalist-campaign-shaping-mainstream-indonesian-islamic-discourse/ (accessed 5 July 2022).

Watson, C.W. 2005. "A Popular Indonesian Preacher: The Significance of Aa Gymnastiar". *Journal of the Royal Anthropological Institute* 11, no. 4: 773–92.

Wilson, Ian Douglas. 2008. "'As Long as it's Halal': Islamic Preman in Jakarta". In *Political, Social and Legal Expressions of Islam*, edited by Greg Fealy and Sally White, pp. 192–210. Singapore: ISEAS – Yusof Ishak Institute.

3

THE SALAFI-JIHADI IDENTITY AND MALAYSIA'S BATTLE WITH ISLAMIST EXTREMISM

Ahmad Fauzi Abdul Hamid

Introduction

The puritan form of Islamic ideology, salafi-jihadism, sanctions the use of violence to accomplish its objective of erecting an Islamic state that enforces the ideals of Salafism, which calls for a return to the Prophet's puritanical teachings as exemplified in his *hadith* (oral and practical traditions), *sunna* (trodden path), and the lives of his companions and *al-salaf al-salih* (pious predecessors), i.e. early generations of Muslims who survived Muhammad (peace be upon him) until three-hundred years of his death. Underlying the violence approved by terrorist network Al-Qaeda's jihadist ideology was its indiscriminate call to kill both civilian and military enemies anywhere in the world, thus catapulting armed jihad to the global stage (Amin 2014, pp. 118–19). Salafi-jihadism became the driving doctrine behind the active recruitment of jihadist fighters into Al-Qaeda franchises all over the world and large-scale movements of transnational *jihadist* funds (Hegghammer 2009, pp. 251–57, Zulkarnain and Nordin 2013, pp. 22–25).

The rise since mid-2014 of the Islamic State of Iraq and Syria (ISIS), a terrorist group otherwise known as the Islamic State of Iraq and the Levant (ISIL), the Islamic State (IS) or Daesh (after its Arabic acronym), at one point seemed to have eclipsed other manifestations of global Islamist violence. ISIS's notoriety was attributable to, among other things, its spectacular brutality, territorial gains, and apocalyptic ideology. ISIS intentionally employed violence as a political weapon and showcased grisly online images to cow populations under its control and convince the large viewing public of its invincibility. What many did not realize was that ISIS tapped into sentiments that had been fostered by extremist policies of many Muslim governments and leaders themselves as an outgrowth of decades of authoritarian rule following post-colonial upheavals in many Muslim societies. The lack of a civic culture and human rights regime in Muslim polities is legitimized by the identification of such forms of governance with secular, liberal, and hence ungodly values, driven as it is by a bipolar view of the world pitting the *umma* against belligerent forces. In ISIS, Muslims were lulled into believing that a promised utopia was in the offing, underlined by its territorial control and imposition of a political order ostensibly based on Islam, and fuelled by eschatological convictions founded upon a misreading of Prophetic traditions dealing with events near the end of time.

ISIS's violent ideology drew support from a handful of Muslims in Southeast Asia. Some were sympathetic to its cause; others were willing to leave behind their families and fight alongside ISIS militants in the Middle East. By contrast, this chapter argues that violent ideology has had minimal penetration in Malaysia, although Salafism as an ideology has taken root in the country and is trending. Given this context, this chapter proposes some educational antidotes to the menace of violent Islamist extremism.

A Peculiar Salafi-Jihadi Identity: ISIS's Appropriation of Violent Extremism

The storming of ISIS into positions of power in swathes of territory in Iraq and Syria took place within an overall post-Arab Spring political milieu that witnessed increasing politicization of Salafi-based groups and individuals throughout the Arab world (Al-Anani and Maszlee 2013; Hassan 2016, p. 6). Hitherto associated with political quietism that abhorred rebellion against authority, Salafists in countries such as Egypt, Libya, and Tunisia gained unprecedented attention in the jostling for influence among the masses following the downfalls of their countries' dictatorial regimes.[1]

ISIS's strategy was premised on a deliberate provocation of warlike conditions, arising from which were rampant chaos, misery, and helplessness that they were prepared to exploit. Sectarian hatred was raised to extreme levels, with displaced Sunni Arabs becoming as much victims of atrocities committed by Iran-backed Shi'ite militias, as they later turned vengeful aggressors in ISIS-sponsored killing sprees (International Crisis Group 2016, pp. 9–11).[2]

On the one hand, pin-pointing Salafism as the single explanatory cause for ISIS's extraordinary gravitation towards violent extremism can be unduly reductionist. ISIS deliberately employs gratuitous violence and sensationalizes it to instil fear, anger, and hopelessness among populations under its control worldwide. Emotional trauma is intentionally inflicted on the large viewing public to convey impressions of ISIS's invincibility and supposed destiny as the group that would usher in Muslims' ultimate victory in the *Al-Malhamah al-Kubra*—the Great War between good and evil, or the Battle of Armageddon in Islamic eschatology.[3]

Without discounting other motivating factors, the appeal to the end of times narrative plays no less an important role in attracting large numbers of Muslim youth from as far as Europe, Southeast Asia, and Australia to embark on a lifetime journey of *hijrah* (emigration) to ISIS-administered regions in the Middle East (Johnston et al. 2016, p. xxii; Chalk 2015; Sholeh 2016, pp. 101–2). Nevertheless, with new instructions in 2016 from the ISIS leadership to prospective jihadists that they need not emigrate should prohibitive circumstances arise (MEMRI 2015), there has been rising concern that the gory violence ISIS is infamous for will be exported to the fighters' home countries through not only the "blowback effect" of returning fighters, but also lone wolves whose only source of radicalization might be social media (Vidino 2014).[4]

On the other hand, violence as a corollary of the *takfiri* culture has been a bane in the history of Salafism as a whole and its Wahhabi version in particular.[5] Such leading scholars of the Saudi religious establishment as Aadel al-Kalbani, former imam of the Grand Mosque in Mecca, and Hatim al-'Awni of Umm al-Qura University, also in Mecca, have admitted the troubling fact that ISIS draws upon a strict reading of Wahhabi-Salafi texts to justify violence perpetrated in the name of Islam (MEMRI 2014; al-Hashemi 2014). What has effectively taken place in the *umma* over the past forty years or so is the Wahhabi co-optation of Salafism, marshalled by such Saudi-connected scholars as Nasiruddin al-Albani (1914–99), Abd al-Aziz ibn Baz (1910–99), Muhammad ibn Salih al-Uthaymeen (1925–2001), Saleh al-Fawzan (b. 1933), Safar al-Hawali (b. 1950), and Salman al-'Awda (b. 1956) (Olidort 2015, pp. 12–13; Brown 2015, pp. 139–42). The earlier *salafiyyah* trend associated with the Al-Manar modernist school of Jamaluddin Al-Afghani (1838–97), Muhammad Abduh (1849–1905), and Rashid Rida (1865–1935) has largely been shunned by contemporary Salafis for being too rationalist in orientation (Wiktorowicz 2006, p. 212). Saudi Arabia's petrodollar-powered dissemination of Wahhabi thought under the guise of Salafism has proceeded with evangelical fervour since the 1970s.

Since the 1980s, Salafism has become by far the most dominant Islamist trend worldwide. The term "Salafi" as now *ummatically* employed refers almost exclusively to the Wahhabi-Salafi trend (El Fadl 2005, pp. 86–87). Under the guise of *ummatic* unity, such Saudi institutions as the Rabitat al-'Alam al-Islami (Muslim World League, MWL), the World Assembly of Muslim Youth (WAMY), and the Islamic University of Madinah have served as conduits to export Wahhabi dogma worldwide. In the process, Wahhabi-Salafi influence has permeated Muslim state institutions, ruling parties, charity associations, non-governmental organizations (NGOs), Islamist movements, and educational networks (Algar 2002, pp. 47–53; Dorsey 2016). According to a commissioned study of five countries viz. Egypt, Tunisia, Bosnia, Pakistan, and Indonesia by a European Parliament Committee on Foreign Affairs, Wahhabi-Salafi financial aid, whether via institutional or private networks, "systematically pursue a goal of political influence" (Directorate-General for External Policies, Policy Department 2013, p. 1).

Global ISIS Threat

In ISIS's scheme, such horrid feats as bloody military conquest, enslavement of the vanquished, legalized rapes of non-conformist women, and decimation of heretics such as the Yazidis and recalcitrant Shi'ite and Sunni populations alike are no longer tolerated as collateral damage but rather rejoiced over as signs of triumph. They find religious justifications for their savagery in disputed Prophetic traditions and storytelling of gruesome battlefield encounters between companions of the Prophet and enemies of Islam, especially renegade Muslims such as during the Apostasy Wars launched by Caliph Abu Bakr (573–634) against rebellious tribes (Hassan 2016, pp. 17–19). For example, quoting Ibn Tayimiyyah and claiming justification from the precedence established by Caliph Abu Bakr, which El Fadl (2005, p. 54) however contends to be apocryphal, ISIS practises the burning alive of prisoners of war, beginning with that of the Jordanian pilot Muath al-Kasasbeh in January 2015 (Shoebat 2015; Miqal 2015). The cruel method of execution did not stop despite setbacks that ISIS had to endure on its battlefronts.[6]

Yet, it was reported that Qatar, another state with Wahhabi leaning—though not as conservative as Saudi Arabia with whom it has broken ranks since June 2017 over allegations of supporting terrorist groups (Economist 2016; Dorsey 2017)—had issued an official *fatwa* in 2006 permitting the burning alive of apostates, only to take it down from its *Islam Web* website once news of Muath al-Kasasbeh's murder went viral online. What is striking is also the fact that the Qatar *fatwa* and ISIS conveniently chose to dismiss the Prophet's caution: "No one punishes with fire except the Lord of fire", as a mere sign of humility rather than expressing prohibition (Ibrahim 2015). Large-scale slavery and multiple rapes of unbelieving female "slaves"—the other crimes against humanity that ISIS was notorious for—also drew sanction from past edicts issued by the Wahhabi-Salafi religious establishment not necessarily drawn to ISIS's type of violence (Report of the Independent International Commission of Inquiry on the Syrian Arab Republic 2014, pp. 8–10; Callimachi 2015). An example is Saleh al-Fawzan's infamous advocacy of slavery as "part of Islam" and "part of jihad", pronouncing those Muslims who outlaw slavery as "ignorant" and "infidel" (Al-Ahmed 2003). Al-Fawzan was a principal author of Saudi Arabia's educational curriculum which ISIS later adopted, albeit temporarily.

In its appropriation of violence as a political weapon, ISIS has gone further than Al-Qaeda in its application of *takfirism* within *takfirism*, whereby even mainstream Wahhabi-Salafists such as the ones aligned to the Saudi state are selectively singled out as apostates (Hassan 2016, pp. 10, 14). To ISIS, violence is to be managed to derive maximum political capital, which includes striking fear in the hearts of its opponents. Two authors had endeavoured to offer justifications for ISIS's uncompromising brutality against especially renegade Muslims, viz. Abu Abdullah al-Muhajir and Abu Bakr Naji, who wrote treatises entitled *Questions About the Jurisprudence of Jihad*[7] (also known as *The Jurisprudence of Blood*) and *The Management of Savagery*[8] respectively (Hassan 2016, p. 17; Manne 2016). In contrast with Al-Qaeda who had concentrated on war against the "far enemy", ISIS shifted the focus of its belligerence to the "near enemy", meaning apostate Muslim regimes, Shi'ites, allegedly deviant sects such as the Sufis and Yazidis, rival jihadists, and fellow Muslims complicit with the aforementioned groups. This is based on the doctrine, inherited from Al-Qaeda's Abdullah Azzam (1941–89) and Egyptian Al-Jihad radical theoretician Muhammad Abd al-Salam Faraj (1954–82), that Islam's worst enemies are those within the fold (McGregor 2003, pp. 96–98; Byman and Williams 2015; Hassan 2016, p. 9). ISIS's visceral abomination of the Shi'ites ran directly to Ibn Taimiyya's warning: "The origin of all sedition and calamity is Shia and their allies, and many of the swords unleashed against Islam come from them" (quoted in Hassan 2016, p. 15).[9]

Ambivalence Between Moderate and Extremist Islamist Identities in Malaysia[10]

Large-scale violence as perpetrated by Al-Qaeda and ISIS quintessentially represents a retreat of the moderation agenda in contemporary Islam as couched in the Arabic term *wasatiyyah*, derived from the word *wasat* or a state of being intermediate or in the middle. *Wasatiyyah* connotes the idea of moderation, without lapsing into negligence (Arabic: *tafrit*) or transgressing beyond acceptable borders into excess (Arabic: *ifrat*). Both negligence and excess are manifestations of extremities at one or the other end. The contemporary phenomenon of Muslim extremism is traced to exaggeration (Arabic: *ghuluw*) in doctrinal understanding and religious practices that essentialize Islam in such a manner that its institutions and categories lose their attribute of being just (Arabic: *'adl*). To be moderate is therefore also to be fair or just. As God proclaims in the Qur'an (2: 143): "Thus have We made of you an *umma* justly balanced (Arabic: *ummatan wasatan*), that ye might be witnesses over the nations ...." (Yusuf Ali n.d., p. 57). Failure to adhere to *wasatiyyah* would lead to the malaise of fanaticism (Arabic: *taasub*), which breeds bigotry, intolerance, and ultimately violence. As Bangladeshi rural development activist Mamoon al-Rasheed (2001, p. 61) reminds us, "Injustice is the spawning ground of violence." In the propagation, practice and dispensation of peace and justice regardless of race, colour and creed, Muslims have arguably the best example in the life of Prophet Muhammad (peace be upon him) (Ahmad Fauzi and Shaik Abdullah 2009–10, pp. 154–71). His Medina Charter conferred political, cultural, and religious rights on non-Muslims, proclaiming them to be de facto members of the *umma* within the context of one nation (Arabic: *umma wahidah*) despite their different religious beliefs (Morrison 2001, pp. 2–3; Considine 2016).

Implementation of the ideals of peaceful coexistence between peoples of diverse religions has been hailed as one of the most glittering achievements of Islamic civilization, as exemplified by the *convivencia* of medieval Spain—a concept which has been integral to the Islamic-oriented pluralist worldview of reformist Muslim democrats such as Anwar Ibrahim, Malaysia's iconic Islamist who rose to become Deputy Prime Minister (1994–98) and tenth Prime Minister since 24 November 2022 (Allers 2013, pp. 106, 200, 234).[11] In peaceful times, classical Muslim rulers meted out justice to non-Muslim minorities as a matter of principle, fully acknowledging the Qur'anic vision of a pluralist world (Filali-Ansary 2009). They even not unusually accorded their non-Muslim subjects better treatment over Muslim dissidents (Al-Azmeh 2009, pp. 11–12). Generally, wherever and whenever Muslim leaders were pluralistic enough to adopt "a flexible and differentiated approach in matters of governance, culture and society", dominions under their rule thrived (Hefner 2005, p. 23). The pluralistic nature of Islam is testified by its historic tolerance and even encouragement of multiple interpretations of its many religious texts and scriptural sources which trace their origins to the Qur'an and the *sunna*, both of which are believed by Muslims to be of divine quality. Since the Prophet's demise, the Islamic intellectual tradition has seen the emergence and passing of various schools of thought in different branches of religious knowledge such as *tawhid* (oneness of God or monotheism), *fiqh* (jurisprudence), *tasawwuf* (spirituality or Sufism), *tafsir* (Quranic exegesis) and *hadith*.[12]

Moderation and pluralism go hand in hand, yet many Muslim-majority countries have failed to internalize values and ideals based on justice, inadvertently lending credence to Lewis' (1990, p. 56) claim that "Islam was never prepared, either in theory or in practice, to accord full equality to those who held other beliefs and practice other forms of worship." Injustice, both inter-religious and intra-religious, is prevalent in many Muslim societies, despite the rhetoric spewed by their political establishments. According to ElKaleh and Samier (2013, pp. 190–91), one of the reasons for the yawning gap that exists between Islamic beliefs and work practices is the influence of Ibn Taymiyyah's writings on Islamic leadership. The Salafi influence gained momentum worldwide through the popularity in Islamist circles of the Muslim Brotherhood (MB), which, notwithstanding its founder Hassan al-Banna's (1906–49) Sufi roots, underwent a process of Salafization when many of its leaders and scholars adopted Saudi Arabia as their safe haven in the wake of regime-orchestrated repression in Egypt. The radical doctrines of Sayyid Qutb and Maududi came to dominate MB thinking as a result of Al-Banna's failure to instil credible scholarly foundations among his followers, in addition to his premature assassination (Lynch 2010, pp. 469–70, 473; Al-Azhari 2014). It was Qutb-cum-Maududi's *tawhidic* formulations within the context of the obligation to fight for a syariah-based Islamic state that dominated *usra*[13] sessions—frequently more powerful in impact than classroom-based religious lessons—in schools, colleges, and universities throughout the *umma* from the 1970s to 1990s. With regard to formal education, Saudi largesse influenced many governments to reorient their religious curriculum away from orthodox Sunni theology of the Ashaarite-Maturidite traditions[14] towards a Salafi-centric theology derived from the teachings of Ibn Taymiyyah.

This was the case for instance with the International Islamic University of Malaysia (IIUM), on whose governing board sits the Saudi ambassador in Malaysia as a permanent member and whose rectorship in 1988–99 was held by Saudi citizen-cum-MB activist Dr Abdul Hameed Abu Sulayman (1936–2021) (Asmady 2015, pp. 195–99). The founding of IIUM in 1983 as a model university for the Muslim world was the intellectual legacy of Maududi and Ismail Raji Al-Faruqi (1921–86) (Moten 2006, pp. 190–91). Al-Faruqi in 1981 had established the USA-based International Institute of Islamic Thought (IIIT), of which IIUM's Abdul Hameed Abu Sulayman also served as President, out of a US$25 million grant from the Saudi-based Islamic Development Bank (IDB) (Tasnim et al. 2015, p. 239). Al-Faruqi was a cardinal protagonist of Wahhabi-Salafi thought, as shown by his enthusiasm in translating three of Muhammad ibn Abd al-Wahhab's treatises and his exclusion of Sufism from his Islamization of knowledge scheme (Algar 2002, pp. 14–15, 50–52; Rosnani and Imron 2000, pp. 35–36). Al-Faruqi exerted enormous influence on both Anwar Ibrahim and Dr Mahathir Mohamad, under whose first premiership (1981–2003) Malaysia's Islamization agenda proceeded apace (Allers 2013, p. 72; Schottmann 2013, p. 61).

IIUM has played a pivotal role in churning out new cohorts of syariah-based lawyers, consultants, economists, judges and religious functionaries intent on Islamizing (read: Salafizing) Malaysia's legal, political, social, economic, and cultural landscape. Recent research on the teaching of comparative religion at IIUM reveals its unidirectional orientation that inevitably essentializes the religious "Other", with emphasis more on reinforcing conviction in the moral inferiority of non-Muslim religious traditions than appreciatively exploring them, aggravated by the uncritical pedagogy employed by course instructors (Kenney 2015, pp. 282–85). In Malaysia, Salafi-centric theology penetrates deep into the heart of the once moderate Malaysian Islam, supplanting orthodox Sunni theology as taught in state-funded religious education right from primary until university level, not restricted to only IIUM (Syed Hadzrullathfi and Muhammad Rashidi 2012, p. 58).

The impact of Salafization has been deadly to the type of tolerant Islamic discourse that once distinguished Malaysia from other versions of Islam that we encounter in the Middle East, Africa, and South Asia (Ahmad Fauzi 2016). The tenor of both inter-religious and intra-Islamic relations have been marred as a result of policy-making with respect to Islam becoming hardened in sync with the increasing penetration of the ever-expanding Islamic bureaucracy by religious officials who have been effectively Salafized, perhaps without their even realizing it. A more extreme face of Malaysian Islam seems to be asserting itself as indicated by the release of recent statistics compiled by the USA-based Pew Research Centre. For example, a relatively high 11 per cent of Malaysian Muslims surveyed in 2015 expressed a favourable view of ISIS (Poushter 2015). A 2013 sample puts Malaysian Muslim support for suicide bombing as justifiable at a surprisingly 18 per cent high, and while only 8 per cent express worry about Muslim extremist groups, a staggering 31 per cent worry more about Christian extremists (Pew Research Center 2013). Such disturbing trends have prompted concerned academics such as Shad Saleem Faruqi, Emeritus Professor of Law at the MARA Technology Institute University (Universiti Teknologi MARA, UiTM), to bemoan Malaysia's apparent decline from "an admirable rainbow-hued nation…going down the path of Ziaul Haque's Pakistan",[15] and Nader Hashemi, Director of the Centre for Middle East Studies at the University of Denver in the United States, to lament Malaysia's failure to live up to its potential as the *umma*'s "beacon of hope" in countering radical and extremist Islam (Sheith Khidhir 2016).

For all the voices of apprehension about extremism, in terms of actual physical violence, terrorist incidents in Malaysia are very rare. The only successful ISIS-related attack on Malaysian soil was the grenade bombing of the Movida night-club in Puchong, Selangor, on 28 June 2016 by Imam Wahyudin Karjono, 22, and Jonius Ondie@Jahali, 25, purportedly acting under the instructions of Malaysian chief ISIS recruiter Muhammad Wanndy Mohamed Jedi in Syria (Dass and Singh 2022). The latest Global Terrorism Index estimates Malaysia's terrorism impact to be at a low 2.247 (country rank: 63), in contrast with its Southeast Asian neighbours: the Philippines' 6.79 (high, country rank: 16), Thailand's 5.723 (medium, country rank: 22), and Indonesia's 5.5 (medium, country rank: 24) (Institute for Economics and Peace 2022). This seemingly belies the startlingly high rates of extremism among the country's Malay-Muslims. It masks the uncomfortable fact that low numbers of violent extremism do not indicate an absence of non-violent extremist attitudes among the youth. In fact, Mohd Mizan (2017), for instance, revealed that ISIS ideology was penetrating schools, colleges and universities, leading to at least forty arrests until the time he submitted his commissioned report to the Ministry of Higher Education in 2016. Later, Thomas Koruth Samuel of the Southeast Asia Regional Centre for Counter-Terrorism (SEARCCT), Ministry of Foreign Affairs, disclosed that out of 2,116 undergraduates studying at five different public universities he surveyed, 21 per cent confessed to holding to the belief that terrorism was an effective tool in achieving an objective. Furthermore, 33 per cent were of the opinion that there was nothing wrong with embracing radical violent ideas so long as they did not engage in terrorism (Samuel 2018).

Analysts have drawn attention and offered tentative explanations to the apparent "low violence versus high extremism" discrepancy (cf. Chan 2018). Taking cues from deceptive statistics, those unfamiliar with the intricacies of Malaysian domestic politics may be tempted to offer frightening prognostications concerning possibilities of large-scale Islamist terrorist attacks in the country targeting among others non-Muslim figures and establishments and Muslim leaders regarded as accomplices of the secular state's *taghut* (false god) systems (Liow 2015). News that the government was allowing the return home of foreign terrorist fighters (FTFs) among its citizens abroad similarly raised jitters among Malaysians (Mohd Mizan 2021).

Alarm bells were especially sounded when then Special Branch Counter Terrorism Division chief Ayob Khan revealed that from 2013 until 2019, Malaysia's counter-terrorism squads managed to foil 25 attempted terror attacks in the country (Bernama 2019). Figures of Malaysians directly involved in ISIS have varied over time, from 137 detained until October 2016, as given by then Deputy Prime Minister Ahmad Zahid Hamidi (Kanyakumari 2016), to 240, as mentioned by Youth and Sports Minister Khairy Jamaluddin in November 2016 (Cheng 2016). According to Ayob Khan, at the turn of 2017, 264 militants were in jail for ISIS-related offences, with sixty remaining in Iraq and Syria. Numbers joining ISIS from Malaysia, however, have been rising, and part of the blame was to be found in religious authorities, private and public institutions of higher learning, NGOs, and government departments for continually patronizing preachers with clear Wahhabi-Salafi sympathies (Farik 2017; Muzliza 2017). Corroborating Ayob's claims were arrests of two students of the Malaysian branch of Al-Madinah International University (MEDIU)—duly identified as a Wahhabi-Salafi conduit—for suspected ISIS links (Farik 2016; Skuad Khas Harian Metro 2016). In January 2017, it was reported that Mercy Mission Malaysia, an Islamic-based relief NGO, would establish a university in the country by 2018 (Bernama 2017). Yet, a background check of its founder-cum-chairperson who made the announcement, Dr Tawfique Chowdhury, revealed that he has a record of giving lectures that pronounce non-Salafi Muslims as deviant, including those of the Ashaarite-Maturidite school to which the majority of Malaysian Muslims adhere.[16]

To top it all, Malaysia's deradicalization programme for ISIS-related detainees seeks to learn from Saudi Arabia's experience (Bernama

2016), which makes it almost certain that it will not extinguish the Wahhabi-Salafi roots from which Salafi-jihadist groups like ISIS sprouted. Yet, this is hardly surprising given that so many Islamist-minded Malay-Muslims have grown up admiring the father of Salafi-jihadism, Sayyid Qutb, his compatriot Maududi, and by default the progenitor of Wahhabism, Muhammad ibn Abd al-Wahhab, who influenced them both (Mohamad Fauzi 2007; Kamal Hassan 2003, pp. 430–40). ISIS's intellectual pedigree has been succinctly spelt out in a statement ascribed to the Yemeni journalist Abdulelah Haider Shaye: "The Islamic State was drafted by Sayyid Qutb, taught by Abdullah Azzam, globalized by Osama bin Laden, transferred to reality by Abu Musab al-Zarqawi, and implemented by al-Baghdadis: Abu Omar and Abu Bakr" (quoted in Manne 2016; Hassan 2016, p. 19).[17]

From Salafism to Salafi-Jihadism to Terrorism: A Slippery Slope?

In Malaysia, although Wahhabi-Salafism had made its presence felt since the tenures of Mahathir Mohamad and Abdullah Ahmad Badawi (2003–9) as Prime Minister, it was only during Najib Razak's premiership that a conscious attempt at state capture was made (Ahmad Fauzi and Che Hamdan 2015, pp. 312–21). In retrospect, perhaps Malaysia's decline could have been better anticipated. Unfortunately, when concerned stakeholders came to realize that Islamization was opening the pathway for radicalization, their positions in civil society were counterpoised by Salafi-centric figures, institutions, and discourses. That these Salafi elements do not themselves whip up support for ISIS is secondary to the very exclusionary nature of their message.

Malaysia's mainstreaming of Salafism, while not amounting to an approbation of Salafi-jihadism per se, nurtured an environment in which the same exclusivist religious precepts responsible for spawning militant groups were being gradually legitimized in all layers of Malay-Muslim society. Despite the existence of a national *fatwa* pronouncing Wahhabism as unsuitable for Malaysian society (Malay Mail Online 2015), then Deputy Minister in the Prime Minister's Department Asyraf Wajdi Dusuki (2016) defended Wahhabism in parliament as being part of mainstream Sunni Islam. In order to safeguard its bilateral relations with Saudi Arabia—from whom Malaysia gets generous pilgrimage quotas and other pecuniary benefits—an outright ban on Wahhabi-Salafism was out of the question (Asmady 2015, p. 187). Of all people, Prime Minister Najib Razak (2009–18) himself, whose cordial ties with Saudi Arabia had by then been the subject of global headlines (Coughlin 2016), commended the valour of ISIS fighters during a function of the ruling United Malays National Organisation (UMNO) party (Chi 2014). The Prime Minister's Office was quick to exonerate Najib as having been unfairly quoted out of context, mentioning his continuous advocacy of moderation and rejection of extremism as indicated by the Global Movement of Moderates he initiated in 2010 (Malay Mail Online 2014). As Malaysia continues to pay lip-service to *wasatiyyah* as the main plank in combating terrorism (El-Muhammady 2015), the whole country received shocking news between 2014 and 2016 of how the normally "gentle" Malay-Muslims joined ISIS and its affiliates, emerging as more than capable of committing suicide attacks and killing in the most gruesome manner (Tan 2014; El-Muhammady 2016; Utusan Malaysia 2016).

Malaysia's decreasing levels of religious tolerance is palpable from the many court cases that have pitted Muslims against non-Muslims, and state-inclined conservative Muslims against fellow unorthodox Muslims for more than a decade (2006–17), wrecking societal cohesiveness that has previously been a hallmark of Malaysia's plural society (Ahmad Fauzi and Muhamad Takiyuddin 2014). In contemporary Malaysia's Islamicized surroundings, the Wahhabi-Salafi doctrine of *al-wala' wa al-bara'* has been integrated with Malay ethnocentrism under the banner of *ketuanan Melayu* (Malay supremacy)—lately repackaged as "Islamic supremacy" (*Ketuanan Islam*) (Chin 2016)—to create in the Malay-Muslim psyche a siege mentality which thrives on insecurity and fears of especially non-Muslim economic prowess. Under such an environment, Islamism exhorts Muslims to undergo as separate lives as possible from those of non-Muslims, whose un-Islamic mores are shunned if not fought altogether as if in a state of perpetual war (El Fadl 2005, pp. 206–7, 224–49). On the ground, the debilitating impact of Islamism shows in the manifest decline of interfaith initiatives (Osman 2009, p. 69; Rahimin Affandi et al. 2011, pp. 95–97). The lukewarm response of Malay-Muslims towards calls for more social engagement with non-Muslims stems from a state-orchestrated discouragement of non-Muslims from participating in public discussion of Islam, further reinforcing the exclusionary character of the Islamization narrative (Hunt 2009, p. 588). Non-Muslims have also voiced their concern at the subtle Islamization of public education, as manifested for instance in curriculum changes that downplay the contributions of non-Muslims in nation-building (Barr and Govindasamy 2010).

In order to safeguard vested political and economic interests, Malaysia's ruling Muslim establishment has willingly allowed itself to be led into a Faustian pact with Wahhabi-Salafism in both the *ummatic* and domestic arenas. Malaysia's much-cherished multiculturalism and pluralism are gradually becoming inevitable victims of this unholy alliance, with non-Muslims and unorthodox Muslims being systematically marginalized in the emerging Islamist body politic. This phase of Islamization ostensibly still bases its agenda on Islam, when it is really Islamism or political Islam that is being upheld, in the same way that the ideals of purist Salafism have been overwhelmed by Wahhabi-driven political Islam, to which a little addition of jihadism paves the way towards ISIS-type extremism. Commenting on Malaysia's struggle in stemming Malay-Muslim youths' attraction to ISIS, Hunter (2016) rightly notes, "There needs to be a national vision for a virtuous society based upon *tawhidic* principles—the oneness of God—something inclusive for all." Such a theology could be developed along the lines of an anthropocentric framework of *tawhid* as proposed by the Indonesian scholar Sumanto Al Qurtuby (2013).

In Malaysia, unfortunately, such adventurous scholarly initiatives in Islamic studies are lacking, contributed no doubt by the Wahhabi-Salafi antipathy towards philosophy and rationalist theology. Malaysia's Islamic educational curriculum invariably places emphasis on Islam's legalistic and creed-related aspects, relegating its higher order thinking, spiritual, civilizational, and philosophical aspects to the periphery. Comparative religion hardly features in the syllabi, and where it is taught at all such as at IIUM, the way it is delivered seeks to justify Muslim cultural, social-economic, and political supremacy over non-Muslims (Kenney 2015; Ahmad Fauzi and Mohd Haris Zuan 2018, p. 42). As for students who do not specialize in Islamic studies, there has been an inordinate amount of attention given to the science, technology, engineering, and mathematics (STEM) content such as to ostensibly prepare them for high-paying jobs in the industrial labour market.

Such bias towards the applied sciences has alarmed educationists for not only neglecting civilizational aspects which contribute immensely to producing holistic graduates (Mohamed Ghouse and Azeem Fazwan 2017; Merican 2017), but perhaps more importantly lay open the door towards extremism taking hold of them in the event that they undergo religious awakening at some point in their lives. This is consistent with Gambetta and Hertog's (2016) findings that non-religious stream graduates make up a disproportionately large number of violent Islamist extremists throughout the years—a point which the media has picked up in interviews with experts (Sheith Khidhir 2017; Soo 2022).

Conclusion

The example of Malaysia above is not insignificant as a barometer of the *umma* as a whole. Long known as a bright spot amidst the generally sorry state of affairs in the Muslim world, Malaysia used to be admired for its uncharacteristic success in combining Islam with modernity, with its attendant economic and political development, within the context of a plural society. Barring hiccups such as some racialist aspects of its nation-building (Muhammad Haniff 2007), Malaysia was generally touted as an exemplary model of a rapidly developing Muslim-majority state (Siddiqi 1995, pp. 20–21, 24). Such claims are verified by statistical figures. In the Islamicity indices developed by Professors Hossein Askari and Scheherazade Rehman of George Washington University, for instance, Malaysia emerges top among Muslim-majority countries in internalizing Qur'anic values in spheres of real lives such as economic achievement, social progress, human rights, governance, and justice (Rehman and Askari 2010; McElroy 2014). If even in such a modern nation-state the youth now gravitate towards ISIS, one can imagine the situation in other less developed Muslim countries, where factors such as economic deprivation, family breakdowns, cultural vacuousness, and political despotism fuse to generate conditions ripe for radicalization. In reality, the bitter fact to swallow is that Muslim regimes and governments themselves bear a huge responsibility for the rise in militancy by appropriating Islamist symbols and programmes for selfish political purposes, thus opening up spaces and opportunities for the Salafization of communities, often accompanied by material benefits.

NOTES

1. For some Western observers, to dismiss the geopolitical significance of this newly found Salafi activism would have been unwise (Wright 2012; Caryl 2012). Bearing in mind the turmoil still engulfing the Middle East and North Africa, a scenario in which the Salafists gained access to power either absolutely or in collaboration with other political actors was not far-fetched. ISIS, after all, had capitalized on wide feelings of victimization among Sunnis in Iraq and Syria to boost its credibility and attract support.
2. Ever since Abu Musab al-Zarqawi's days, AQI and then ISIS's tactic was to radicalize the Sunnis with Salafi-jihadist aspirations once they had gravitated towards it. In ISIS's appropriation of violence, loyalists of Saddam Hussain's (1937–2006) regime, some trained in the art of brutality, initially played important roles but in due course saw their influence eclipsed by the clout of Salafi-jihadist extremists (Johnston et al. 2016, pp. 14, 30). It is safe to assume that former Saddam loyalists who went on to become right-hand men of Abu Bakr al-Baghdadi, for example Abu Muslim al-Turkmani (1959–2015) and Abu Ali al-Anbari aka Abd ar-Rahman Mustafa al-Qaduli (1957/59–2016) who oversaw ISIS's Iraqi and Syrian territories respectively on behalf of al-Baghdadi, had converted to the Salafi-jihadist cause, interest in which they might have harboured since their days in Saddam's administration and which simply hardened during incarceration in USA-operated detention centres such as Camp Bucca in southern Iraq (Lister 2014; Sherlock 2014; Thompson and Suri 2014).
3. A significant number of ISIS's accoutrements takes their cue from Islam's apocalyptic traditions, however skewed their interpretations might be to fit their narrative (Muhammad Haniff 2015). ISIS's official online journal, *Dabiq*, for instance, is named after a northern Syrian town which features in eschatological traditions as one of the battlefield sites. ISIS's black flag is supposed to represent the banner due to be waved by Islam's promised redeemer near the end of time, Imam al-Mahdi, who will lead Muslims into a series of doomsday battles against unbelievers (McCants 2015, 2016).
4. For many of these latter types of *jihadists*, recruitment into militant Islamism is attributable less to religion than to a host of social, cultural and psychological factors (Krisch 2015; Dearden 2016). The fact that young recruits join ISIS due to a melange of factors does not diminish the powerful sense of the "in-group versus out-group" type of mentality mentioned by Lewis (1990, p. 49), that can so easily boil down to fanaticism and eventually to violence (Graham 2015).
5. On the association between *takfir* ideology and violence, see the video "Takfiri Ideology: Warning Very Graphic Content", 31 May 2016, https://www.youtube.com/watch?v=RoisZpruRtU (accessed 13 January 2017).

6 See for example, "SHOCKING NEW VIDEO (see below) Released by the Islamic State (ISIS) Shows 4 Prisoners Chained Upside Down and then Savagely Burned to Death", *Bare Naked Islam*, 31 August 2015, http://www.barenakedislam.com/2015/08/31/shocking-new-video-released-by-the-islamic-state-isis-shows-4-prisoners-chained-upside-down-and-then-savagely-burned-to-death/ (accessed 15 December 2017); and "WATCH: ISIS Releases Video of Burning 2 Caged Turkish Soldiers to Death in English", *Heavy*, 1 January 2017, http://heavy.com/news/2017/01/isis-islamic-state-amaq-news-the-cross-of-the-shield-turkey-turkish-soldiers-burned-to-death-execution-wilayat-halab-aleppo-syria-english-translation-subtitles-video/ (accessed 13 January 2017).

7 Al-Muhajir's lectures which form the basis of the book are available online at https://archive.org/details/FIFTH-SERISE-PRESENTAION-OF-FIQH-EL-JIHAD (accessed 5 January 2023).

8 The version translated by Brookings scholar William McCants is available online at https://azelin.files.wordpress.com/2010/08/abu-bakr-naji-the-management-of-savagery-the-most-critical-stage-through-which-the-umma-will-pass.pdf (accessed 15 December 2017).

9 Coercion and fear are essential to ensure obedience of populations under ISIS's control, as bluntly conveyed to researcher Hassan Hassan in his interview with an ISIS official: 'If you think people will accept the Islamic project [voluntarily], you're wrong. They have to be forced at first. The other groups think they can convince people and win them over but they're wrong" (quoted in Hassan 2016, p. 7). But within one year of the proclamation of its caliphate in Mosul in June 2014, ISIS's blood-thirsty antics were too much even for Al-Qaeda to bear, so much so that its spokesmen such as American convert Adam Gadahn (1978–2015) began denouncing openly the nature and extent of ISIS's draconian punishments (Lee 2015). Although sharing the same Salafi-jihadi roots with Al-Qaeda, ISIS clearly opted for interpretations that maximize pain and suffering of its victims. As discussed for instance by Wagemakers (2016), regarding the two Quranic verses which appear to legalize beheading (Yusuf Ali n.d., pp. 472, 1560), ISIS's interpretation of "smiting enemies" necks' condones slaughtering, whereas Al-Qaeda understands it in the more "merciful" manner of separating the head from the body quickly with a single blow, avoiding torture. The rationale for the more gory choice lay in its allegedly greater effectiveness as a means to sow fear in the hearts of enemies, as supposedly enjoined by the verses in concern. Other atrocious methods of execution practised by ISIS were drowning, detonating explosives tied around the neck, close range shooting, crucifixion, stabbing right into the middle of the heart and throwing down from high buildings for those found guilty of homosexuality (Raqqa is Being Slaughtered Silently 2016).

10 "Malaysia" here refers to the nation state which came about as a result of the merger in 1963 between then Malaya i.e. the area which encompasses present-day Peninsular Malaysia, Sarawak and Sabah—both on Borneo island, and Singapore, who subsequently left the federation in 1965.
11 Sacked on 2 September 1998 by then Prime Minister Dr Mahathir Mohamad, Anwar was imprisoned from 1999 to 2004 on what were widely believed to be trumped-up charges of corruption and sodomy. Having had his conviction quashed by the Federal Court, Anwar was freed, upon which he set up to unite an opposition pact that managed to twice deny the ruling National Front coalition a two-thirds parliamentary majority in 2008 and 2013. In 2014, however, Anwar lost his appeal against another conviction for sodomy allegedly committed in 2008, after which he served his second jail term.
12 These fundamentals of religious knowledge, but especially *tawhid*, *fiqh* and *tasawwuf* are collectively recognized as *fard 'ain* (individual obligation) disciplines, meaning doctrinal and ritual obligations which must be acknowledged and practised by every adult male and female Muslim.
13 Literally meaning "family" in Arabic, *usra* refers to Muslim Brotherhood-inherited cell-like groups to discuss ways and means of acting on Islam as a way of life, often conducted outside of official working hours. For details, see Nabisah et al. (2015).
14 The schools of thought developed along the lines of theological principles formulated by the classical scholars Abu Hassan al-Ashaari (874–936) of Iraq and Abu Mansur al-Maturidi (853–944) of Samarkand.
15 Personal email to the present author, 25 July 2016.
16 See the video "History of Deviance ¦ Ash'ari - Maturudi - Deobandi - Shia - Shaikh Tawfique Chowdhury", 10 August 2016, https://www.youtube.com/watch?v=zjPW62gzVDw&list=PLgXaG9inyxm4EpttZZywJbKx1nqaa_bDR&index=75 (accessed 5 January 2023).
17 See https://abdulela.wordpress.com/2014/08/04/ for the original quote in Arabic, dated 4 August 2014 (accessed 5 January 2023).

REFERENCES

Ahmad Fauzi Abdul Hamid. 2016. *The Extensive Salafization of Malaysian Islam*. Trends in Southeast Asia, no. 9/2016. Singapore: ISEAS – Yusof Ishak Institute.

Ahmad Fauzi Abdul Hamid and Che Hamdan Che Mohd. Razali. 2015. "The Changing Face of Political Islam in Malaysia in the Era of Najib Razak, 2009–2013". *Sojourn: Journal of Social Issues in Southeast Asia* 30, no. 2: 301–37. https://doi.org/10.1355/SJ30-2A (accessed 5 January 2023).

Ahmad Fauzi Abdul Hamid and Mohd Haris Zuan Jaharudin. 2018. "Islamic Education in Malaysia: Between Neoliberalism and Political Priorities in Light of the Malaysia Education Blueprint 2013–2015". In *Policies and Politics in Malaysian Education: Education Reforms, Nationalism and Neoliberalism*, edited by Cynthia Joseph, pp. 31–53. London and New York: Routledge.

Ahmad Fauzi Abdul Hamid and Muhamad Takiyuddin Ismail. 2014. "Islamist Conservatism and the Demise of Islam Hadhari in Malaysia". *Islam and Christian-Muslim Relations* 25, no. 2: 159–80. https://doi.org/10.1080/09596410.2014.880549 (accessed 5 January 2023).

Ahmad Fauzi Abdul Hamid and Shaik Abdullah Hassan Mydin. 2009–10. "The Prophet (peace be on him) as a Model for Universal Peace and Justice". *Insights: Quarterly Focused on Faith Studies* 2, nos. 2–3: 153–78.

Al Qurtuby, Sumanto. 2013. "The Islamic Roots of Liberation, Justice, and Peace: An Anthropocentric Analysis of the Concept of Tawhid". *Islamic Studies* 53, nos. 3–4: 297-325.

Al-Ahmed, Ali. 2003. "Author of Saudi Curriculums Advocates Slavery". *Saudi Information Agency*, 7 November 2003. https://swap.stanford.edu/was/20090418061718/http://www.arabianews.org/english/article.cfm?qid=132&sid=2 (accessed 5 January 2023).

Al-Anani, Khalil and Maszlee Malik. 2013. "Pious Way to Politics: The Rise of Political Salafism in Post-Mubarak Egypt". *Digest of Middle East Studies* 22, no. 1: 57–73. https://doi.org/10.1111/dome.12012 (accessed 5 January 2023).

Al-Azhari, Syekh Usamah Sayyid. 2014. "Menelusuri Krisis Mesir dan Peran Teknologi" [Retracing the Egyptian Crisis and the Role of Technology]. *Muslimedianews.com*, 21 January 2014. http://www.muslimedianews.com/2014/01/syekh-usamah-sayyid-al-azhari.html (accessed 15 December 2017).

Al-Azmeh, Aziz. 2009. "Pluralism in Muslim Societies". In *Pluralism in Muslim Contexts*, edited by Abdou Filali-Ansary and Sikeena Karmali, pp. 9–15. Edinburgh: Edinburgh University Press.

Al-Hashemi, Hanan. 2014. "Wahhabism at the Heart of the Controversy". *Shafaqna*, 30 November 2014. https://en.shafaqna.com/13577/al-akhbar-com-wahhabism-at-the-heart-of-the-controversy/ (accessed 5 January 2023).

Al-Rasheed, Mamoon. 2001. "Islam, Nonviolence, and Social Transformation". In *Islam and Nonviolence*, edited by Glenn D. Paige, Chaiwat Satha-Anand (Qader Muheideen) and Sarah Gilliatt, pp. 59–108. Honolulu: Centre for Global Nonviolence.

Algar, Hamid. 2002. *Wahhabism: A Critical Essay*. New York: Islamic Publications International.

Allers, Charles. 2013. *The Evolution of a Muslim Democrat: The Life of Malaysia's Anwar Ibrahim*. New York: Peter Lang.

Amin, ElSayed M.A. 2014. *Reclaiming Jihad: A Qur'anic Critique of Terrorism*. Leicester: The Islamic Foundation.

Asmady Idris. 2015. *Malaysia's Relations with Saudi Arabia 1957–2003*. Kota Kinabalu: UMS Press.

Asyraf Wajdi Dusuki. 2016. "Wahabi Bukan Ajaran Sesat" [Wahhabism is Not a Deviant Teaching]. Facebook, 28 April 2016, https://www.facebook.com/drasyrafwajdidusuki/photos/a.148660531830669.27045.116331768396879/1313553488674695/?type=3&theater (accessed 5 January 2023).

Barr, Michael D. and Anantha Raman Govindasamy. 2010. "The Islamisation of Malaysia: Religious Nationalism in the Service of Ethnonationalism". *Australian Journal of International Affairs* 64, no. 3: 293–311. https://doi.org/10.1080/10357711003736469 (accessed 5 January 2023).

Bernama. 2016. "M'sia Aims to Help End Conflict in Syria". *The Star Online*, 17 October 2016. https://www.thestar.com.my/news/nation/2016/10/17/msia-aims-to-help-end-conflict-in-syria/ (accessed 5 January 2023).

———. 2017. "Mercy Mission to Set Up its Own University by 2018". *Malaysiakini*, 1 January 2017. https://www.malaysiakini.com/news/367817 (accessed 5 January 2023).

———. 2019. "PDRM Kekang 25 Cubaan Serangan Pengganas" [Royal Malaysian Police Foils 25 Attempted Terror Attacks]. *Berita Harian Online*, 2 October 2019. https://www.bharian.com.my/berita/kes/2019/10/613121/pdrm-kekang-25-cubaan-serangan-pengganas (accessed 5 January 2023).

Brown, Jonathan A.C. 2015. "Is Islam Easy to Understand or Not? Salafis, the Democratization of Interpretation and the Need for the Ulema". *Journal of Islamic Studies* 26, no. 2: 117–44. https://doi.org/10.1093/jis/etu081 (accessed 5 January 2023).

Byman, Daniel L. and Jennifer R. Williams. 2015. "ISIS vs. Al Qaeda: Jihadism's Global Civil War". *Brookings*, 24 February 2015. https://www.brookings.edu/articles/isis-vs-al-qaeda-jihadisms-global-civil-war/ (accessed 5 January 2023).

Callimachi, Rukmini. 2015. "ISIS Enshrines a Theology of Rape". *New York Times*, 13 August 2015. https://www.nytimes.com/2015/08/14/world/middleeast/isis-enshrines-a-theology-of-rape.html (accessed 5 January 2023).

Caryl, Christian. 2012. "The Salafi Moment". *Foreign Policy*, 12 September 2012. https://foreignpolicy.com/2012/09/12/the-salafi-moment/ (accessed 5 January 2023).

Chalk, Peter. 2015. *Black Flag Rising: ISIL in Southeast Asia and Australia*. Barton: ASPI.

Chan, Nicholas. 2018. "The Malaysian 'Islamic' State versus the Islamic State (IS): Evolving Definitions of 'Terror' in an 'Islamising' Nation-State". *Critical Studies on Terrorism* 11, no. 3: 415–37. https://doi.org/10.1080/17539153.2018.1447217 (accessed 5 January 2023).

Cheng, Nicholas. 2016. "Khairy: Youths Make Up 80% of Those Arrested for IS Involvement". *The Star Online*, 14 November 2016. https://www.thestar.com.my/news/nation/2016/11/14/parliament-youth-involvement-is/ (accessed 5 January 2023).

Chi, Melissa. 2014. "Be Brave Like ISIL Fighters, Najib Tells Umno". *Malay Mail Online*, 24 June 2014. https://www.malaymail.com/news/malaysia/2014/06/24/be-brave-like-isil-fighters-najib-tells-umno/693209 (accessed 5 January 2023).

Chin, James. 2016. "From *Ketuanan Melayu* to *Ketuanan Islam*: UMNO and the Malaysian Chinese". In *The End of UMNO? Essays on Malaysia's Dominant Party*, edited by Bridget Welsh, pp. 171–212. London: Routledge.

Considine, Craig. 2016. "Religious Pluralism and Civic Rights in a 'Muslim Nation': An Analysis of Prophet Muhammad's Covenants with Christians". *Religions* 7, no. 15: 1–21. https://doi.org/10.3390/rel7020015 (accessed 5 January 2023).

Coughlin, Con. 2016. "Saudi Arabia Funds Moderate Muslims, Not Isil". *The Telegraph*, 28 January 2016. https://www.telegraph.co.uk/news/worldnews/middleeast/saudiarabia/12127916/Saudi-Arabia-funds-moderate-Muslims-not-Isil.html (accessed 5 January 2023).

Dass, Rueben and Jasminder Singh. 2022. "Pathways to the Caliphate: Mapping Malaysian Foreign Fighter Networks in Iraq and Syria from 2012–2019". *Terrorism and Political Violence*: 1–34. https://doi.org/10.1080/09546553.2022.2059352 (accessed 5 January 2023).

Dearden, Lizzie. 2016. "Isis: Islam is 'Not Strongest Factor' Behind Foreign Fighters Joining Extremist Groups in Syria and Iraq – Report". *Independent*, 17 November 2016. https://www.independent.co.uk/news/world/europe/isis-foreign-fighters-british-european-western-dying-radicalised-islam-not-strongest-factor-cultural-online-propaganda-a7421711.html (accessed 5 January 2023).

Directorate-General for External Policies, Policy Department. 2013. *Salafist/Wahhabite Financial Support to Educational, Social and Religious Institutions*. Brussels: European Union.

Dorsey, James M. 2016. "Creating Frankenstein: The Saudi Export of Wahhabism – OpEd". *Eurasia Review*, 7 March 2016. https://www.eurasiareview.com/07032016-creating-frankenstein-the-saudi-export-of-wahhabism-oped/ (accessed 5 January 2023).

_____. 2017. "Qatari Wahhabism vs. Saudi Wahhabism and the Perils of Top-down Change". *Huffpost*, 4 December 2017. https://www.huffingtonpost.com/entry/qatari-wahhabism-vs-saudi-wahhabism-and-the-perils_us_5a257240e4b05072e8b56b29 (accessed 5 January 2023).

Economist. 2016. "The Other Wahhabi State". *The Economist*, 2 June 2016. https://www.economist.com/middle-east-and-africa/2016/06/02/the-other-wahhabi-state (accessed 5 January 2023).

El Fadl, Khaled Abou. 2005. *The Great Theft: Wrestling Islam from the Extremists*. New York: HarperOne.

El-Muhammady, Ahmad. 2015. "Applying Wasatiyah within Malaysian Religio-Political Context". *American Journal of Islamic Social Sciences* 32, no. 3: 134–40.

———. 2016. "Countering the Threats of Daesh in Malaysia". In *Countering Daesh Extremism: European and Asian Responses*, edited by Beatrice Gorawantschy, Rohan Gunaratna, Megha Sarmah, and Patrick Rueppel, pp. 105–22. Singapore: Konrad-Adenauer-Stiftung and RSIS.

ElKaleh, Eman and Eugenie A. Samier. 2013. "The Ethics of Islamic Leadership: A Cross-Cultural Approach for Public Administration". *Administrative Culture* 42, no. 2: 188–211.

Farik Zolkepli. 2016. "Foreign Students Among Seven IS Militants Nabbed". *The Star Online*, 20 December 2016. https://www.thestar.com.my/news/nation/2016/12/20/foreign-students-among-seven-is-militants-nabbed/ (accessed 5 January 2023).

———. 2017. "Still Many Joining IS". *The Star Online*, 1 January 2017. https://www.thestar.com.my/news/nation/2017/01/01/still-many-joining-is-the-threat-of-terror-group-islamic-state-must-never-be-underestimated-down-pla/ (accessed 5 January 2023).

Filali-Ansary, Abdou. 2009. "Introduction: Theoretical Approaches to Cultural Diversity". In *Pluralism in Muslim Contexts*, edited by Abdou Filali-Ansary and Sikeena Karmali, pp. 1–6. Edinburgh: Edinburgh University Press.

Gambetta, Diego and Steffen Hertog. 2016. *Engineers of Jihad: The Curious Connection between Violent Extremism and Education*. Princeton and Oxford: Princeton University Press.

Graham, John. 2015. "Who Joins ISIS and Why?" *Huffpost*, 29 December 2015. https://www.huffpost.com/entry/who-joins-isis-and-why_b_8881810 (accessed 5 January 2023).

Hassan, Hassan. 2016. *The Sectarianism of the Islamic State: Ideological Roots and Political Context*. Washington, D.C.: Carnegie Endowment for International Peace. https://carnegieendowment.org/2016/06/13/sectarianism-of-islamic-state-ideological-roots-and-political-context-pub-63746 (accessed 5 January 2023).

Hefner, Robert W. 2005. "Introduction: Modernity and the Remaking of Muslim Politics". In *Remaking Muslim Politics: Pluralism, Contestation, Democratization*, edited by Robert W. Hefner, pp. 1–36. New Jersey: Princeton University Press.

Hegghammer, Thomas. 2009. "Jihadi-Salafis or Revolutionaries? On Religion and Politics in the Study of Militant Islamism". In *Global Salafism: Islam's New Religious Movement*, edited by Roel Meijer. pp. 244–66. London: Hurst.

Hunt, Robert. 2009. "Can Muslims Engage in Interreligious Dialogue: A Study of Malay Muslim Identity in Contemporary Malaysia". *The Muslim*

World 99, no. 4: 581–607. https://doi.org/10.1111/j.1478-1913.2009.01289.x (accessed 5 January 2023).

Hunter, Murray. 2016. "Islamic State's Appeal in Malaysia". *Asia Sentinel*, 22 January 2016. https://www.asiasentinel.com/society/islamic-state-appeal-malaysia/ (accessed 5 January 2023).

Ibrahim, Raymond. 2015. "Qatar Published Fatwa In 2006 Permitting Burning People — Removes It After ISIS Burns Pilot". *Raymond Ibrahim*, 7 February 2015. https://www.raymondibrahim.com/2015/02/07/qatar-published-fatwa-in-2006-permitting-burning-people-removes-it-after-is-burns-pilot/ (accessed 5 January 2023).

Institute for Economics and Peace. 2022. *Global Terrorism Index 2022: Measuring the Impact of Terrorism*. Sydney: IEP. https://www.visionofhumanity.org/wp-content/uploads/2022/03/GTI-2022-web-04112022.pdf (accessed 5 January 2023).

International Crisis Group. 2016. *Exploiting Disorder: Al-Qaeda and the Islamic State*. Crisis Group Special Report, 14 March 2016. Brussels: ICG.

Johnston, Patrick B., Jacob N. Shapiro, Howard J. Shatz, Benjamin Bahney, Danielle F. Jung, Patrcik K. Ryan, and Jonathan Wallace. 2016. *Foundations of the Islamic State: Management, Money, and Terror in Iraq, 2005–2010*. Santa Monica: RAND Corporation.

Kamal Hassan, M. 2003. "The Influence of Mawdudi's Thought on Muslims in Southeast Asia: A Brief Survey". *The Muslim World* 93, nos. 3–4: 429–64. https://doi.org/10.1111/1478-1913.00031 (accessed 5 January 2023).

Kanyakumari, D. 2016. "Zahid: 137 Detained So Far Over IS Terror Links". *The Star Online*, 18 October 2016. https://www.thestar.com.my/news/nation/2016/10/18/zahid-parliament-is/ (accessed 5 January 2023).

Kenney, Jeffrey T. 2015. "Teaching Religious Studies at the International Islamic University Malaysia". *Teaching Theology & Religion* 18, no. 3: 280–85. https://doi.org/10.1111/teth.12296 (accessed 5 January 2023).

Krisch, Joshua A. 2015. "The Psychology of a Terrorist: How ISIS Wins Hearts and Minds". *Vocativ*, 16 November 2015. https://www.vocativ.com/251306/psychology-terrorist/ (accessed 5 January 2023).

Lee, Ferran. 2015. "American Al Qaeda to ISIS: No Paradise for You". *ABC News*, 28 June 2015. https://abcnews.go.com/International/american-al-qaeda-isis-paradise/story?id=32036802 (accessed 5 January 2023).

Lewis, Bernard. 1990. "The Roots of Muslim Rage". *The Atlantic*, September 1990. https://www.theatlantic.com/magazine/archive/1990/09/the-roots-of-muslim-rage/304643/ (accessed 5 January 2023).

Liow, Joseph Chinyong. 2015. "Malaysia's ISIS Conundrum". *Brookings*, 21 April 2015. https://www.brookings.edu/opinions/malaysias-isis-conundrum/ (accessed 5 January 2023).

Lister, Charles. 2014. "Islamic State Senior Leadership: Who's Who". *Brookings*, 20 October 2014. https://www.brookings.edu/wp-content/uploads/2014/12/en_whos_who.pdf (accessed 5 January 2023).

Lynch, Marc. 2010. "Islam Divided Between *Salafi-jihad* and the *Ikhwan*". *Studies in Conflict & Terrorism* 3, no. 6: 467–87. https://doi.org/10.1080/10576101003752622 (accessed 5 January 2023).

Malay Mail Online. 2014. "Najib in No Way Supports Militant Group ISIL, Says Prime Minister's Office". *Malay Mail Online*, 26 June 2014. https://www.malaymail.com/news/malaysia/2014/06/26/najib-in-no-way-supports-militant-group-isil-says-prime-ministers-office/694947 (accessed 5 January 2023).

———. 2015. "No Place for Wahhabism in Malaysia, Fatwa Council Says". *Malay Mail Online*, 1 March 2015. https://www.malaymail.com/news/malaysia/2015/03/01/no-place-for-wahhabism-in-malaysia-fatwa-council-says/850279 (accessed 5 January 2023).

Manne, Robert. 2016. "The Mind of Islamic State: More Coherent and Consistent Than Nazism". *The Guardian*, 3 November 2016. https://www.theguardian.com/world/2016/nov/04/the-mind-of-islamic-state-more-coherent-and-consistent-than-nazism (accessed 5 January 2023).

McCants, William. 2015. "How ISIS Got Its Flag". *The Atlantic*, 22 September 2015. https://www.theatlantic.com/international/archive/2015/09/isis-flag-apocalypse/406498/ (accessed 5 January 2023).

———. 2016. "Apocalypse Delayed". *Jihadica*, 16 October 2016. https://www.jihadica.com/apocalypse-delayed/ (accessed 5 January 2023).

McElroy, Damien. 2014. "Ireland 'Leads the World in Islamic Values as Muslim States Lag'". *The Telegraph*, 10 June 2014. http://www.telegraph.co.uk/news/worldnews/europe/ireland/10888707/Ireland-leads-the-world-in-Islamic-values-as-Muslim-states-lag.html (accessed 5 January 2023).

McGregor, Andrew. 2003. "'Jihad and the Rifle Alone': 'Abdullah 'Azzam and the Islamist Revolution". *The Journal of Conflict Studies* 23, no. 2: 92–113.

MEMRI. 2014. "Senior Saudi Salafi Cleric: 'ISIS is a True Product of Salafism'". MEMRI Inquiry & Analysis Series No. 5872, 3 November 2014. https://www.memri.org/reports/senior-saudi-salafi-cleric-isis-true-product-salafism (accessed 5 January 2023).

———. 2015. "Issue 11 of ISIS's English Language Magazine 'Dabiq': A General Review". *Middle East Media Research Institute Jihad and Terrorism Threat Monitor*, 9 September 2015. http://www.memrijttm.org/content/view_print/blog/8723 (accessed 12 January 2017).

Merican, A Murad. 2017. "World Philosophy Day: The European Gaze on the Other". *New Straits Times*, 29 November 2017. https://www.nst.com.my/education/2017/11/308715/world-philosophy-day-european-gaze-other (accessed 5 January 2023).

Miqal, Sidq. 2015. "From Ibn Taymiyyah To Daish (ISIS/ISIL) – by Sidq Miqal". *Shiapac*, 7 February 2015. http://www.shiapac.org/2015/02/07/from-ibn-e-taymiyyah-to-daish-isisisil-by-sidq-miqal/ (accessed 5 January 2023).

Mohamad Fauzi Zakaria. 2007. *Pengaruh Pemikiran Sayyid Qutb Terhadap Gerakan Islam di Malaysia* [The Influence of Sayyid Qutb's Thoughts on Islamic Movements in Malaysia]. Kuala Lumpur: Jundi Resources.

Mohamed Ghouse Nasuruddin and Azeem Fazwan Ahmad Farouk. 2017. "Irrelevant Courses? Think Again". *The Sun Daily*, 26 September 2017. http://www.thesundaily.my/news/2017/09/26/irrelevant-courses-think-again (accessed 5 January 2023).

Mohd Mizan, M.A. 2017. "Evolving Global Threat Landscape Requires Continued Vigilance". *Counter Terrorist Trends and Analyses* 9, no. 4: 13–17.

———. 2021. "Fake Paradise for Malaysian Foreign Terrorist Fighters". *MEI@75*, 16 February 2021. https://www.mei.edu/publications/fake-paradise-malaysian-foreign-terrorist-fighters (accessed 5 January 2023).

Morrison, Scott. 2001. "The Genealogy and Contemporary Significance of the Islamic *Ummah*". *Islamic Culture* 75, no. 3: 1–30.

Moten, Abdul Rashid. 2006. "Islamic Thought in Contemporary Pakistan: The Legacy of 'Allama Mawdudi". In *The Blackwell Companion to Contemporary Islamic Thought*, edited by Ibrahim M. Abu-Rabi', pp. 175–94. Malden and Oxford: Blackwell Publishing.

Muhammad Haniff Bin Hassan. 2007. "Explaining Islam's Special Position and the Politic of Islam in Malaysia". *The Muslim World* 97, no. 2: 287–316. https://doi.org/10.1111/j.1478-1913.2007.00174.x (accessed 5 January 2023).

———. 2015. "Selective Nature of Islamic State's Armageddon Narrative". *Eurasia Review*, 9 February 2015. https://www.eurasiareview.com/09022015-selective-nature-isis-armageddon-narrative-analysis/ (accessed 5 January 2023).

Muzliza Mustafa. 2017. "Polis: Jabatan Agama Tak Cukup Gagah Tangani Ekstremisme" [Police: Religious Departments Not Strong Enough to Handle Extremism]. *Free Malaysia Today*, 7 January 2017. https://www.freemalaysiatoday.com/category/bahasa/2017/01/07/polis-jabatan-agama-tak-cukup-gagah-tangani-ekstremisme/ (accessed 5 January 2023).

Nabisah Ibrahim, Siti Rozaina Kamsani, and Julia Champe. 2015. "Understanding the Islamic Concept of *Usrah* and Its Application to Group Work". *The Journal for Specialists in Group Work* 40, no. 2: 163–86. https://doi.org/10.1 080/01933922.2015.1017067 (accessed 5 January 2023).

Olidort, Jacob. 2015. *The Politics of "Quietist" Salafism*. The Brookings Project on U.S. Relations with the Islamic World; Analysis Paper No. 18, February 2015. Washington, D.C.: Brookings. https://www.brookings.edu/wp-content/uploads/2016/07/Brookings-Analysis-Paper_Jacob-Olidort-Inside_Final_Web.pdf (accessed 5 January 2023).

Osman Bakar. 2009. "Islam and the Challenge of Diversity and Pluralism: Must Islam Reform Itself?" *Islam and Civlisational Renewal* 1, no. 1: 55–73. https://doi.org/10.52282/icr.v1i1.13 (accessed 5 January 2023).

Pew Research Center. 2013. "The World's Muslims: Religion, Politics and Society, Chapter 2: Religion and Politics". *Pew Research Center's Forum on Religion & Public Life*, 30 April 2013. https://www.pewresearch.org/religion/2013/04/30/the-worlds-muslims-religion-politics-society-religion-and-politics/ (accessed 5 January 2023).

Poushter, Jacob. 2015. "In Nations with Significant Muslim Populations, Much Disdain for ISIS". *Pew Research Center Fact Tank*, 17 November 2015. https://www.pewresearch.org/fact-tank/2015/11/17/in-nations-with-significant-muslim-populations-much-disdain-for-isis/ (accessed 5 January 2023).

Rahimin Affandi Abd Rahim, Mohd Anuar Ramli, Paizah Ismail, and Nor Hayati Mohd Dahlal. 2011. "Dialog Antara Agama: Realiti dan Prospek di Malaysia" [Religious Dialogue: Its Reality and Prospects in Malaysia]. *Kajian Malaysia: Journal of Malaysian Studies* 29, no. 2: 87–106.

Raqqa is Being Slaughtered Silently. 2016. "Between the Jurisprudence of Blood and the Management of Savagery: Islamic State Advances Terror Methods". *Atlantic Council*, 2 June 2016. https://www.atlanticcouncil.org/blogs/syriasource/between-the-jurisprudence-of-blood-and-the-management-of-savagery-islamic-state-advances-terror-methods/ (accessed 5 January 2023).

Rehman, Scheherazade S. and Hossein Askari. 2010. "An Economic Islamicity Index (EI2)". *Global Economy Journal* 10, no. 3: 1–39. http://hossein-askari.com/wordpress/wp-content/uploads/islamicity-index.pdf (accessed 5 January 2023).

Report of the Independent International Commission of Inquiry on the Syrian Arab Republic. 2014. *Rule of Terror: Living under ISIS in Syria*. New York: United Nations.

Rosnani Hashim and Imron Rossidy. 2000. "Islamization of Knowledge: A Comparative Analysis of the Conceptions of Al-Attas and Al-Faruqi". *Intellectual Discourse* 8, no. 1: 19–44.

Samuel, Thomas K. 2018. *Undergraduate Radicalisation in Selected Countries in Southeast Asia: A Comparative Quantitative Analysis on the Perception of Terrorism and Counter-Terrorism Among Undergraduates in Indonesia, Malaysia, the Philippines, Singapore and Thailand*. Kuala Lumpur: SEARCCT.

Schottmann, Sven Alexander. 2013. "God Helps Those Who Help Themselves: Islam According to Mahathir Mohamad". *Islam and Christian-Muslim Relations* 24, no. 1: 57–69. https://doi.org/10.1080/09596410.2012.712454 (accessed 5 January 2023).

Sheith Khidhir bin Abu Bakar. 2016. "Malaysia No Longer a Torch for Islam". *Free Malaysia Today*, 29 July 2016. https://www.freemalaysiatoday.

com/category/nation/2016/07/29/malaysia-no-longer-a-torch-for-islam/ (accessed 5 January 2023).

———. 2017. "Education System Partly to Blame for Rise of Extremism, Says Prof". *Free Malaysia Today*, 21 November 2017. http://www.freemalaysiatoday.com/category/nation/2017/11/21/education-system-partly-to-blame-for-rise-of-extremism-says-prof/ (accessed 5 January 2023).

Sherlock, Ruth. 2014. "Inside the Leadership of Islamic State: How the New 'Caliphate' is Run". *The Telegraph*, 9 July 2014. https://www.telegraph.co.uk/news/worldnews/middleeast/iraq/10956280/Inside-the-leadership-of-Islamic-State-how-the-new-caliphate-is-run.html (accessed 5 January 2023).

Shoebat, Walid. 2015. "Watch the Most Horrific Video by ISIS Burning POW Jordanian Pilot". *Shoebat.com*, 3 February 2015. https://shoebat.com/2015/02/03/watch-horrific-video-isis-burning-pow-jordanian-pilot/ (accessed 5 January 2023).

Sholeh, Badrus. 2016. "Daesh in Europe and Southeast Asia: An Indonesian Perspective". In *Countering Daesh Extremism: European and Asian Responses*, edited by Beatrice Gorawantschy, Rohan Gunaratna, Megha Sarmah and Patrick Rueppel, pp. 95–104. Singapore: Konrad-Adenauer-Stiftung and RSIS.

Siddiqi, Muhammad Nejatullah. 1995. "Towards Regeneration: Shifting Priorities in Islamic Movements". *Encounters: Journal of Inter-Cultural Perspectives* 1, no. 2: 3–29.

Skuad Khas Harian Metro. 2016. "Universiti Kebencian" [University of Hatred]. *Harian Metro*, 16 December 2016.

Soo, Wern Jun. 2022. "Prevention is Better than Cure: How Malaysian Experts Are Moving to Nip Extremism in the Bud". *Malay Mail Online*, 31 December 2022. https://www.malaymail.com/news/malaysia/2022/12/31/prevention-is-better-than-cure-how-malaysian-experts-are-moving-to-nip-extremism-in-the-bud/35307 (accessed 5 January 2023).

Syed Hadzrullathfi bin Syed Omar and Muhammad Rashidi bin Haji Wahab. 2012. "Konsep Pengajian Tauhid Tiga: Satu Analisis" [The Concept of Triple Tawhid: An Analysis]. *Jurnal Kefahaman Ahli Sunnah Waljamaah* 2: 55–84.

Tan Yi Liang. 2014. "Wisma Putra Denounces Acts of Terror by Malaysians in Syria and Iraq". *The Star Online*, 24 June 2014. https://www.thestar.com.my/News/Nation/2014/06/24/Malaysia-Denouce-terrorism/ (accessed 5 January 2023).

Tasnim Abdul Rahman, Wan Sabri Wan Yusof, Zuriati Mohd Rashid, and Ahmad Nabil Amir. 2015. "Al-Faruqi's Fundamental Ideas and Philosophy of Education". *Dinamika Ilmu* 15, no. 2: 235–48.

Thompson, Andrew and Jeremi Suri. 2014. "How America Helped ISIS". *New York Times*, 1 October 2014. https://www.nytimes.com/2014/10/02/opinion/how-america-helped-isis.html (accessed 5 January 2023).

Utusan Malaysia. 2016. "Mohd. Rafi Jadi Pengganas Hasil Pengaruh Buku" [Mohd. Rafi Became a Terrorist as a Result of Influence from Books]. *Utusan Online*, 27 June 2016. http://www.utusan.com.my/berita/nasional/mohd-rafi-jadi-pengganas-hasil-pengaruh-buku-1.347533 (accessed 15 December 2017).

Vidino, Lorenzo. 2014. "European Jihadists in Syria: Profiles, Travel Patterns and Governmental Responses". In *New (And Old) Patterns of Jihadism: Al-Qa'ida, the Islamic State and Beyond*, edited by Andrea Plebani, pp. 27–43. Milan: ISPI.

Wagemakers, Joas. 2016. "Salafi Source Readings Between Al-Qaeda and IS". *Oasis* 12, no. 23 (July): 55–62.

Wiktorowicz, Quintan. 2006. "Anatomy of the Salafi Movement". *Studies in Conflict & Terrorism* 29, no. 3: 207–39. https://doi.org/10.1080/10576100500497004 (accessed 5 January 2023).

Wright, Robin. 2012. "Don't Fear All Islamists, Fear Salafis". *New York Times*, 19 August 2012. https://www.nytimes.com/2012/08/20/opinion/dont-fear-all-islamists-fear-salafis.html (accessed 5 January 2023).

Yusuf Ali, Abdullah. n.d. *The Holy Qur'an: English Translation of the Meanings and Commentary*. Madinah: King Fahd Holy Quran Printing Complex.

Zulkarnain Haron and Nordin Hussin. 2013. "A Study of the Salafi Jihadist Doctrine and the Interpretation of Jihad by Al Jama'ah Al Islamiyah". *KEMANUSIAAN: Asian Journal of Humanities* 20, no. 2: 15–37.

PART II

States and Organizations Driving Trends

4

EXTREMISM IN MALAYSIA: CIVIL SERVANTS AS TRENDSETTERS AND CONDUITS OF TRENDS

*Mohd Faizal Musa**

Introduction

In discussions on trending Islamic ideas, focus has been given to the role of charismatic personalities or popular mediums, namely the Internet and social media, but not on the role played by administrators. In Malaysia, the role of public administrators is equally important, especially on matters related to Islam, as religion has become intertwined with public policy. Malaysia's civil service is estimated to employ a million staff members, and for a country with a population of 32.7 million, the number of civil servants signifies "strength and influence" (Ahmad Faiz Yaakob et al. 2012, p. 133). Majority of the civil servants are Malay by ethnicity and this does not accurately reflect Malaysia's multiethnic composition. According to Malaysia's 2020 census, the three major ethnic groups in the country are Malay or Bumiputera (69.4 per cent), Chinese (7.3 per cent), and Indian (0.7 per cent) (Launching of Report on the Key Findings Population and Housing Census of Malaysia 2020).[1]

Prijono Tjiptoherijanto (2012) states that the "indigenous Bumiputeras which are largely ethnic Malays" have "87 per cent of government jobs". Prijono further adds that "the biggest loser in the current system is Indians, who, according to government statistics make up 9 per cent of the labor force but hold 16 per cent of menial jobs and control just 1.2 per cent of equity in registered company in the country". In 2022, the Prime Minister's Office (PMO) admitted that 89.23 per cent of the top posts in Malaysia's public service are Malay, and that those from Sabah and Sarawak are also least represented (Malaysiakini 2022).[2]

As most civil servants are Malay-Muslim, scrutinizing their role and impact in society is important, especially since those serving in religious institutions are also considered civil servants. Moreover, religious authorities have been allocated a large amount of funds from Malaysia's national budget. The previous administration provided a RM1.5 billion budget allocation for the management and development of Islam, and this was heavily criticized especially since the religious authorities are regarded as largely incompetent (Imran Ariff 2021).

This chapter aims to analyse the significance of a Malay-Muslim dominant civil service. Arguably, as Muslims, the Malays are very much influenced by current Islamic trends. The civil servants' way of thinking about certain issues can be carefully predicted according to contemporary trends. For instance, they could potentially be radicalized or inclined to extreme ideas if radical thinking and extremism become more dominant in society and if left unchecked. Without proper guidance and leadership, civil servants can also use their position to promote their own understanding of Islam. The civil service can hypothetically develop into a space for the breeding of extremism and could consequently lead to unintended outcomes in society.

The civil service therefore acts as a medium of transmission of Islamic trends and ideas. It is therefore crucial to examine their behavioural conduct, especially since there are serious allegations of mismanagement, ill treatment, and radicalism.[3] Furthermore, the threat of extremism within the civil service does not just affect Muslims but is also a growing concern for religious minorities and their right to the freedom of religion.[4] The aim of this chapter is to understand how civil servants, as receivers and transmitters of certain ideas, have trespassed the boundaries protecting the rights of religious minorities, and have begun to illustrate tendencies towards non-violent extremism.

The Anatomy of the System

Article 132 of the Federal Constitution specifies that the public service shall consist of the Federal and State General Public Service, the Joint Public Services, the Education Service, the Judiciary and the Legal Service and the Armed Forces (Shad Saleem Faruqi 2011). This explains why Malaysia's public service is bloated and why civil servants can be very influential in crafting public policy, as they are involved in all realms of public life. Malaysia's public service is headed by the Ketua Setiausaha Negara (Chief Secretary to the Government, KSN). A very prominent group of civil servants under the KSN is the Pegawai Tadbir dan Diplomatik (Malaysian Administrative and Diplomatic Officers). They are an exclusive group of civil servants who run the top management, serve in the federal government, and are also seconded to state governments. The public service is expected to be partial and neutral in its governance and is often thought to be loyal to the government of the day. However, the General Order based on Act 132 (2) states that the top management and professional groups are not allowed to be involved in political activities, although they can be ordinary members of political parties on the condition that they have informed their superiors or respective departmental heads. According to Abdul Aziz Bari (2009), civil servants must be loyal to the country, not the government.

To harness their professionalism, the Federal Constitution stipulates several clauses to protect civil servants. This includes Article 144 which provides for the formation of a Special Commission responsible for matters relating to appointment, promotion, discipline and dismissal, and the guarantee of service term; and an impediment to dismissal and demotion; as well as the opportunity to self-defend upon legal conviction as provided by Article 135 (Ahmad Faiz Yaakob et al. 2012).

The public service is also shaped by policies introduced by the government of the day. For instance, civil servants are expected to abide by government policies in handling public affairs which are within their power and capacity. These policies include Dasar Penerapan Nilai-Nilai Islam (Inculcation of Islamic Values Policy, introduced in 1985 by former Prime Minister Mahathir Mohamad); Islam Hadhari (Civilisational Islam, introduced in 2003 by former Prime Minister Abdullah Badawi); Islam Wasatiyyah (Moderate Islam, introduced in 2016 by former Prime Minister Najib Razak); and Keluarga Malaysia (Malaysian Family, introduced in 2021 by former Prime Minister Ismail Sabri).

Lim Heng Seng (2016), a law practitioner, said that the promotion of Islam in civil administration was introduced to balance the increasing demands of the proponents of an Islamic state at the time, and that these policies eventually shaped Malaysian Islam:

> ... the concept of an Islamic state is premised on Islam as a political ideology and the supremacy of Syariah. In the post-Merdeka period from the early 1980s, demands by Islamic state proponents and activists as well as the political responses of Umno set the stage for a unique form of Malaysian-style Islamisation and the erosion of the basic structure and character of the Malaysian polity. In 1982, the Umno-led government under then prime minister Tun Dr Mahathir Mohamad announced the policy of inculcating 10 Islamic values that are universal in nature in the administration. These universal values are: trust, responsibility, honesty, dedication, moderation, diligence, discipline, cooperation, honourable behaviour and thanksgiving. The initiative was hardly pursued with any degree of commitment or vigour. It became the launching pad and platform for gradualist Islamisation of national policies, systems and institutions as conceived by the religious bureaucrats which have scant, if any, significance to the promotion of universal values. This was followed by former prime minister Tun Abdullah Ahmad Badawi's concept of "Islam Hadhari" and current prime minister Dato' Sri Najib Tun Razak's "Islam Wasatiyyah".

However, there are no fundamental differences between these administrations' various visions of Islam. Nevertheless, the sources of inspiration, frameworks, and approaches of these visions are worth scrutinizing as they did make a difference to the country's foreign policy. For example, during Mahathir Mohamad's and Abdullah Badawi's premiership, Malaysia had a warm relationship with member states of the Organization of Islamic Cooperation (OIC) such as Turkey, Iran and Pakistan, while Najib Razak appeared to have paid more attention to the Gulf states, including Saudi Arabia.[5]

Malaysia's government has expended resources to cultivate Islamic approaches to governance, and civil servants are involved in this both directly and indirectly. The civil service is increasingly dominated by religious authorities, and religious institutions are provided with extensive funding. Therefore, any worrying trends propagated in the name of Islam, such as radicalism or sectarianism, must be kept in check (Shiozaki and Kushimoto 2014).[6]

In Malaysia, two groups of civil servants speak for Islam. The first is Jabatan Kemajuan Islam Malaysia (Department of Islamic Development Malaysia, JAKIM) and the second are the 14 state religious authorities. Before JAKIM was established on 1 January 1997, Bahagian Hal Ehwal Agama Islam (Islamic Affairs Division, BAHEIS) was responsible for ensuring the proper teaching of Islam in Malaysia and protecting the purity of Muslims' faith. JAKIM is entrusted "with reasons to mobilize the development and progress of Muslims in Malaysia" (Jabatan Kemajuan Islam Malaysia 2015). Other than JAKIM, Islam is also under the jurisdiction of the states. Each state and the Federal Territories have their own Majlis Agama Islam (Islamic Religious Council), mufti, syariah courts and religious administrative officers, including their own officers responsible for the administration of justice.

Murray Hunter (2019), a senior journalist focusing on Southeast Asia, underlined a few issues regarding Malaysia's civil service. Besides being mono-ethnic, the civil service is male-dominated and also plagued with corruption and bureaucracy. Corruption is an especially big issue:

> Corruption is endemic, with numerous methods used to profit from public funds. Some officers in areas close to the procurement process set up small trading companies which supply items not subject to tender such as office furniture, fixtures, stationary, printing, and computer equipment at inflated prices to their respective departments or ministries... in 2018 the Malaysian Anti-Corruption Commission (MACC) prosecuted only 418 civil servants out of 1.7 million employees for fraud and corruption, with 13 from top management. This year to September 567 have been prosecuted, including eight from top management according to MACC statistics.[7]

As Heiner Bielefeidt (2013) contends, corruption and mono-ethnicity are connected to human rights violations from the aspect of freedom of religion and can lead to chaos in the civil service. This was among some of the issues highlighted by religious minorities during my fieldwork.

Human Rights as an Approach

In studying the freedom of religion in Malaysia, I have chosen to approach the issue through a human rights lens. Approaching the issue from a human rights perspective enables us to understand the limits or boundaries that have been trespassed, and to pay attention to the grievances of religious minorities. This will also provide greater elucidation on the role of civil servants in this issue. Ultimately, I argue that the issue of the freedom of religion can only be understood by examining the risks that arise from the lack of the freedom of religion. Thus, the negative experiences of religious minorities must be addressed.

On 11 March 2014, Bielefeidt, Special Rapporteur on freedom of religion or belief at the United Nations (UN) presented his annual report on collective religious hatred. He stressed that collective religious hatred is not a natural occurrence but can be avoided. According to him, collective religious hatred occurs because of fear or anxiety. The feeling is the opposite of love and compassion which should be fostered by religion and its followers. Based on his observations of the reports and complaints involving freedom of religion from the member states of the UN, he expressed that collective religious hatred occurs as a result of political situations, and therefore can actually be avoided.

To refer to Bielefeidt (2013, pp. 7–8) directly, there are three reasons for collective religious hatred being widespread: (1) the outbreak of corruption as the main cause of collective religious hatred; (2) a climate of political authoritarianism which causes the spread of collective religious hatred and; (3) a narrow concept of political identity also causes collective religious hatred. There are governments who use religion to establish or assert a mould for national identity.

From my standpoint, all three symptoms are observable in Malaysian society. There is increasing concern about civil servants being involved in corruption, and that they wield a lot of power, especially if they have links to religious institutions. This is also linked to political authoritarianism and a rigid political identity which has been embedded in Malaysia's social fabric. The pervasiveness of political authoritarianism and a rigid political identity could also be due to the hybrid regime which has characterized Malaysia for a long time. William Case (2019) states, "Hybrid regimes use calibrated controls that culminate in an 'uneven playing field' by working systemically to promote favoured sets of ethno-religious identities over the maligned, stigmatised and dreaded social 'other'." Therefore, the interviews I conducted aimed at understanding and combating these issues.

After highlighting these causes, Bielefeidt outlines several approaches to overcome collective religious hatred. He calls for mutual respect regarding the right to the freedom of religion and emphasizes that a strong trust between people must be built, especially at the federal level.

This requires an infrastructure essentially defined by respect, the keyword in human rights discourse. While a country has the right to have an official religion, it should make no room for discrimination and disrespect of other religions. Bielefeidt also stresses that a strong trust between the government and religious minorities can only be established if there is prompt communication between both parties. In this case, communication could refer to: (1) interaction between all inter- and intra-religious groups; (2) consistent outreach efforts by the government to religious minorities and; (3) the smooth running and nurturing of multilateral public debates about religious issues. For example, in the context of Malaysia, if a Sunni Muslim group is allowed to campaign, tour, and conduct seminar series on the perceived menace of Shi'a Muslims; the religious minority, in this case the Shi'as, also need to be empowered and given an equal space to respond. The government only needs to monitor the situation of the public debate and ensure that it does not affect national stability.

With this framework in mind, I conducted my study on the freedom of religion in Malaysia. Twenty-three individuals who were called authorities, representatives, icons, seniors, or the sole voice or guardian of religion or belief were interviewed. These individuals or parties are adherents of the following beliefs: Sunni Islam, Ahmadi Islam, Shi'a Islam (Twelver), Shi'a Islam (Bohra), Sufi Islam, "Liberal Islam", Sikhism, Catholic Christianity, Protestant Christianity, Anglican Christianity, Evangelical Christianity, Millah Ibrahim (Abrahamic

Faith), Paganism (ancestral religion), Baha'i faith, Hinduism, Taoism, and Atheism. In addition, a total of 35 adherents of various religions were also interviewed to allow for a better understanding of issues concerning religious freedom in the country.[8]

Civil Servants: The Threat of Extremism

The religious minorities I spoke to expressed their grievances about Malay-Muslim civil servants who use their position to promote Islam, while at the same time encroaching on the freedom of religion of others. Ideally, a civil servant must be neutral. A Muslim convert from Sabah expressed that officers at the Jabatan Pendaftaran Negara (National Registration Department, JPN) in Sabah would easily assist any individual who was willing to convert to Islam, but would complicate the efforts of those of other faiths:

> And I was surprised because a civil servant, an officer, you wouldn't say that. "The easiest way you get a citizenship certificate later, you convert to Islam, confirm you will get it." I don't know to what extent this NRD, this should be exposed. This is a very sensitive issue. And yet, an officer, a civil servant, someone who implements our daily administrative policies says so. – A Muslim convert from Sabah

Racism is intertwined with encroachments on the freedom of religion and belief. Another Muslim convert from Sabah shared that receiving assistance during the COVID-19 pandemic was very selective, and was dependent on race and religion, which in turn was dependent on the government of the day. The quote below describes how assistance was given to mainly non-Muslims when Parti Warisan Sabah (Warisan) and Pakatan Harapan (PH) were in power in Sabah:

> The Muslims do not care about or do not fight for the rights of the Dusun people. The Dusuns, we all know lah, are Christians, things like that. So, we see this trend is indeed happening. Because I went to the ground, when I went to these villages, we saw there was segregation or even division between, let's say, these villages. Like yesterday I went to Nabawan, the complainant told me, for example, the food assistance, NGO aid, NGOs that people say are pro-government, only help the Christian Dusun people. – A Muslim convert from Sabah

My findings also revealed that there have been complaints that civil servants attempt to pursue their own personal agenda and beliefs.

These 1.6 million civil servants, who are mostly Malay-Muslim, are among the key beneficiaries of the annual financial budget, receiving generous handouts from the government. However, since these findings are based on anecdotes, further investigation is needed to see how pervasive this trend is in the civil service (given its sheer size spreading across East and West Malaysia).

As most of them are Muslim, there are several allegations from religious minorities that the civil servants use their position to promote their own understanding of Islam. Most of the allegations are directed towards officers from JPN, religious authorities, and school teachers. It can be argued that they are merely applying government policies, in this case, the Policy for the Inculcation of Islamic Values, or their own interpretation of Islam as an "official religion". However, there have also been allegations of forced conversion by these officials:

> So, the issue of statelessness in Sabah ... he said it's easy, you just pay between 8,000 to 15,000 (ringgit), we're talking about corruption, so you become a Sabahan; five things you become, you become Malaysian, so you become Sabahan, you get Malay Muslim rights, you get Bumiputera rights, and get the right for whatever it is, so you can buy land and everything. – A female Iban Anglican

> The act of converting to a different faith. I think ... besides Islam, I think, you know, conversion from Christianity to Hinduism, Hinduism to Buddhism, you don't see so much an issue or a problem because there isn't a requirement that will affect your status, you know. I think, I think the difficulty here is also because it ties in with our identity card. You know, our identity card is the maker of our beliefs. I think with the National Registration Department also, not an issue if somebody come and say, you know, "semalam saya Buddhist, hari ini saya Christian, [yesterday I was Buddhist, today I'm Christian] I have to change" ... I have not heard actually of the people changing to Buddhist. Islam, when it comes to Islam, and obviously, you want you have the right, you have no faith in this religion at all, and you want to openly declare yourself as, you know, a Christian or Hindu or whatever, and proceed to carry on your life in that ... that way, but this makes it impossible for you to do that. – A female Sunni Muslim

Another example was an Orang Asli respondent who stated how their religion and even their names are often determined by the officer at the JPN, sometimes without their knowledge or consent. This arbitrary act often creates a lot of confusion and conflict especially during defining moments, such as when the individuals are about to get married or give birth, and even during funerals:

> According to the trend, Orang Asli have mostly Malay names, but they are not Muslims. The story is ... when going to JPN to register the child's name in the birth certificate, the JPN officer usually encourages giving Malay names because the first reason, it's good to hear. It's easy to spell ... if in the 60s, Orang Asli names were (authentic) Orang Asli names. We have not been recognised to decide our own name, our own faith ... In the early 2000s they always told me that this university student from ... I don't know which university, maybe UIA or whichever university, has a major in Islamic Studies, went to the village to sit there to preach and one of the rewards was ... I don't know whether it is true, what kind of money is zakat? Alms (for the poor)? Or whatever money, they can get monthly income, they are happy to get help, they are happy to ... what is it that they have a standing for help or whatever, they can be happy compared to the Orang Asli who do not believe in Islam. So, I think if we want to convert people to join a religion, don't use that angle, show that the religion is good, and one day when his mind, when his faith is open to follow the religion, he will enter naturally, not with ... like there is bait, [as if] there is a shrimp behind the noodles [a hidden motive] or something like that, that's all. – An Orang Asli Temuan from Bidor, Perak

A Shi'a leader also complained about religious authorities complicating matters by allegedly creating false narratives and spreading propaganda about their teachings:

> Negative propaganda from religious authorities. The problem is the religious center, in the mosque, there are *ustaz* [teachers] who come and lambast, [spread] negative propaganda in the *surau* [small mosque].
> – A Twelver Shi'a leader

On the other hand, an Atheist respondent suggested that civil servants can make a difference if they are willing to be objective:

> Majlis Perbandaran [Town Council] ... you would be considering your political affiliation, your political expediency rather than what the local community means. So, it is unlikely that you want to speak up for the ten Buddhists and be at loggerheads ... potential loggerheads with 1,000 Muslims who are there. So, this notion of inclusive, this notion of solidarity with the 10 non-Muslims, does not come into it. This

means at the end you are denied representation, places of worship, and even a seat on the table, right? This is from the governance point of view. – An Atheist

Most teachers in Malaysia are also civil servants. Apart from claims that teachers discriminate against Ahmadi students, there are also allegations that those who are sent to Sarawak to teach are involved in converting indigenous children to Islam:

> Those who are strong in religion, go and spread Islam. Majority of them will lead, in all communities he will be the *Imam*...Yes, so many of them are married to locals, so these people become converts. So, there are two groups that give us a headache from before; first, are the soldiers, because the soldiers who came first, that's the real problem. Then after that ... the second group is teachers. So, the teachers who came at that time were most of us who felt, right or wrong, I don't know, it was these other people who may not have been the best, to be sent to Sabah, Sarawak, and have very little understanding of our community, you know, so they don't interact with the people. – An Iban female Anglican

These civil servants have been perceived as utilizing the Policy on the Inculcation of Islamic Values and their special position as Malay-Bumiputera in regulating religion. For example, a pastor compared this situation to the state of Christianity in Malaysia, which does not face similar regulation in terms of a national policy:

> ... in the case of Islam in Malaysia, is highly regulated. Now, it is not supposed to be like that, but it's highly regulated. So, you face a lot of constraints whilst comparing to Christianity in Malaysia, Christianity is not regulated at all. There are traditions, there are bound by certain traditions or sacred traditions of churches and all. But because of that, there are no liberties for a Muslim to do a lot of things. – A Protestant

Nevertheless, the minorities I spoke to also cited some positive experiences, mostly due to a few open-minded individuals or civil servants. For example, an Ahmadi leader shared how a director of religious authorities in Selangor managed to stop a message of religious hatred from being exhibited publicly:

> But I salute that Datuk Azib [Datuk Mohamad Azib Mohd Isa]. MAIS [Majlis Agama Islam Selangor, Selangor Islamic Religious Council] has a director who is very open-minded. Very open-minded. Because when

they started installing those signboards, the first were installed near Shah Alam. Near the roundabout. Near Shah Alam Mosque. When they installed, the day they installed the thing, it just so happened that a member of our congregation passed by that way. Then the next day I went to see Datuk Azib. I did not go to JAIS (Jabatan Agama Islam Selangor, Selangor Islamic Religious Department), I went to see MAIS. I talked to him. He was surprised. 'I did not direct that installation. What did they write there?' He must not have known what was written on those signboards. That's up to him. But that's my experience with him. On the spot, he ordered it to be brought back down. – An Ahmadi leader

One of the religious officials I spoke to clearly stated that the government's attitude towards religious minorities does not solve any issues. He questioned their approach of harassing the minorities, especially the Shi'as and Ahmadis:

When we settle matters with force, arrests and so on, not only does it do nothing to solve the problem, but it also gives more strength to the friends who have been arrested. – A Sunni official from Perak

Issues regarding the demolition of houses of worship can also create tension and lead to violence. There have been proposals from religious minorities themselves requesting that this sensitive issue be resolved from a town planning perspective, instead of looking at it from the perspective of an illegal construction on government land. However, to do so, it would require a lot of discussion, a handsome amount of funds as fees and compensation, proper relocation of the houses of worship, and the application of a human rights framework to the issue:

To give one good example, this unit majority I think over 80 percent are Chinese. They are Taoists, Christians, Buddhists, but there's no place for worship. There is only one [not audible] and a Muslim *surau*, it is not being used. JAIP [Jabatan Agama Islam Perak, Perak Islamic Religious Department] ah? It has not been used because there's no number. You built a *surau* or masjid [mosque], you must have the people there, otherwise, you built [using] so much money and then there are no people to pray. So that piece of land is still there, but there's not a single piece of land for other than Islam. Come on man when you use the money, it is our money. But it is the government, the government is for the nation, the government is not for one race. It happens that the majority of the ministers are Malay and Muslim but it shouldn't be the [inaudible]. When you are the minister, you put your religion aside. Religion and government must be separated. When they believe that religion and government are the same, then it will be a problem. Some will say, "I cannot help you with the lot of the land because I'm a Muslim I cannot help another religion," you know, people said it like that you know. Those from the land office ... Majlis Daerah [District Council], they cannot do that because they (are) doing work you know, it is not, "I'm doing Muslim work," No! They do that as a *pentadbir tanah* [land administrator] you know. *"Pentadbir tanah' bukan 'pentadbir tanah Muslim"*, [land administrator, not Muslim land administrator] no ... *pentadbir tanah ajer* [merely land administrator], *ataupun Majlis Daerah* [or the District Council] and that you as a minister for the whole district. And district doesn't mean Muslim only, district means everybody, and this is us in Malaysia. Today it is something that has to be righted you know because they are getting the wrong idea. [inaudible] many things also Muslim Muslim Muslim, and maybe they forget that we are here for other religions. – A Taoist leader

... there is also a problem with this shrine which it [is], operated by individuals. What those people do is supposed they live in that area. They build a shrine opposite the house, and then open it just under the tree. That will be a problem. I think they didn't have to study it. That is the reason why the location of the temple as well is different in Malaysia because when Indians came to work here. Especially in Klang Valley. The reason why there are so many temples here is because they won't be able to go back. That is why they built a home here and feel more comfortable living here. One of the things that they want to be is very close to one religion, so they study and make connections between other temples like in *ladang* [plantation], and [they] show an effort to make themselves to be wanted here and to start fresh. I think a lot of them made peace with the fact that they won't go back. They really don't have enough money to go back. So, I don't think the issue is emotional itself. Purely because of the fact that faith is attached to it. I think it's a lot of connotations we should respect, and there is really something that is supposed to be developed and entirely properly. I think people will be ok with demolishing but you have to do it respectfully. I guess so, ya... – Participant from a focus group discussion with Hindus

A self-proclaimed progressive Sunni Muslim that was part of the PH administration (2018–20) serving as an official stated how important it is to first engage civil servants when addressing such an issue:

Whether it's big or small, anywhere you can just build the mosque. But when it comes to this issue, totally concerned about the Hindu temple. Concern, why? Because most of the time, it was built on illegal land that's obviously owned by the government. And people will see this conflict between the Hindus and the authorities on this. But actually, it's about land issue. Land issue, yes, definitely, ya. Since, there is this Minister of Religious Affairs, kan? It is not named as Islamic authority or anything. So, being a Malay-Muslim in the majority country, I mean, the biggest reform could change if it happens, if the, what we call that, Islamic authority is changed. Because why, because they are the majority. Because any reform that they make will, will have an impact whether it's good or bad to people as a whole, you know. So, that's what I see the time during Mujahid [Mujahid Yusof Rawa, Minister in the Prime Minister's Department in charge of Religious Affairs in the PH administration from July 2018 to February 2020]. Coming from a political leader like him as a minister, he came and met Nisha who is a transgender and explained that Islam doesn't discriminate, and all these kinds of messages are really important. But unfortunately, in Malaysia it's always [about] political will, that is one. The second is to leave the institution. And unfortunately, now, our associates are not ready for that reform, and that has been proven during Pakatan Harapan of 22 months during the process. Just people don't see that they have much time to do the reforms, but the 22 months is proven, it shows enough that the institution itself is not ready to change. I know that one thing we should engage is civil servant. – A Sunni Muslim

Ideals of Civil Servants

During my fieldwork, a number of religious minorities expressed that they perceive the government and civil servants with fear. The following are some anecdotes describing this sentiment:

> I think a lot of fear. Fear of repercussions, fear of not either legal repercussions or even just being attack bully. I think that in Malaysia, there is fear to even share about Baha'ism faith to Muslims. So Baha'i in general for some reason there is fear to even share my own belief to other Muslims. So, in that sense, I think it is psychological fear. – A Baha'i

> We keep ourselves to ourselves even in private groups on social media. Even a lot of those views that are expressed on private groups are held back per se cause fear of persecution. – An Atheist

> I remembered that one time that I went to Masjid Negara. [A prominent foreign preacher] was speaking there. So, the beginning part of his lecture was actually okay. But only, but when it comes to

questions and answers. Remember this is our National Mosque, ya. And I can't remember how many hundreds or even thousands of people were there to listen to him speaking. But when someone asked about LGBT, there with his megaphone, he [openly criticized the group]. And this is National Mosque. – A Muslim leader

We can practise our faith, but there, I would say that the space given to us seems to be shrinking. – A Catholic leader in Peninsular Malaysia

I do remember was somewhere in the 2009/2010 I think when the Allah issue erupted, I think there were several churches that were bombed ... somebody threw molotov cocktail at it, I think mine is #### church, which is Protestant Church in ... and also of course recently Sri Lankan Easter, which is at the point of time at least my church is very concern, and actually we raised security on Sunday morning to ensure that we don't have like ... suddenly some ... persons just appearing out from nowhere you know, causing security and things like that, so we are affected both internally and also externally out of Malaysia, out of what we actually read. – A Protestant follower

I am also a bit worried are the incident of the freedom fighters who are going to the Middle East to fight, I mean if they are willing to go there and kill for in the name of religion, nothing is stopping them for being the same here. – A Catholic

Kalau saya sendiri, di zaman sekolah saya pernah dibuang asrama. Lagi satu, bukan sekadar ejek. Kemudian sampai kena penjara ada di Malaysia ini. Kena lokap. Di Baitussalam kita sendiri. Di Kampung Baru kena lempang.
Translation: As for myself, during my school days, I was once expelled from the boarding school. And it was not just the insults. We were later imprisoned and put in lockup. It happened here in our own premises, the Baitussalam. I was also slapped in Kampung Baru. – An Ahmadi remembering how he was dismissed from boarding school

Manusia takkan diculik eh semata-mata untuk dihilangkan apa, dengan perkara yang remeh. Jadi, dari segi inkues tu sendiri menyatakan adalah hubungan dengan mazhabnya. Jadi, kalau itu boleh berlaku, saya fikir tidak ada satu orangpun boleh berasa selamat selagi mana mereka menyatakan mereka menganut mazhab Jafari. Kerana, kalau betullah perkara itu berlaku, ini bukti sejauhmana orang yang memegang kuasa boleh pergi dan itu parah. Parah dari segi hak asasi manusia tu sendiri mungkin paling rendah.
Translation: Citizens should not be abducted or put through an enforced disappearance for trivial reasons. The [SUHAKAM; Suruhanjaya Hak Asasi Manusia Malaysia, Human Rights Commission of Malaysia]

inquest itself explained that the disappearance was in connection with his [Amri Che Mat] school of thought. So, if this can happen, I don't think even one person would feel safe as long as we adhere to the Jafari school of thought. Because, if it's true that this happened, it proves how far those in power are willing to go, and that is horrible. It's horrible because from the perspective of human rights, it's probably at the lowest level. – A Twelver Shi'a commenting on Amri Che Mat's enforced disappearance

The above quotes from the interviews and focus group discussions highlight that civil servants are loathed for their behaviour. I believe Malaysia's civil servants have not been exposed to a human rights perspective. As a result, such an approach is not considered when they craft policies or standard operating procedures, leaving citizens in fear whenever they encounter civil servants in certain situations. As most civil servants are Muslims, the religious minorities whom I met with tended to speak about the religious hatred that they experience.

As evident from the quotes above, religious minorities are worried about how the attitudes of some civil servants were infringing on their rights. Having said that, I argue that the power which the civil servants wield facilitates their role in spreading discourses and practices that could influence the development of non-violent extremism. If left unchecked, these behaviours could easily develop into violence. In other words, civil servants are impactful in influencing Islamic trends, and given the power that they enjoy, they can sow the seeds of chaos.

However, there are ways to contain this threat. For example, Bielefeidt refers to the Rabat Plan of Action 2013 to identify the types of speech, conduct, and action that may sow or cause discrimination, violence and hatred, and which are serious enough for precautions to be taken. The Rabat Plan of Action 2013 also provides guidelines and policies for government and civil society in preventing collective religious hatred.

I recommend that Malaysian civil servants refer to the Rabat Plan of Action 2013 as a fundamental guide on the freedom of religion and expression. Not only does it set the benchmark for dealing with the freedom of religion, but it also lays out how certain forms of "freedom of expression" could actually be regarded as collective religious hatred. It describes collective religious hatred as involving:

I. Context; for example, by doing an in-depth analysis of the context of a speech alone, its social and political background can be determined,

and it can be ascertained whether the speech is directed at target groups such as Christians, or Shi'as.
II. Speaker; it is essential that the position of the individual expressing the hate speech is identified.
III. Intent; in this case, intention and not negligence or recklessness should be given focus.
IV. Content or form; analysis of the content and form of speech is also critical in determining if it is, in fact, a violation of human rights.
V. Extent of the speech; whether the speech is done in public, what the size of the audience is, the means of dissemination, whether it is through broadcasting or printed leaflets, and also whether the statement or publication is widely accessible to the general public.
VI. Potential risks; finally, incitement and defamations cultivating collective religious hatred are determined based on the potential risks that may occur as a result of the speech or broadcast in question.

The Rabat Plan of Action 2013 can therefore serve as a necessary guide for the demarcation of a threshold in relation to hate speech, intolerance, and unsympathetic expressions, all of which are starting points for the development of non-violent extremism (Norshahril et al. 2021).

If civil servants adopt this human rights framework in their operations, Malaysian religious minorities will not be at the receiving end of discriminatory fatwas, the denial of the rights of their children, and the abuse of power by civil servants pursuing their own agenda. Instead, civil servants would adopt a human rights approach when addressing issues such as forced faith conversions, the illegal construction of houses of worship, and even alleviating the endemic racism and corruption in the country. As there is no concrete mechanism in the Malaysian civil service to measure non-violent extremism, it is hopeful that this human rights approach can also be developed and inculcated among civil servants so as to prevent the infiltration of potential extremists into the civil service.

Another important step would be for civil servants to engage with the Congress of Union of Employees in the Public and Civil Services Malaysia (CUEPACS), which is a national trade union coalition in Malaysia that has a membership of 1.2 million. Engaging with CUEPACS, who is responsible for engaging with government authorities on various issues, might lead to greater discussion and implementation of a human rights approach at the policy level.

Conclusion

Malaysia's civil servants are mostly Malay-Muslim and are therefore very important as a vote bank for any political party. Because of their awareness of their importance, these civil servants may feel immune or shielded from being reprimanded for their actions. It is therefore crucial to enhance regulations and laws concerning corruption, as the integrity and dishonesty of the public sector has been a cause for concern among religious minorities. There is therefore a need to re-look at the role and practice of civil servants, and their unlimited power, as well as their role in engaging in corruption and the infringement on the rights of religious minorities. For this to be done, Malaysia needs a strong leader committed to reforming the civil service.

One thing for sure is that these infringements are a form of non-violent extremism and can possibly develop into physical violence. All the findings from the ground suggest that Malaysia's civil service is a double-edged sword: it can either address radicalization or extremism and reprimand those involved or play a nurturing role. As such, it is imperative that the frustrations of the religious minorities that have been documented above are not ignored, and should be a catalyst for greater engagement with a human rights approach.

NOTES

*My fieldwork was funded by the American Bar Association and the IMAN Research Center. I also benefitted from my time as a Visiting Fellow at ISEAS – Yusof Ishak Institute, Singapore.

1. In Malaysia, Malays are constitutionally defined as Muslim; Article 160 of the Federal Constitution defines a Malay as "a person who professes the religion of Islam, habitually speaks the Malay language, conforms to Malay custom..." As Rosli Dahlan and Mohammad Afif Daud (2016) put it, this oft-quoted definition of what it means to be *Malay* "tends to suggest that: anyone could by religious conversion and adoption of custom and language belong; anyone born a Malay is compelled by law to be a Muslim. Strictly speaking, this provides not so much a racial as a tribal distinction".
2. Shad Saleem Faruqi (2011) in explaining the racial quotas stated above noted that "in Malaysia, the issue of race discrimination is complicated". This is evident from the juxtaposition of Article 136 which states that

"all persons of whatever race in the same grade in the service of the Federation shall be treated impartially", and Article 153 which "permits reservations and quotas in favour of Malays and the natives of Sabah and Sarawak".

3 Ali Hamsa, the former Chief Secretary to the Government, responded with a warning that if any of the 1.6 million civil servants were influenced by terrorism and arrested by police, they will not be tolerated (Harian Metro 2015). There have also been discussions about how civil servants pose a threat to public policies, laws, and even the federal constitution. In this sense, the civil service has been described as a "deep state" in which the executive branch is pitted against unelected bureaucrats and civil servants. The allegations of the civil service being a deep state were a topic of serious debate during the 22 months that Pakatan Harapan was in power (New Straits Times 2019).

4 For instance, Ayob Khan Mydin Pitchay, the previous chief of the counter-terrorism unit under the Malaysian Special Branch, once warned that religious authorities (and hence, civil servants) are lenient towards foreign preachers who end up radicalizing students, military personnel, and civil servants: "I think, our country's religious authorities need to be more aggressive in screening and investigating the backgrounds of foreign preachers who come to this country. Do not let foreign preachers freely preach in this country because some of them are leaders of militant groups, recruiting our people like university students, members of the government and security forces as happened in the case of JI before" (Mohd Azis Ngah and Mohd Anwar Patho Rohman 2015).

5 I have discussed this topic at length in my other writings. See for example Mohd Faizal Musa (2018, 2020, 2022) and Mohd Faizal Musa and Siti Syazwani Zainal Abidin (2021).

6 This dynamic has been carefully researched by two Japanese academics. According to them:

> The education sector has been the largest employer of ulama, but the ulama's involvement with the state has extended beyond that. Religious leaders also found themselves increasingly more deeply engaged with the state, such as in the federal government where ulama were employed as public servants, especially in Jabatan Kemajuan Islam Malaysia (JAKIM), or the Department of Islamic Development. This department, which was established in 1997, is housed in the Prime Minister's Office. In state governments, ulama are commonly employed in Majlis Agama Islam, or the state's Islamic Religious Council, as well as in the Department of Islamic Affairs, the Mufti's Office and the Sharia Courts. Religious affairs in Malaysia have thus increasingly been mediated by a regulatory regime that has started to define and delimit the nature and space for religious

practice and leadership. According to Article 3 of the Federal Constitution, the Head of State in each state—upon whom the titles such as "Sultan" are bestowed—are defined as the Heads of the Religion of Islam, and have authority over the management of Islamic affairs. Therefore, the state, rather than the ulama, have been identified as responsible for overseeing the administration and leadership of the Muslim community.

7 For additional reading on Malay domination of the civil service, see Woo (2015). On gender imbalance in the civil service, see Lim (2019). On Malaysia's bureaucracy, see Lim (2007).

8 Since 2019, I have had the privilege of being a Principal Researcher for a project led by the American Bar Association and IMAN Research Centre on "Aspects of Freedom of Religion in Malaysia", during which I have been gathering data through my engagements with heads of various religious communities and focus groups discussions with their adherents. The data included in this chapter was gathered through the work that I did for the above project. It is believed that this is the first such comprehensive study which aims to understand the approaches of both religious minorities and the majority in understanding an existing problem and crafting possible solutions.

REFERENCES

Abdul Aziz Bari. 2006. *Politik Perlembagaan: Suatu Perbincangan tentang Isu-Isu Semasa dari Sudut Perlembagaan dan Undang-Undang* [Politics of the Constitution: A Discourse of Current Issues from the Perspective of Constitutional and Legal Aspects]. Kuala Lumpur: Institut Kajian Dasar.

_____. 2009. "Dilema Pegawai Kerajaan: Antara Politik, Kerjaya" [Dilemma of Civil Servants: Between Politics and Career]. *Sinar Harian* 17.

Ahmad Atory Hussain. 2006. "Islam Hadhari: Suatu Kesinambungan Dasar Penerapan Nilai-Nilai Islam Selepas Era Tun Dr. Mahathir Mohamad". *REKAYASA – Journal of Ethics, Legal and Governance* 1, no. 2: 1–10. http://jgd.uum.edu.my/images/vol2_2006/1.rekayasa-2006-ahmad%20atory-ed%20pz-1.pdf.

Ahmad Faiz Yaakob, Asri Salleh, Kamaruzaman Jusoff, and Mohamad Khairul Anwar Hussain. 2012. "Malaysian Civil Service: Problems and Challenges". *UiTM Trengganu E-Academia Journal* 1, no. 1: 132–46. https://ir.uitm.edu.my/id/eprint/14080/ (accessed 12 June 2022).

Bielefeldt, Heiner. 2013. "Report of the Special Rapporteur on Freedom of Religion or Belief, Heiner Bielefeldt". A/HRC/25/58, 2013. http://ap.ohchr.org/documents/dpage_e.aspx?m=86, 7-8.

Case, William. 2019. "Malaysia Today: The Demise of a Hybrid? Not So Fast...". *The Asia Dialogue*, 14 May 2019. https://theasiadialogue.com/2019/05/14/malaysia-today-the-demise-of-a-hybrid-not-so-fast/ (accessed 13 July 2022).

Harian Metro. 2015. "Penjawat Awam Terlibat IS Tak Akan Dibantu", 8 March 2015. https://www.hmetro.com.my/mutakhir/2015/03/35445/penjawat-awam-terlibat-tak-akan-dibantu (accessed 12 February 2018).

Hunter, Murray. 2019. "Malaysian Civil Service's Cancerous Culture". *Asia Sentinel*, 24 October 2019. https://www.asiasentinel.com/p/malaysian-civil-service-cancerous-culture (accessed 17 June 2022).

Imran Ariff. 2021. "Too Much Money for Religious Authorities, Say Critics". *FreeMalaysiaToday*, 29 October 2021. https://www.freemalaysiatoday.com/category/nation/2021/10/29/too-much-money-for-religious-authorities-say-critics/ (accessed 15 March 2022).

Jabatan Kemajuan Islam Malaysia. 2015. "Fungsi JAKIM". http://www.islam.gov.my/node/1211 (accessed 18 November 2016).

Lim Fui Yee Beatrice. 2019. "Women Left Behind? Closing the Gender Gap in Malaysia". *Japan Labour Issues* 3, no. 17: 22–29.

Lim Heng Seng. 2016. "The Federal Constitution, Islamisation and the Malaysian Legal Order". *Legal Herald*, May 2016. https://krisispraxis.com/wp-content/uploads/2016/10/Islamization-Federal-Constitution.pdf (accessed 1 August 2022).

Lim Hong-Hai. 2007. "Improving Administrative Performance in Malaysia: The More Difficult Next Steps". *Reform, Policy and Society* 26, no. 2: 33–59.

Malaysiakini. 2022. "89.23% Penjawat Awam Gred 56 dan Ke Bawah Bumiputera" [89.23% Civil Servants of Grade 56 below are Malays]. *Malaysiakini*, 21 July 2022. https://m.malaysiakini.com/news/629071 (accessed 1 August 2022).

Mohd Azis Ngah and Mohd Anwar Patho Rohman. 2015. "Tidak Tegas Punca Ideologi IS Mudah Meresap" [Permeation of IS Ideology a Cause of Leniency]. *Berita Harian*, 3 May 2015. https://www.bharian.com.my/bhplus-old/2015/05/52452/tidak-tegas-punca-ideologi-mudah-meresap (accessed 24 April 2022).

Mohd Faizal Musa. 2018. "The Riyal and Ringgit of Petro-Islam: Investing Salafism in Education". In *Islam in Southeast Asia: Negotiating Modernity*, edited by Norshahril Saat, pp. 63–87. Singapore: ISEAS – Yusof Ishak Institute.

_____. 2020. "Sunni-Shia Reconciliation in Malaysia". In *Alternative Voices in Muslim Southeast Asia: Discourses and Struggles*, edited by Norshahril Saat and Azhar Ibrahim, pp. 156–82. Singapore: ISEAS – Yusof Ishak Institute.

_____. 2022. *Muslim Sectarianism Versus the De-escalation of Sectarianism in Malaysia*. Trends in Southeast Asia, no. 10/2022. Singapore: ISEAS – Yusof Ishak Institute.

Mohd Faizal Musa and Siti Syazwani Zainal Abidin. 2021. "Longer Term External Conditions Behind Legal Conservatism in Malaysian Islam". *ISEAS Perspective*, no. 2021/23, 4 March 2021.

New Straits Times. 2019. "Dr M to Look into Claims of 'Deep State' in the Civil Service". *New Straits Times*, 8 December 2019. https://www.nst.com.my/news/nation/2019/12/546003/dr-m-look-claims-deep-state-civil-service (accessed 1 August 2022).

Norshahril Saat, Nur Syafiqah Mohd Taufek, and Afra Alatas. 2021. "Rethinking Extremism Beyond Physical Violence: Anti-Shia Hostility in Malaysia". *ISEAS Perspective*, no. 2021/81, 16 June 2021.

Prime Minister's Office. "Dasar Penerapan Nilai-Nilai Islam Dalam Pentadbiran". https://www.pmo.gov.my/dokumenattached/Dasar/10DASAR_PENERAPAN_NILAI.pdf (accessed 17 June 2022).

Rosli Dahlan and Mohammad Afif Daud. 2016. "Malaysia: Who is the Malay". In *Mondaq: Lee Hishammuddin Allen & Gledhill*. https://www.mondaq.com/indigenous-peoples/469128/who-is-the-malay.

Shad Saleem Faruqi. 2011. "Safeguards for Public Servants". *Malaysian Bar*, 19 October 2011. https://www.malaysianbar.org.my/article/news/legal-and-general-news/legal-news/safeguards-for-public-servants.

Shiozaki Yuki and Kushimoto Hiroko. 2014. "Reconfigurations of Islamic Authority in Malaysia". *Asian Journal of Social Science* 42, no. 5: 602–19.

Tjiptoherijanto, Prijono. 2012. "Civil Service Reform in Malaysia: Commitment and Consistency". Working Paper in Economics and Business II (4). Department of Economics, Faculty of Economics, University of Indonesia. https://www.lpem.org/repec/lpe/papers/201204.pdf#page10.

Woo, Kuan Heong. 2015. "Recruitment Practices in the Malaysian Public Sector: Innovations or Political Responses?" *Journal of Public Affairs Education* 21, no. 2: 229–46.

5

DIGITAL ANTI-ISLAMIST ACTIVISM AT THE FOREFRONT OF POLITICAL POLARIZATION IN INDONESIA

Yuji Mizuno[1]

Introduction

Following its democratic transition in 1998 which saw the lifting of the state's grip on religious affairs, there is a broad scholarly agreement that liberal and progressive Islam in Indonesia is on a decline (Fealy 2019; van Bruinessen 2013). Taking advantage of this political opening in the post-Suharto era, Islamist actors have expanded their influence with their majoritarian agenda to normalize religious conservatism at the expense of the country's pluralist fabric (Hefner 2021; Jones 2021) and challenge liberal Islamic intellectuals' "power to define the terms of [religious] debate" (van Bruinessen 2013, p. 4). However, under the Joko Widodo presidency whose political platform embraces religious pluralism, the government has pushed back on Islamism, albeit accompanied by repressive measures, relying on heightened government authority (Mietzner 2018; Fealy 2020; Setijadi 2021). This development is closely associated with the broader trend of "democratic backsliding" or "illiberal turn" under the Widodo government (Power and Warburton 2020; Diprose et al. 2019). Scholars argue that the political elites today are creatively implementing "authoritarian innovations" (Curato and Fossati 2020) to assist such developments, among which increasingly prominent is the use of social media campaigns to stifle opponents and critics as well as to justify controversial government policies (Wijayanto and Berenschot 2021; Sastramidjaja and Wijayanto 2022).

Under such conditions, I argue in this chapter that proponents and sympathizers of liberal Islamic activism have found a new life by incorporating new forms of online media and adapting to the political opportunities, evolving into frontline critics in the war against religious conservatism on cyberspace. In the process, these "digital anti-Islamist activists" as I frame them which include members of the renowned but now-inactive Jaringan Islam Liberal (Liberal Islamic Network, JIL) community, have managed to amass substantial online followings as opinion leaders, spreading their views through highly polemical rhetoric by attracting mainstream media coverage and rattling the Islamist communities and grassroots. In an era characterized by political polarization and democratic regression, however, the use of polarizing rhetoric and prioritizing the defence of the Widodo government's controversial policies have invited scrutiny from the other end of the spectrum of civil society, which emphasizes the preservation of democratic principles.

Based on digital ethnography and original data obtained through interviews,[2] the following sections will shed light on the current wave of resistance by liberal Islamic activists against Islamism, which has unfolded in the digital realm. By examining these actors, this chapter aims not only to update the latest development concerning liberal Islamic actors in Indonesia, but also contribute to understanding the fluid and volatile world of politics in cyberspace and its continuity with the recent political trend such as polarization and democratic backsliding. After detailing the prominent liberal Islamic actors and their forms of activism and public reception towards them, this chapter will examine how Islamists have attempted to silence their activism, albeit generally with little success. Lastly, it will explore how such activism has been received by leftist civil society, in the context of the ongoing discussion concerning the illiberal shift under the Widodo government.

A New Wave of Anti-Islamist Counter-Activism Following the 2017 Election

As cyberspace develops into the "frontier of political communication in Indonesia" (Genta and Wihartono 2018, p. 47), scholars have paid great attention to the preponderance of Islamist and conservative Islamic narratives online (Kirana and Garadian 2021; Sugihartati et al. 2020). For instance, some scholars have examined the disinformation campaign deployed by Islamist grassroots (Facal 2020; Seto 2019) or the underground network of "buzzers"[3] designed to aid Islamist-backed political candidates during elections (Rakhmani and Saraswati 2021). On the other hand, scholars note that moderate Islamic organizations such as Nahdlatul Ulama (NU) were "relatively late to join the online competition for religious authority" (Hoesterey 2021, p. 88). The foremost targets of these Islamist social media operations have been the "vanguard" liberal Islamic actors and groups,[4] most notably the JIL (Ardhianto 2018). Following the rise of Islamism which capitalized on Indonesia's political liberalization in the late 1990s to early 2000s, JIL was formed in 2002 as a countermovement inspired by the *pembaharuan* or Islamic reformism of the 1980s and 1990s to oppose the Islamists by vocally and provocatively advocating for a reinterpretation of the Islamic orthodoxy (Ali 2005; Fealy 2007). However, due to the overwhelming Islamist pressure (offline and online) that disrupted and threatened JIL's activities, its influence significantly declined in the mid-2000s and became effectively inactive by the early 2010s.[5]

Meanwhile, on the other end of the spectrum, grassroots supporters of Joko Widodo and Basuki Tjahaja Purnama (Ahok)'s pluralist platform started organizing social media campaign teams following the 2012 Jakarta election. This was enabled by the coordination and organization provided by political parties, polling agencies, and private actors with know-how concerning online campaigning, which constituted what Saraswati (2020) termed as a "political campaign industry". Several prominent pro-Widodo/Ahok social media influencers emerged from the campaign grassroots in subsequent elections, most notably Denny

Siregar, Eko Kuntadhi, and Permadi Arya (ibid.). Siregar, for example, is one of the most followed pro-Widodo social media influencers, and as of August 2018, he already has more than 625,000 and 560,000 followers on Facebook and Twitter, respectively (Lipson 2018).[6]

Having witnessed the Islamist show of force during the 2016 Aksi Bela Islam (Action to Defend Islam) rally and the 2017 Jakarta gubernatorial election, these pro-Widodo social media influencers ramped up their activism to fight against the Islamist influencers and buzzers in the run-up to the 2019 presidential election. By joining forces with these prominent players involved in the social media campaign ecosystem, some former JIL activists and sympathizers have found new channels to communicate their ideas. Among them are Mohamad Guntur Romli, a JIL activism veteran who also ran for the pluralist pro-Widodo and pro-Ahok Partai Solidaritas Indonesia (Indonesian Solidarity Party, PSI) in 2019. There is also Ade Armando, a JIL sympathizer and an academic based at the University of Indonesia (UI), who emerged as one of the most vocal online supporters of Widodo and Ahok. In addition to building a presence through their own social media accounts, these former JIL activists and sympathizers also built an organized online media channel with the pro-Widodo influencers.

Notably, in 2018, the founders of the JIL, Nong Darol Mahmada and Akhmad Sahal, together with Denny Siregar launched a YouTube channel named *CokroTV*, a pro-Widodo online media platform with a strong orientation toward the defence of religious pluralism. The channel focuses on providing regular commentary on current political and religious topics, many of which pertain to Islam. The commentaries feature hosts from varying backgrounds, ranging from pro-Widodo social media influencers with micro-celebrity statuses such as Siregar and Eko Kuntadhi, as well as figures from the JIL community such as Darol Mahmada, Akhmad Sahal, Armando and Guntur Romli, to prominent academics in the field of Islamic studies such as Syafiq Hasyim and Luthfi Assyaukanie. Moreover, the channel has previously invited the participation of high-profile guests such as Airlangga Hartarto, the chairman of Golkar party and a member of Widodo's cabinet, and Yaqut Cholil Qoumas, the previously leader of the NU's youth organization's paramilitary wing Banser who later assumed the Minister of Religious Affairs office.[7] The channel also regularly invites contributions from PSI politicians with a liberal political outlook, such as Grace Natalie, Rian Ernest, and Faldo Maldini.[8] As of September 2022, the number of subscribers to the channel has reached 1.9 million, which is not far off the numbers of subscribers to channels fronted by conservative celebrity Islamic preachers such as Abdul Somad (2.9 million), Khalid Basalamah (2.3 million), and Felix Siauw (1.2 million), or those run by popular opposition political commentators such as Refly Harun (2.3 million).

The social media activists coalescing around *CokroTV* unite on their shared mission to confront conservative interpretations of Islam and Islamist political narratives. Their polemic attacks ultraconservative Islamic practices that increasingly take hold in Indonesia, including polygamy, the forced use of the veil, the "haramization" of cultural practices with non-Islamic religious origins, and adherence to the puritanical Salafi Islamic movement accompanied by "Arabization" or an equation of Arabic culture and traditions with Islamic authenticity. In addition, they heavily scrutinize the Islamist actors, namely the Islamist political party Partai Keadilan Sejahtera (Prosperous Justice Party, PKS) and the Islamist vigilante group Front Pembela Islam (Islamic Defenders Front, FPI) as well as its leaders Rizieq Shihab and Bahar bin Smith, and even more mainstream figures and institutions, including the controversial clerical body Majelis Ulama Indonesia (Council of Indonesian Islamic Scholars, MUI) and celebrity preachers with a history of making religiously exclusivist statements in their sermons, such as Abdul Somad, Khalid Basalamah, and Felix Siauw. In addition, they are strong backers of the Widodo government's policy of cracking down on extremist Islamist groups such as Hizbut Tahrir Indonesia (HTI) and regulating Islamic affairs (e.g., a volume cap on mosque loudspeakers, regulation of halal certification), and staunch critics to Islamist-backed Anies Baswedan's governance in Jakarta as well as his political manoeuvres for the upcoming 2024 election. In the process, they do not shy away from employing provocative rhetoric that reminisces the controversy caused by JIL in its time. Armando, for example, is known for this, exemplified by his social media post in 2017 that questioned the sacredness of *hadith* (sayings of the Prophet Muhammad) loosely based on classical debate on its authenticity, and a post in 2018 which he claimed that the *adzan* (the call for prayer) is not sacred, both of which were widely covered by the mainstream media and reported to the police by grassroots Islamist activists for alleged blasphemy. The controversy intensified in 2021 after Armando's statement on a *CokroTV* video that he prays the obligatory five times per day even though doing so is not directly prescribed in the Qur'an (detikNews 2021), in addition to his view that Muslims do not need to follow the sharia (Terkini.id 2021). Such statements sparked outrage from high-profile Islamic scholars, including the MUI personnel and imam Shamsi Ali based in New York City.

The use of provocative rhetoric by Armando and his colleagues that attracts mainstream media coverage comes in line with what Tapsell (2015) points out as "spreadability", quoting the concept used by Jenkins, Ford and Green (2009), in his analysis on pro-Widodo/ Ahok social media campaign grassroots. Accordingly, the popular or controversial YouTube or other social media content can influence the broader public debate, as "[television] programs either broadcast the videos or covered the videos' popularity as news or entertainment" (Tapsell 2015, p. 39), and the same dynamics can be observed for print and online news media, thus considerably enwidening the reach of content. While Tapsell discussed this in the context of the "Jokowi phenomenon" during election campaigns, I argue that the same logic can be applied to provocative statements by these influencers in their cyber campaign against Islamist groups. Armando acknowledges that "this is about the domino effect. Or chain reaction. People will look at us, saying what we want to say freely, and this will influence others who feel injustice and dissatisfaction to speak up".[9]

The use of such a polemical style, however, often invites criticism from observers due to the possibility of sustaining or even worsening post-electoral political polarization (Nathaniel 2022). Indeed, their position as influencers and opinion leaders places them at the hub in the pro-Widodo "algorithmic enclave" (Lim 2017, 2021), equipping them with a powerful capacity to reinforce "affective polarization" (Iyengar et al. 2012) between Widodo's supporters and oppositions. Similarly, the use of agitational terms such as *kadrun*,[10] which is frequently used by these influencers, is often scorned for not being productive when having political and religious dialogues.[11] The members of *CokroTV*, on the other hand, echo the view of academic observers who consider that in today's political climate, the "slightest criticism against Islam is already impossible" (Sebastian et al. 2020, p. 2) without provoking a major backlash. As such, they believe in the need for vocal activism to push the boundaries of taboos and inspire people to speak up, with the style that sometimes receives praise for being "delightfully bold and refreshing" in the current climate of religious conversation (Suryakusuma 2020). In addition, members of the channel believe that "the channel is well received by the public, shown by the number of subscribers" and the "societal demand for counter-Islamist activism is rising among the Indonesian public", as people wish to hear from public intellectuals and activists who can "confront the issue of Islamic conservatism with straightforward criticism".[12]

In light of *CokroTV's* increasing popularity, stakeholders of *CokroTV* are expanding its presence beyond cyberspace and seeking to enhance its connectivity "offline". In February 2022, Armando and other former JIL activists and CokroTV participants Nong Darol Mahmada, Mohamad Guntur Romli, and Akhmad Sahal established a non-governmental organisation (NGO) named Pergerakan Indonesia Untuk Semua (Indonesia for All Movement, PIS). Over 130 high-profile individuals signed up as declarators, including politicians from Partai Demokrasi Indonesia Perjuangan (Indonesian Democratic Party of Struggle, PDI-P) and PSI, journalists, academics, artists, clerics and leaders of various religions, and familiar faces such as Denny Siregar and Eko Kuntadhi. In the organization's declaration, Darol Mahmada also specifically thanked prominent politicians such as Wishnutama Kusubandio, a heavyweight in the media industry and a former minister in the Widodo cabinet, and Jeffrie Geovanie, a business mogul who is also the chairman of the PSI's board of trustees (CokroTV 2022), which suggests a strong backing by the political elites. The organization remains small in scale, with members and declarators being recruited directly through invitations by Armando himself. Yet, as he calls it, it is still an "unprecedented" attempt to create a pluralist movement originating from digital activism in Indonesia. The members believe that such an attempt could serve as a starting point for more people to speak up on the issue of religious intolerance, especially in rural areas, which they believe represents the next frontier for advocacy.[13] In the words of Darol Mahmada, the founder of the PIS,

> In many places we go, from Bali to Kupang, we are warmly greeted by the people from local communities who follow our channel. There have been local NGOs and activists in different regions asking us how they

can help in our mission and work together, not only through financial means, but also through networking and activism. This is one of the reasons why we established the PIS, we want to try to embrace these demands.[14]

Islamists' Lacklustre Response

Facing the rise of *CokroTV* and the seemingly unstoppable wave of social media posts by Armando and Siregar, grassroots Islamist activists have grown increasingly anxious about their online presence and called for any available options to halt their activities. For example, *suaraislam.id*, a prominent Islamist online media, referred to *CokroTV* as "a gang of destroyers of Islam" who defend Islamophobia with the government's backing and urged readers to resist them by never accessing their videos (Hidayat 2021). Unlike the time of the JIL, during which Islamist forces could easily dominate the movement through sheer force, Islamists today have a hard time stopping anti-Islamist narratives from spreading online, largely due to the Widodo government's crackdown on extremist Islamist groups and buzzer operations.

Due to these government crackdowns which have weakened their capacity to promote their social cause, both online and offline, Islamists have turned to laws to repress *CokroTV*. Among the most used instruments are Article 28(2) of the Electronic Information and Transactions (ITE) Law, which forbids the spreading of information online that may incite enmity on issues concerning religion, ethnicity, race, and inter-group relations (SARA), and Article 156a of the Criminal Code, which prohibits the defamation of religion. Both articles are highly controversial due to their history of being used to legally justify the "blasphemy ban" and restrict open conversation on religious issues (Amnesty International 2014). For several years, online-based anti-Islamist and pro-Widodo activists and influencers such as Guntur Romli, Armando, Siregar, Kuntadhi, Arya, Muannas Alaidid,[15] and Husin Shihab[16] all have become targets of police reports by grassroots Islamist activists.[17] However, none of these attempted prosecutions have been successful.[18] Islamist leaders such as Novel Bamukmin as well as opposition social media activists such as Refly Harun have repeatedly criticized the failure of these prosecutions by highlighting examples of the police's quick responses against Islamist leaders such as Rizieq Shihab, Bahar bin Smith, and Maaher At-Thuwailibi, alleging an uneven application of the law by the state apparatus against this particular group of activists, who represent the government's interests. This situation has contributed to the activists being labelled *"buzzer istana"* (palace buzzers) or shills paid to manufacture particular public opinions and sentiments in favour of the government's interest.[19] Former JIL activists argue that such an accusation is baseless. Darol Mahmada, for instance, stated that *CokroTV* operates based on a YouTube Partner Program, which enables content creators to earn revenue from advertisements included in their videos, with the revenue being split between the speakers and the compensation to the guests. While the channel does receive donations from unnamed supporters who endorse its activism against religious intolerance, such donations do not come from the government, nor are the amounts involved huge, and the money is mostly spent on fees to rent the studio.[20] Unlike the original JIL community, which relied on donations from foreign development agencies such as the United States Agency for International Development (USAID) (Fealy 2019; Gillespie 2007), the current online media monetization system has ensured the continuity of the channel's activism and simultaneously rendered the "paid shill" and "foreign agent" accusations ineffective.

Considering their inability to legally persecute liberal activists, the grassroots Islamist activists have continued to explore the possibility of violently suppressing such activism through other measures. For example, in November 2020, Rizieq Shihab, the head honcho of FPI, asserted that the police's failure to take the "blasphemy" of these anti-Islamist activists seriously is "intolerable" and could lead to an explosive outcome. "Why is Denny Siregar being left untouched, Ade Armando being left untouched, Abu Janda [Permadi Arya] being left untouched? ... This could be a ticking time bomb that can explode at any time", decried Rizieq (CNN Indonesia 2020). In November 2021, following the aftermath of Armando's "five-time prayers" controversy, Novel Bamukmin, a former cadre of the FPI and the leader of the PA212,[21] stated there will be "street justice" against Armando in the form of violent reprisals if the government is slow to implement the appropriate legal procedure (Suara.com 2021). Fast forward to 11 April 2022, a vicious incident occurred during a student protest against the

Widodo government's alleged attempt to extend the presidential limit as well as the rising prices of basic commodities. Armando, while himself a Widodo supporter, was present in front of the parliament building with the PIS crew to support the students' demands and shoot a video for his social media. However, after he argued with some women regarding his social media content, a crowd gathered around him while a group of men brutally assaulted Armando. When the police finally rescued him, he was covered in blood (Kompas 2022a). Despite calls by pro-government politicians for the national Student Executive Body (BEM SI) to take responsibility for the incident (Tempo 2022), the police later confirmed that the assailants were not from among the student protesters; rather, they were motivated by their fury at Armando's social media content (Kompas 2022b). Supporters of Armando such as Grace Natalie publicly suggested that the attackers came from the grassroots of the now-disbanded FPI and HTI, who happened to be at the scene of the assault and managed to exploit the opportunity (Suara.com 2022).

This incident added to the long history of threats experienced by liberal Islamic activists, harkening back to past incidents such as the death penalty fatwa in 2002 and the attempted bomb assassination in 2011 against the chief coordinator of the JIL, Ulil Abshar Abdalla. It also echoed the "Monas Incident" on 1 June 2008, the Pancasila Day, which witnessed an attack by the FPI against liberal Islamic activists including Darol Mahmada and Guntur Romli, who rallied under the banner of a civil coalition known as the National Alliance for Freedom of Religion and Belief (AKKBB). Contrary to the intentions of grassroots Islamist activists, however, the incident and the subsequent media coverage of it caused Armando to garner both popular sympathy and political support. For instance, Mahfud MD, one of the coordinating ministers in the Widodo cabinet, expressed regret on behalf of the government and urged the police to act decisively against the perpetrators (detikNews 2022b). Before long, the assailants were identified and apprehended by the police, while Armando recovered and returned to *CokroTV* after around a month of hospitalization. Recalling the incident and the government's firm handling, *CokroTV* activists reaffirmed the importance of government protection. "Unlike during the time of the Susilo Bambang Yudhoyono government, the state apparatus today is decisive, and that is why against all odds, we are still here".[22]

"The Jokowi government, police, and military are all united in their opposition to Islamist groups" and despite the adversity, "we feel protected, and we are not afraid. We are optimistic about the future of our activity".[23]

Mutual Suspicion Between Progressive Civil Society Organizations

The Widodo administration, particularly in its second term, has invited heightened public scrutiny for enacting policies that have curtailed civil liberty and eroded institutional mechanisms to ensure horizontal accountability (Mujani and Liddle 2021). In the face of mounting criticism, supporters of the ruling elites have geared up their social media campaign machinery to conduct wide scale political manipulation to suppress political opponents and critics to its governance (Sastramidjaja and Wijayanto 2022). As key players in the pro-Widodo algorithmic enclaves, anti-Islamist influencers, with their absolute trust in Widodo as the champion of religious pluralism, also played their part in apologetics of the controversial policies and denouncing critics. They occasionally involve political Islam in issues with no direct relevance to it, attempting to "poison the well". Among the most documented is the Widodo government and its social media army's sustained effort to spread the "Taliban infiltration" allegation in the Komisi Pemberantasan Korupsi (Corruption Eradication Commission, KPK). The leading pro-Widodo influencer, Denny Siregar, was among this conspiracy's earliest and most enthusiastic grassroots propagators[24] (Saraswati 2020), and *CokroTV* hosted his commentary in August 2019 before the ratification of the revised KPK bill. The allegation proved popular among the partisan Widodo supporters, with many other anti-Islamist activists also approving this theory. He delved down on this allegation in the channel again later when the issue became a boiling topic in May 2021 after the dismissal of high-ranking KPK investigators including Novel Baswedan, known for his outward Islamic piety and being a cousin of Islamist-friendly Anies Baswedan.

In addition, the *CokroTV* collective has consistently shown a heightened sensitivity to NGOs with critical views towards the Widodo administration. For instance, Siregar has attacked anti-corruption NGOs for defending the KPK for allegedly being collusive with

Baswedan. However, this became more visible in June 2021 when Armando, Darol Mahmada, and others announced the establishment of Civil Society Watch (CSW) as a channel division. In Armando's own words, the mission of CSW is "[to be] watchful of civil society that can be categorized as harmful to the interest of the people of Indonesia" (Civil Society Watch 2021). This initiative invited widespread scrutiny by leftist civil society, with members of NGOs such as the Setara Institute, Legal Aid Foundation of Indonesia (YLBHI), Institute for Criminal Justice Reform, and many more voicing criticisms or scepticism regarding the CSW endangering the already shrinking room available for criticism of the state. In clarifying his meaning, Armando argued that "civil society" in this context can mean many things, ranging from mass organizations such as Pemuda Pancasila, clerical organizations such as the MUI, labour unions, to the mass media. Before the announcement of the CSW, however, in a session that discussed the issue of the heightening Papuan insurgency, Armando criticized a diverse group of NGOs by name, including Amnesty International, KontraS, WALHI, Setara Institute, ICW, and Lembaga Bantuan Hukum (Legal Aid Institute, LBH) for signing a petition to reject the government's attempt to designate the insurgents previously known by the Indonesian government as the Papuan Armed Criminal Group (KKB) as a terrorist organization (Suparman 2021). This represented a follow up to his prior statement that there are "evil NGOs and media" and encouragement of citizens to provide information to "expose" these unnamed entities (Armando 2021). The apologetics concerning the Widodo government's illiberal policies and the stance that can be seen to be undermining the horizontal accountability have made leftist civil society highly suspicious of CSW's aims. Transparency International Indonesia (TII), for example, commented that an effort by one civil society group to monitor other civil society groups is not urgently required in the current climate of Indonesian politics. In contrast, it is much more critical to hold the government accountable against the backdrop of the worsening quality of democracy and declining scores on democracy indices (CNN Indonesia 2021). Others have voiced much stronger views. For instance, an academic stated that CSW's work is "no different to the intelligence unit" or "Pam Swakarsa" (voluntary security guards working for the state intelligence) (Abdil 2021).

The anti-Islamist activists continued to back controversial actions by government officials on other occasions, including the arrest of two human rights activists—Haris Azhar and Fatia Maulidiyanti—for accusing Coordinating Minister of Maritime Affairs and Investment, Luhut Binsar Pandjaitan, of violating the ITE law. In one case, however, an influencer "crossed the line" by engaging in a direct lawsuit. This came in November 2021, when Husin Alwi Shihab, a former PSI politician[25] and declarator of PIS with an extensive track record of reporting high-profile Islamist leaders such as Bahar bin Smith to the police, premeditatively attempted to sue Greenpeace Indonesia, after their criticism of Widodo's speech on deforestation at the COP26 Climate Summit, on the ground that "they were paid to make noise" and to spread misinformation. Shihab echoed the belief held by Luhut that NGOs need to be audited and monitored by the government to prevent them from "provoking" the community (Noor 2021). He only withdrew the lawsuit after public outcry, and Greenpeace denounced him that such an action will "destroy the climate of democracy" (Rohana 2021).[26]

The liberal anti-Islamist activists' alignment with the Widodo government's illiberal policies, and the mutual suspicion between the progressive civil society, comes in line with the scholars' several frameworks on civil society's fragmented response towards Widodo's authoritarian turn. In his observation, Mietzner (2020) argued that the democratic erosion in Indonesia has been enabled by the rupture of civil society and the weakening of its capacity to ensure the diagonal accountability mechanisms, as primordial and identity-based cleavages have created divisions between the components of civil society. Bourchier and Jusuf (2022), in their historical analysis of liberal political thought in Indonesia, pointed out that the liberals, without its strong societal basis, have had "limited political choices when they have had to defend their interests" and frequently relied on stronger allies and patrons, including the authoritarian state. From the Marxist standpoint, Abdil (2022) viewed this as the symptom of the "bourgeois reformism" resulting from the absence of class-based organized left, which exposes the fundamental limitation of civil society activism in Indonesia. As the cycle of strengthening Islamist majoritarianism and the state's repressive response continues, the phenomenon points to the need for continued scholarly attention and theorizing on the mechanism of societal support to the heightened state authority.

Conclusion

Focusing on social media-based anti-Islamist influencers, this chapter has shown that the contours of vanguard liberal Islamic activism during the second term of the Widodo government has been characterized by rising Islamic conservatism and the state's repressive response. It has also illustrated the unceasing political polarization of civil society (especially within the cyberspace), and the increasingly illiberal tendency of government policies that put some progressives in a dilemmatic position between a "rock (of state authoritarianism) and a hard place (Islamic radicalism)" (Suryakusuma 2020).

This chapter has also shown that activists and influencers who coalesce around *CokroTV* have been vocal in pushing the boundaries of conversations surrounding Islamic conservatism, including using a highly provocative style that invites mainstream media coverage, enabled by the muted response by the Islamist activists whose strength has been dwindling after the state clampdown. However, responses to their activism have varied widely. On one hand, these anti-Influencers enjoy strong support from the public as observed by the increasing number of followers on their social media which suggests that counter-activism against Islamism has a strong societal demand despite the decline of organizations such as the JIL during the previous generation. In fact, it is possible to see a further increased presence if the collective continues to expand its reach, potentially through collaborations with the community-based liberal Islamic NGOs and the sophistication of religious arguments through the participation of scholars and activists versed in Islamic tradition. However, on the other hand, their uncompromising stance on using provocative methods to counter Islamism has ignited an increased call by grassroots Islamist activists for their activism to be silenced. Furthermore, the group's staunch pro-Widodo stance, which has brought them to the defence of some of the government's controversial policies, has occasionally led to mutual suspicion between them and the leftist segment of civil society.

NOTES

1 The author wishes to thank the conveners and participants of the ISEAS workshop on the "Trendsetters of Islam in Maritime Southeast Asia: Emerging Discourses and Trending Ideologues" for their valuable comments,

Fachry Aidulsyah for his helpful advice during the course of research, and Iqra Anugrah for his constructive feedback on the draft manuscript.

2 The interviews were conducted in June 2022, with the main actors of the *CokroTV*.

3 "Buzzers" are the operators of fake or anonymous accounts that support a certain political agenda in exchange for monetary compensation. They should be distinguished from "social media influencers", who include celebrities and high-profile activists working for particular political interests under their real names, with or without monetary incentives. However, people often use "buzzer" as a catch-all term for any social media users alleged to be working for particular political clients. Pro-government influencers, for example, are often derided as "palace buzzers" (*buzzer istana*) who are paid by the government elites to propagate pro-government views. For more on buzzers and influencers, see Wijayanto and Berenschot (2021), Rasidi and Sukmani (2021) and Sastramidjaja and Wijayanto (2022).

4 Fealy (2019) distinguishes between the different approaches of liberal and progressive Islamic activism in Indonesia. The "vanguard" activists lead the public discourse and influence policymaking, and in the process, they often employ polemics against conservative Islamic groups. This tactic is best exemplified by the Liberal Islamic Network (JIL). The other main approach is "community-based" activism, which constitutes the majority of liberal grassroots activism in Indonesia. It is best exemplified by non-governmental organizations and think tanks such as the Wahid Institute and Maarif Institute (which are affiliated with the moderate Islamic mass organizations Nahdlatul Ulama and Muhammadiyah, respectively). Community-based activists are generally more cautious concerning backlash and so adopt strategies such as education and community building to ensure the acceptance of religious tolerance among the wider public.

5 The package bomb attack against the JIL office in the 68H Utan Kayu street in March 2011, aimed at the chief coordinator of the JIL Ulil Abshar Abdalla, marked the turning point for the JIL's activity. In the interview with the author (7 June 2022), one of the founding members of the JIL Nong Darol Mahmada recalled that the incident forced the JIL to halt its activity to prevent further disturbance against the broader Utan Kayu cultural community.

6 As of June 2022, Denny Siregar boasts 1.7 million followers on Twitter and almost 1 million followers on Facebook, making him one of the giants in the social media scenes.

7 Both shows aired in 2018. Other high-profile guests included Mahfud MD, who in 2018 was still contesting his nomination as a vice presidential candidate paired with Widodo for the 2019 election.

8   Observers find the strong influence of JIL activists and their ideas to the birth of the PSI, and as such it is not surprising to see the intertwinement between the PSI politicians and the *CokroTV* and its organizational body PIS. For more on the JIL's influence to the PSI, see Savirani et al. (2021).
9   Interview with Ade Armando (8 June 2022).
10 *"Kadrun"* is shorthand for *"kadal gurun"*, which refers to the dabb lizard that inhabits North Africa and the Middle East. The term is widely used online as an agitational label with racist undertones against perceived supporters of the Islamist agenda (Heriyanto 2019).
11 The view was shared by the founder of the JIL, Ulil Abshar Abdalla, among others (Republika 2022).
12 Interviews with Nong Darol Mahmada (7 June 2022) and Ade Armando (8 June 2022). According to Darol Mahmada, initially *CokroTV* mostly featured a discussion with invited guests, although this format did not take off. The channel then switched to a much more confrontational style whereby the hosts does not mince words and instead offered straightforward commentary, which garnered much more significant user traffic.
13 Interview with Ade Armando (8 June 2022).
14 Interview with Nong Darol Mahmada (7 June 2022).
15 A lawyer of Siregar and Armando.
16 A former PSI politician and a declarator of PIS. More on Shihab in the next section.
17 In many of these cases, the anti-Islamist activists retaliate against their Islamist opponents by also reporting them to the police based on the ITE Law.
18 A recent example of a pro-Widodo influencer who was convicted under this law is Ferdinand Hutahaean, a former Democrat Party member. Hutahaean was sentenced to five months in prison by the Central Jakarta District Court on 19 April 2022, for violating Article 14(1) of Law No. 1 of 1946 regarding the Regulation of Criminal Law, which prohibits spreading fake information or intentionally causing public unrest. The case was based on a series of social media posts that included the statement "your God is weak" in January 2022 in the context of Bahar bin Smith's case. This post invited an allegation of incitement based on SARA by grassroots Islamist activists (detikNews 2022a).
19 For example, JPNN (2021).
20 Interview with Nong Darol Mahmada (7 June 2022).
21 PA212 or the 212 Alumni Brotherhood is an organization that mostly consists of the remnants of the 2016 *Aksi Bela Islam* rally organizers, chiefly the ex-FPI cadres.
22 Interview with Nong Darol Mahmada (7 June 2022).
23 Interview with Ade Armando (8 June 2022).

24 The term "Taliban" in reference to the KPK investigators first circulated in May 2019 after a journalist Neta S. Pane's comment on alleged division within the KPK between the "India" faction hailed from the police and the "Taliban" faction led by Novel Baswedan. While initially stayed under the radar, the "Taliban" reference suddenly became viral on both online and mainstream media after being picked up by Denny Siregar on his social media post on June 13. In his post, Siregar spun the "Taliban" context into an issue of radical Islamic infiltration within the KPK, specifically accusing Baswedan and the former KPK commissioner Bambang Widjojanto as the "Taliban" prosecutors (CNN Indonesia 2019).

25 Shihab was dismissed by the PSI in 2018 due to his conflicting viewpoint with PSI's value on the issue of polygamy.

26 In one case, an anti-Islamist activism engaged in "friendly fire", inviting backlash. This came in September 2022 when pro-Widodo influencer Eko Kuntadhi mistakenly insulted a female religious teacher based in a prominent East Javanese Islamic boarding school, mistakenly perceived to be an Islamic radical, inviting fierce protest by the members of NU community. Kuntadhi took responsibility by making a public apology and visit to the school, and resigning from his position as the head of a volunteer organization for Ganjar Pranowo's 2024 presidential bid.

REFERENCES

Abdil Mughis Mudhoffir. 2022. "The Limits of Civil Society Activism in Indonesia: The Case of the Weakening of the KPK". *Critical Asian Studies*: 1–21.

Alfian Putra Abdi. 2021. "Kontroversi Civil Society Watch ala Ade Armando yang Menuai Kritik". *Tirto*, 9 June 2021. https://tirto.id/kontroversi-civil-society-watch-ala-ade-armando-yang-menuai-kritik-ggFT (accessed 27 September 2022).

Ali, Muhammad Ali. 2005. "The Rise of the Liberal Islam Network (JIL) in Contemporary Indonesia". *American Journal of Islamic Social Sciences* 22, no. 1: 1–27.

Amnesty International. 2014. *Prosecuting Beliefs: Indonesia's Blasphemy Laws*. London: Amnesty International.

Ardhianto, Imam. 2018. "Contemporary Islamic Movement, Popular Culture and Public Sphere in Indonesia: The #IndonesiaTanpaJIL Movement". *Archipel* 95: 151–71.

Armando, Ade. 2021. "Kirim Cerita Anda ke Cokro TV untuk Bongkar LSM dan Media Jahat". *CokroTV*, 27 March 2021. https://cokro.tv/2021/03/27/

kirim-cerita-anda-ke-cokro-tv-untuk-bongkar-lsm-dan-media-jahat/ (accessed 27 September 2022).

Bourchier, David and Windu Jusuf. 2022. "Liberalism in Indonesia: Between Authoritarian Statism and Islamism". *Asian Studies Review*: 1–19.

Civil Society Watch. 2021. "Tentang CSW". Civil Society Watch. https://csw.id/tentang-csw/ (accessed 27 September 2022).

CNN Indonesia. 2019. "Kisruh Polisi Taliban Vs India Jelang Seleksi Pimpinan KPK". *CNN Indonesia*, 2 July 2019. https://www.cnnindonesia.com/nasional/20190702164035-12-408358/kisruh-polisi-taliban-vs-india-jelang-seleksi-pimpinan-kpk (accessed 27 September 2022).

———. 2020. "Rizieq Shihab Ingatkan Bahaya 'Bom Waktu' yang Bakal Meledak". *CNN Indonesia*, 12 November 2020. https://www.cnnindonesia.com/nasional/20201112043836-20-568792/rizieq-shihab-ingatkan-bahaya-bom-waktu-yang-bakal-meledak (accessed 27 September 2022).

———. 2021. "TII Soal Ade Armando Bentuk CSW: Awasi Negara, Bukan Warga". *CNN Indonesia*, 8 June 2021. https://www.cnnindonesia.com/nasional/20210608104544-20-651600/tii-soal-ade-armando-bentuk-csw-awasi-negara-bukan-warga (accessed 27 September 2022).

CokroTV. 2022. "[LIVE] DEKLARASI PERGERAKAN INDONESIA UNTUK SEMUA (PIS) [Video]". YouTube. https://www.youtube.com/watch?v=H4jJrd9fsGU&t=1029s (accessed 27 September 2022).

Curato, Nicole and Diego Fossati. 2020. "Authoritarian Innovations: Crafting Support for a Less Democratic Southeast Asia". *Democratization* 27, no. 6: 1006–20.

detikNews. 2021. "Ade Armando: Perintah Salat 5 Waktu Tidak Ada dalam Al-Qur'an". *detikNews*, 3 November 2021. https://news.detik.com/berita/d-5795034/ade-armando-perintah-salat-5-waktu-tidak-ada-dalam-al-quran (accessed 27 September 2022).

———. 2022a. "Ferdinand Hutahaean Divonis 5 Bulan Bui di Kasus Cuitan 'Allahmu Lemah'!". *detikNews*, 3 November 2021. https://news.detik.com/berita/d-6040167/ferdinand-hutahaean-divonis-5-bulan-bui-di-kasus-cuitan-allahmu-lemah (accessed 27 September 2022).

———. 2022b. "Mahfud Md Minta Penganiaya Ade Armando Ditindak: Bahaya bagi Negara Kita". *detikNews*, 12 April 2022. https://news.detik.com/berita/d-6029562/mahfud-md-minta-penganiaya-ade-armando-ditindak-bahaya-bagi-negara-kita (accessed 27 September 2022).

Diprose, Rachel, Dave McRae and Vedi Hadiz. 2019. "Two Decades of Reformasi in Indonesia: Its Illiberal Turn". *Journal of Contemporary Asia* 49, no. 5: 691–712.

Facal, Gabriel. 2020. "Islamic Defenders Front Militia (Front Pembela Islam) and its Impact on Growing Religious Intolerance in Indonesia". *TRaNS: Trans-Regional and -National Studies of Southeast Asia* 8, no. 1: 7–20.

Fealy, Greg. 2007. "A Conservative Turn". *Inside Indonesia*, 15 July 2007. https://www.insideindonesia.org/a-conservative-turn (accessed 27 September 2022).

———. 2019. "Reformasi and the Decline of Liberal Islam". In *Activists in Transition: Progressive Politics in Democratic Indonesia*, edited by Thushara Dibley and Michele Ford, pp. 117–34. Ithaca: Cornell University Press.

———. 2020. "Jokowi in the Covid-19 era: Repressive Pluralism, Dynasticism and the Overbearing State". *Bulletin of Indonesian Economic Studies* 56, no. 3: 301–23.

Genta, Kuno Yoseph and Wihartono. 2018. "Reconfiguring Post-Ahok Populism, Post-truth, and Cyberspace in Indonesia". In *Proceedings of the 4th International Conference on Contemporary Social and Political Affairs* (ICoCSPA): 47–58.

Gillespie, Piers. 2007. "Current Issues in Indonesian Islam: Analysing the 2005 Council of Indonesian Ulama Fatwa no. 7 Opposing Pluralism, Liberalism and Secularism". *Journal of Islamic Studies* 18, no. 2: 202–40.

Hefner, Robert. 2021. "Islamism and the Struggle for Inclusive Citizenship". In *Religious Pluralism in Indonesia: Threats and Opportunities for Democracy*, edited by Chiara Formichi, pp. 14 –37. Ithaca: Cornell University Press.

Heriyanto, Devina. 2019. "The Rise of 'Kadrun' and 'Togog': Why Political Polarization in Indonesia is Far from Over". *The Jakarta Post*, 20 November 2019. https://www.thejakartapost.com/news/2019/11/19/the-rise-of-kadrun-and-togog-why-political-polarization-in-indonesia-is-far-from-over.html (accessed 15 August 2022).

Hidayat, Nuim. 2021. "Cokro TV, Geng Perusak Islam". *Suaraislam.id*, 4 November 2021. https://suaraislam.id/cokro-tv-geng-perusak-islam/ (accessed 15 August 2022).

Hoesterey, James B. 2021. "Nahdlatul Ulama's 'Funny Brigade': Piety, Satire, and Indonesian Online Divides". *Cyber Orient* 15, no. 1: 85–118.

Iyengar, Shanto, Gaurav Sood and Yphtach Lelkes. 2012. "Affect, Not Ideology: A Social Identity Perspective on Polarization". *Public Opinion Quarterly* 76, no. 3: 405–31.

Jenkins, Henry, Sam Ford and Joshua Green. 2009. *Spreadable Media: Creating Value and Meaning in a Networked Culture*. New York: New York University Press.

Jones, Sidney. 2021. "The Rise of Islamist Majoritarianism". In *Religious Pluralism in Indonesia: Threats and Opportunities for Democracy*, edited by Chiara Formichi, pp. 38–57. Ithaca: Cornell University Press.

JPNN. 2021. "Tuduh Jenderal Dudung Menista Agama, Novel Bandingkan dengan Ade Armando". *JPNN*, 30 January 2022. https://www.jpnn.com/news/tuduh-jenderal-dudung-menista-agama-novel-bandingkan-dengan-ade-armando (accessed 15 August 2022).

Kirana, Dita and Endi Aulia Garadian. 2021. "Religious Trend in Contemporary Indonesia: Conservatism Domination on Social Media". *Studia Islamika* 27, no. 3: 615–22.

Kompas. 2022a. "Kronologi Ade Armando Dikeroyok Setengah Jam, Diklaim Bermula dari Provokasi Ibu-Ibu". *Kompas*, 12 April 2022. https://nasional.kompas.com/read/2022/04/12/08500841/kronologi-ade-armando-dikeroyok-setengah-jam-diklaim-bermula-dari-provokasi?page=all (accessed 15 August 2022).

_____. 2022b. "Motif Pengeroyok Ade Armando, Terprovokasi dan Kesal dengan Pendapat Korban". *Kompas*, 13 April 2022. https://megapolitan.kompas.com/read/2022/04/13/17530901/motif-pengeroyok-ade-armando-terprovokasi-dan-kesal-dengan-pendapat?page=all (accessed 15 August 2022).

Lim, Merlyna. 2017. "Freedom to Hate: Social Media, Algorithmic Enclaves, and the Rise of Tribal Nationalism in Indonesia". *Critical Asian Studies* 49, no. 3: 411–27.

_____. 2021. "Algorithmic Enclaves: Affective Politics and Algorithms in the Neoliberal Social Media Landscape". In *Affective Politics of Digital Media: Propaganda by Other Means*, edited by Megan Bowler and Elizabeth Davis, pp. 186–203. New York: Routledge.

Lipson, David. 2018. "Indonesia's 'Buzzers' Paid to Spread Propaganda as Political Elite Wage War Ahead of Election". *ABC News*, 13 August 2018. https://www.abc.net.au/news/2018-08-13/indonesian-buzzers-paid-to-spread-propaganda-ahead-of-election/9928870 (accessed 15 August 2022).

Mietzner, Marcus. 2018. "Fighting Illiberalism with Illiberalism: Islamist Populism and Democratic Deconsolidation in Indonesia". *Pacific Affairs* 91, no. 2: 261–82.

_____. 2020. "Sources of Resistance to Democratic Decline: Indonesian Civil Society and its Trials". *Democratization* 28, no. 1: 161–78.

Mujani, Saiful and R. William Liddle. 2021. "Indonesia: Jokowi Sidelines Democracy". *Journal of Democracy* 32, no. 4: 72–86.

Nathaniel, Felix. 2022. "Ade Armando dan Polarisasi Politik yang Terus Dipertahankan". *Tirto*, 17 April 2022. https://tirto.id/ade-armando-dan-polarisasi-politik-yang-terus-dipertahankan-grfS (accessed 15 August 2022).

Noor, Wulandari. 2021. "Usai Dipolisikan, Greenpeace Dicecar Husin Shihab: Tak Menutup Kemungkinan Mereka Dibayar untuk Bikin Gaduh". *Pikiran Rakyat*, 15 November 2021. https://depok.pikiran-rakyat.com/nasional/pr-093016973/usai-dipolisikan-greenpeace-dicecar-husin-shihab-tak-menutup-kemungkinan-mereka-dibayar-untuk-bikin-gaduh (accessed 15 August 2022).

Power, Thomas and Eve Warburton. 2020. "The Decline of Indonesian Democracy". In *Democracy in Indonesia: From Stagnation to Regression?*, edited by Thomas Power and Eve Warburton, pp. 1–22. Singapore: ISEAS – Yusof Ishak Institute.

Rakhmani, Inaya and Muninggar Sri Saraswati. 2021. "Authoritarian Populism in Indonesia: The Role of the Political Campaign Industry in Engineering Consent and Coercion". *Journal of Current Southeast Asian Affairs* 40, no. 3: 436–60.

Rasidi, Pradipa P. and Khoirun Nisa Aulia Sukmani. 2021. "Languages of Propaganda". *Inside Indonesia*, 13 October 2021. https://www.insideindonesia.org/languages-of-propaganda (accessed 1 July 2022).

Republika. 2022. "Usai Pengeroyokan Ade Armando, Istilah Kadrun Ramai Lagi di Jagat Maya". *Republika*, 14 April 2022. https://www.republika.co.id/berita/rabo26377/usai-pengeroyokan-ade-armando-istilah-kadrun-ramai-lagi-di-jagat-maya (accessed 1 July 2022).

Rohana. 2021. "Kata Kiki Taufik Soal Husin Shihab Cabut Laporan untuk Greenpeace: Saya Senang, tapi Jelas Kita...". *Pikiran Rakyat*, 16 November 2021. https://depok.pikiran-rakyat.com/nasional/pr-093027695/kata-kiki-taufik-soal-husin-shihab-cabut-laporan-untuk-greenpeace-saya-senang-tapi-jelas-kita (accessed 15 August 2022).

Saraswati, Muninggar Sri. 2020. "The Political Campaign Industry and the Rise of Disinformation in Indonesia". In *From Grassroots Activism to Disinformation: Social Media in Southeast Asia*, edited by Aim Sinpeng and Ross Tapsell, pp. 43–62. Singapore: ISEAS – Yusof Ishak Institute.

Sastramidjaja, Yatun and Wijayanto. 2022. *Cyber Troops, Online Manipulation of Public Opinion and Co-optation of Indonesia's Cyberspace*. Trends in Southeast Asia, no. 7/2022. Singapore: ISEAS – Yusof Ishak Institute.

Savirani, Amalinda, Nuruddin Al Akbar, Ulya Nami Efrina Jamson and Listiana Asworo. 2021. "Floating Liberals: Female Politicians, Progressive Politics, and PSI in the 2019 Indonesian Election". *Journal of Current Southeast Asian Affairs* 40, no. 1: 116–35.

Sebastian, Leonard C., Syafiq Hasyim and Alexander R. Arifianto. 2020. "Introduction: Rising Islamic Conservatism in Indonesia: Islamic Groups and Identity Politics". In *Rising Islamic Conservatism in Indonesia*, edited by Leonard C. Sebastian, Syafiq Hasyim and Alexander R. Arifianto, pp. 1–13. London; New York: Routledge.

Setijadi, Charlotte 2021. "The Pandemic as Political Opportunity: Jokowi's Indonesia in the Time of Covid-19". *Bulletin of Indonesian Economic Studies* 57, no. 3: 297–320.

Seto, Ario. 2019. "Islamist Buzzers: Message Flooding, Offline Outreach, and Astroturfing". *Austrian Journal of South-East Asian Studies* 12, no. 2: 187–208.

Suara.com. 2021. "Novel Bamukmin Desak Aparat Tangkap Ade Armando, Soal Pernyataan Salat Lima Waktu". Suara.com, 7 November 2021. https://banten.suara.com/read/2021/11/07/140154/novel-bamukmin-desak-aparat-tangkap-ade-armando-soal-pernyataan-salat-lima-waktu (accessed 1 July 2022).

_____. 2022. "Sebut-sebut Nama Jenderal Dudung Hingga Ade Armando Dan Abu Janda, Ini 3 Tuntutan Di Aksi PA 212 Siang Ini". Suara.com, 25 March 2022. https://www.suara.com/news/2022/03/25/122248/sebut-sebut-nama-jenderal-dudung-hingga-ade-armando-dan-abu-janda-ini-3-tuntutan-di-aksi-pa-212-siang-ini (accessed 1 July 2022).

Sugihartati, Rahma, Bagong Suyanto and Medhy Aginta Hidayat. 2020. "Channelization Strategies of Radicalism Among Muslim University Students in Indonesia". *Journal of Indonesian Islam* 14, no. 2: 309–34.

Suparman, Fana F. 2021. "Civil Society Watch Sayangkan Sikap Koalisi Masyarakat Tolak Label KKB Teroris." *Berita Satu*, 9 May 2021. https://www.beritasatu.com/archive/771785/civil-society-watch-sayangkan-sikap-koalisi-masyarakat-tolak-label-kkb-teroris (accessed 1 July 2022).

Suryakusuma, Julia. 2020. "Indonesia: Between a Rock and a Hard Place?" *The Jakarta Post*, 5 February 2020. https://www.thejakartapost.com/academia/2020/02/05/indonesia-between-a-rock-and-a-hard-place.html (accessed 1 July 2022).

Tapsell, Ross. 2015. "Indonesia's Media Oligarchy and the 'Jokowi Phenomenon'". *Indonesia* 99 (April): 29–50.

_____. 2020. "The Media and Democratic Decline". In *Democracy in Indonesia: From Stagnation to Regression?*, edited by Thomas Power and Eve Warburton, pp. 210–28. Singapore: ISEAS – Yusof Ishak Institute.

Tempo. 2022. "Ade Armando Dikeroyok, Politisi PDIP Gilbert Simanjuntak Desak BEM SI Minta Maaf". *Tempo*, 13 April 2022. https://metro.tempo.co/read/1581809/ade-armando-dikeroyok-politisi-pdip-gilbert-simanjuntak-desak-bem-si-minta-maaf (accessed 1 July 2022).

Terkini.id. 2021. "Ade Armando: Saya Beragama Islam, tapi Saya Tidak Percaya bahwa Umat Islam Harus Menjalankan Syariat Islam". *Terkini.id*, 16 October 2021. https://makassar.terkini.id/ade-armando-saya-beragama-islam-tapi-saya-tidak-percaya-bahwa-umat-islam-harus-menjalankan-syariat-islam/ (accessed 1 July 2022).

van Bruinessen, Martin. 2013. "Introduction: Contemporary Developments in Indonesian Islam and the 'Conservative Turn' of the Early Twenty First Century". In *Contemporary Developments in Indonesian Islam: Explaining the "Conservative Turn"*, edited by Martin van Bruinessen, pp. 1–20. Singapore: ISEAS – Yusof Ishak Institute.

Wijayanto and Ward Berenschot. 2021. "Organisation and Funding of Social Media Propaganda". *Inside Indonesia*, 13 October 2021. https://www.insideindonesia.org/organisation-and-funding-of-social-media-propaganda (accessed 27 September 2022).

6

SURVEILLANCE CAPITALISM AND DATAIZATION AMONG RELIGIOUS ORGANIZATIONS IN SINGAPORE

Faris Ridzuan and Afra Alatas

Introduction

A religious orientation can be broadly defined as a mode of thinking in relation to religion. According to Karl Mannheim's sociology of knowledge which stipulates that ideas need to be understood within a given socio-historical context, a religious orientation can be more specifically defined as a socio-historically conditioned mode of thinking of a given community or group of people. Religious orientations do not function in a vacuum and can be affected by the political and economic order which governs a given society or community, or the social positioning, roles, functions, and milieus of the group or community in question. For example, the religious orientation(s) of Muslims in Singapore and Malaysia have been affected by feudalism, colonial capitalism, and neoliberal capitalism.

However, change constantly occurs, and the forces affecting religious orientations today may differ. When Karl Marx expounded his critique of capitalism, he studied the scientific and technological advances of his time—steam engines and machines—which are considered rudimentary by today's standards. Instead, today, society is moving towards a new form of capitalism whereby technological and scientific advances have necessitated that artificial intelligence, automation, and bio-technological inventions dominate. As such, we are moving towards a form of capitalism that leverages data as a product, tool, and currency to fuel profits and give advantages to organizations and individuals.

This new form of political economy is called surveillance capitalism, which can be defined as a "new form of information capitalism which aims to predict and modify human behaviour as a means to produce revenue and market control" (Zuboff 2015). It has been further characterized as "the unilateral claiming of private human experience as free raw material for translation into behavioural data" which are then "computed and packaged as prediction products and sold into behavioural futures markets" (Laidler 2019). Companies like Meta, Google, Twitter, TikTok, and other technological giants and even smaller players are the surveillance capitalists in this new political economy. Governments and non-governmental organizations (NGOs) are also involved in using surveillance capabilities developed in the commercial sector even though they might not reap profits from these capabilities (Faris 2022).

Religious organizations are jumping on the bandwagon of surveillance capitalism which busies itself in datafication, which can be defined as the process of converting all information, including individuals' and groups' personalities, behaviour, thoughts, and feelings into data to be analysed and used to influence their behaviour for the organization's desired outcomes or profit (ibid.). We found this to be the case with two religious organizations. Yet, as illustrated below, while they may be progressive in their use of modern tools to conduct their religious outreach and education, the religious orientations of these actors remain rooted in continuity and are perpetuated by their participation in surveillance capitalism and datafication. In the context of a data-driven political economy, these religious actors are complicit in upholding religious orientations and the inequalities of neoliberal capitalism which are reinforced by algorithms. These religious orientations offer little in terms of highlighting the social dimension of Islam which places emphasis on public solutions in lieu of personal salvation and piety in addressing social problems, the latter of which sits well with the neoliberal ideology.

This chapter will begin with a brief introduction to the ideologies of feudalism, colonial capitalism, and neoliberalism in Malay society. It will then briefly discuss the dominant religious orientations among Muslims in Singapore, specifically among the religious elite. Following that, we will discuss how Muslim religious organizations have used social media to conduct their religious outreach and education, and how their activities on specific platforms reflect surveillance capitalism. Finally, we will examine how this upholds a neoliberal ideology in which personal piety trumps the alleviation of social problems via concerted public and social effort, and how this further reinforces religious orientations that prevent systemic or systematic intervention in addressing social problems from a religious perspective.

Focusing on religious organizations in Singapore, we utilized two forms of primary research methodology. The first was to analyse the content which these actors posted on their social media accounts, and to look at the themes which they usually discussed. The second was to conduct in-depth interviews with representatives of these organizations. We spoke to two representatives from the Islamic Religious Council of Singapore (MUIS)—specifically those involved in running the website Muslim.SG—and one representative from the Singapore Islamic Scholars and Religious Teachers Association (PERGAS), who is involved in the organization's marketing strategies.

Feudalism, (Colonial) Capitalism, and Neoliberalism

The Malays' religious orientation took on feudal traits when feudalism defined the Malay world's political economy. Shaharuddin Maaruf (2002/3) lists these traits of feudalism as such:

> (1) a servile attitude towards authority and the acceptance of arbitrary notions of power; (2) the undermining of the positive aspects of individualism, and, therefore, a lack of respect for the human personality; (3) a lack of respect for the rule of law; (4) no distinction between the public domain and personal domains of life; (5) an emphasis on grandeur and an opulent lifestyle; (6) indifference to social justice;

(7) acceptance of unfair privileges for those in position and power; (8) an obsession with power, authority and privilege for their own sake; (9) an undervaluing of rationalism and the philosophical spirit, and encouragement of myths that serve the interests of those in power; and (10) an emphasis on leisure and indulgence of the senses and the simultaneous undervaluing of work.

Despite the transition from feudalism to capitalism, psychological feudalism persists among Muslims in the Malay world today. The traits of feudalism among the Muslim religious and political elite, the religious bureaucracy, and even the masses, still linger in Muslim minds. One such trait of the feudal religious orientation is a blind, almost unquestioning following of religious authority. This is especially prevalent in Malaysia, where feudalism dominates the socio-religious and political spheres (Norshahril 2016).

Succeeding the old feudal order, the advent of colonialism and colonial capitalism facilitated Islam's centralization, administration, and bureaucratization. Structures and systems were put in place, and these helped to perpetuate and fortify the dominant feudal and traditionalist religious orientations at that time while introducing the socio-religious outlook to the influences of capitalism. Before colonialism, one of the defining attributes of Islam was that "religious and customary norms were socially embedded at the local level", and there was no centralized institutional authority to dictate a uniform doctrine, thus resulting in "a pluralistic religio-legal tradition" where "jurists valourised diversity of opinion (*ikhtilaf*) as a generative force in the search for God's truth" (Moustafa 2018). When colonial capitalism and administration were introduced, it "marked an important turning point for the institutionalisation, centralisation, and bureaucratisation of religious authority in the Malay Peninsula" (ibid.). Malay rulers were compelled to receive and act on the advice of the Resident in all matters except those pertaining to Islam and *adat* (custom) (Noor Aisha and Azhar 2017). Although the Malay rulers were the formal guardians of religion and custom, power in these areas was subjected to overriding authority and mediation of the British Residents.

There was also the bureaucratization of administration, in which there was rule based on administrative and procedural laws. For example, State Councils were established to pass laws, including laws relating to Islam. In 1880, the colonial administration made the first provision for regulating marriage and divorce under the Mahomedan

Marriage ordinance, where the government appointed a judge (Taufik and Siddique 1986). However, overall, the administration of Islamic law under colonial capitalism was subjected to the perspective of colonial administrators who tended to dichotomize Islamic law and *adat*, and such binary bifurcations were influenced by a rigid (mis)understanding of both Islamic law and *adat* (Noor Aisha 2006).

Capitalism also had an impact on religion and religious orientations. As Shaharuddin (1988) illustrates, with the introduction of capitalism, there arose a "conflict" between traditional and capitalistic religions. While the former emphasizes blind faith and an uncritical acceptance of intermediate authorities, capitalistic religion advocates for a greater sense of individualism, independent judgement, and a rational and systematic orientation towards life. These traits are necessary in pursuing profit, a defining feature of capitalism (Shaharuddin 1988). While Shaharuddin's analysis of the impact of capitalism on religion appears to be neutral, it is arguable that capitalism, in the form of its neoliberal ideology, has had a negative impact on the practice of religion.

Neoliberalism in modern-day capitalism is an economic model or paradigm that is built upon the classical liberal ideal of the self-regulating market, and it manifests in three ways—as ideology, as a mode of governance, and as a set of policies (Steger and Roy 2010). As an ideology, neoliberalism posits the vision of a single global and globalizing marketplace which puts the production and exchange of material goods at the heart of human experience. As a mode of governance, it is "rooted in entrepreneurial values such as competitiveness, self-interest, and decentralization", and "celebrates individual empowerment and the devolution of central state power to smaller localized units", with the model for good governance being the self-regulating free market (ibid.). As a concrete set of public policies, neoliberalism espouses "(1) deregulation (of the economy); (2) liberalization (of trade and industry); and (3) privatization (of state-owned enterprises)" (ibid.).

In the context of Singapore, neoliberalism is seen as problematic as it espouses a morality which has in place "measures that favour individual over public solutions to social goods" and that "individual merit, hard work, competition, are the best antidotes to social problems" (Teo 2012). However, this has not led to a complete abandonment of public welfare. Yet, the attention to public welfare may be lost in other contexts. For example, in the case of the Muslim community and its religious elite, individual merit, hard work, and competition (in racing to perform ritualistic or personal piety obligations and supplementary acts) are still seen as the prime solutions to addressing social problems, where adherents afflicted by social problems are encouraged and expected to dedicate their time to ritualistic worship and learning about the religion in order to overcome their struggles.

For example, some religious figures still have magico-religious thinking towards mental illness, proposing the performance of specific rituals, the intensification of worship, and deeper learning about Islam and the consequent strengthening of one's *iman* or faith which will result in the alleviation of any mental health problems. These individuals are therefore blamed for their situation. While this is reflective of a traditionalist religious orientation which places emphasis on personal salvation and attention to rituals, it is also a result of neoliberal capitalism in the modern context. Hence, in Singapore's context, traditionalism and neoliberal capitalism reinforce one another.

The link between surveillance capitalism and neoliberalism runs deep, with neoliberalism enabling surveillance capitalism. Neoliberalism, which promotes the superiority of the free and self-regulating market with minimal or zero intervention or regulation from the state, sets conditions ripe for surveillance capitalism to prosper, starting with Google. What is ironic is that the state utilizes the same tools of surveillance capitalism that emerged from the neoliberal market. Amsellem (2022) has called these tools "the neoliberal ear", alluding to the panopticon-like reach of surveillance capitalism.

Traditionalism as the Dominant Religious Orientation

Scholars who have written on religious orientations in Singapore have concluded that traditionalism is the dominant religious orientation among Singapore Muslims. In the general sense, religious traditionalism is "a style of religiousness which holds to the old ways" and is characterized by certainty and unquestioning acceptance (Towler 1984). As Robert Towler put it, "it is not only certain, it is delighted by its certainty, for the stable and secure order which it knows is something to guard and cherish. It affirms and reinforces the present structure of society, resisting every innovation" (ibid.).

In his study on discourses on Islam in Southeast Asia, Azhar Ibrahim examines how Islamic discourse in the region has impacted the Singapore Muslim public and finds that traditionalism is one of the two dominant religious orientations among Muslims in Singapore. In the context of Singapore, the orientation manifests itself in the form of concern with issues such as the practice of rituals and the implementation of laws; determining what is halal (permissible) or haram (impermissible) for use or consumption; women's use of the hijab or head-covering; ways to improve one's acts of devotion and personal piety; and the importance of spreading the religion to Muslims and non-Muslims alike (Azhar 2008). Thus, Muslim piety and morality is the main concern of the traditionalists, and they regard themselves as the authentic protectors and interpreters of Islam who seek to shield Muslim society from "un-Islamic" elements. Consequently, in focusing on piety and the perceived moral degeneration of society, traditionalists tend to give little to no regard to real struggles that Muslims might face in their daily lives and which are rooted in societal structures. This is not helped by the fact that Singaporean Muslim religious elites or intelligentsia are "not at the forefront of the discourse" and that reformist ideas tend to be kept at bay. This is largely because "as gatekeeper and custodian of Islam, the religious circles (*asatizah/ulama*) determine what is a legitimate and authentic discourse", and therefore are responsible for the dominance of a selective Islamic discourse in Singapore Muslim society (ibid.).

Writing in 2021, Nur Fadhlin Sakina, in her undergraduate thesis on Singaporean *asatizah* (religious teachers) use of social media, studies the content which selected *asatizah* post on their social media accounts and concluded that they do indeed approach Islam through a traditionalist lens. Through her study of the social media content of five prominent "*asatizah* influencers", she found that these *asatizah* "remain steeped in traditionalism" (Nur Fadhlin 2021). This is due to their emphasis on issues like personal salvation, the proper performance of prayers, matters of creed, and individual piety. Their efforts are therefore focused on improving the morality and piety of their followers, as opposed to discussing the social issues which have concrete implications for the Muslim community. In other words, the social dimension of religion is missing from their preaching activities. Hence, based on these studies, it appears it is an established observation that traditionalism is the dominant religious orientation of the Muslim religious elite in Singapore and is pervasive even in the online sphere as evinced by the traditionalist social media content of *asatizah* influencers.

Surveillance Capitalism and Religious Organizations

However, it is not just individual influencers who are crucial as study subjects. Religious organizations or institutions are also important members of the religious elite and are equally—if not more—impactful in shaping religious discourse and transmitting knowledge to the public. In the case of Singapore, these organizations would be MUIS, which is a statutory body, as well as PERGAS, which is an NGO. These organizations have also been observed to be traditionalist in their outlook. This has been substantially discussed by Noor Aisha (2008) who analyses the responses of MUIS and PERGAS to a number of socio-religious issues in Singapore. Seeing that these are two key religious organizations regarded as religious authorities for and by the Muslim community, examining how these organizations use data to curate their social media content and maintain a following is imperative. This will shed light on how these organizations partake in surveillance capitalism.

MUIS

The role of MUIS as a statutory body is to advise the President of Singapore on any issues concerning Islam and Muslims in the country. Established in 1968 when the Administration of Muslim Law Act (AMLA) came into effect, MUIS also issues religious guidance to the Muslim public, develops and oversees Islamic education in religious schools, manages the mosques, and administers various activities such as the annual pilgrimage, endowment, halal certification, and the payment of *zakat* (MUIS n.d.). Regarding its social media engagement, MUIS uses various social media platforms and resources to reach out to Singaporean Muslims. These include its Instagram and Facebook pages specifically dedicated to MUIS activities and information, and other initiatives under the organization's ambit. These are Office of the Mufti, Muslim.SG, and SalamSG TV.

During our fieldwork, we spoke to two representatives from the editorial team of Muslim.SG, a "one-stop platform for Muslim millennials"[1] to get quick information on themes like prayer, fasting, halal restaurants, acts of piety and devotion, marriage and relationships, and good character. We spoke about their content creation process during our conversation with the two representatives. We first spoke about their target audience and found that MUIS uses several social media platforms, each with the purpose of reaching out to different age groups. For example, while Muslim.SG is targeted at millennials and is also available on Instagram, Facebook, YouTube, and Spotify in addition to their website, they also have a TikTok account to reach out to "Gen Z".

Regarding other initiatives, MUIS runs a website, Facebook, and Twitter accounts. The Office of the Mufti, which provides jurisprudential guidance, can be found on the MUIS website, and has its own Instagram page. Finally, there is SalamSG TV, a YouTube channel focusing on longer lectures on spirituality and religious observances. These lectures are delivered in English, Malay, and Bengali and target the older generation. Of all these initiatives, it is worth stating that Muslim.SG is one of MUIS's most successful brands, and this is evident from the attention that their content has received. For example, the content they created during the months of Ramadhan and Hari Raya was listed as one of the top five public service campaigns in 2022, and their content has also been featured on the Asia-Pacific YouTube Ads Leaderboard several times (MUIS representatives, personal communication, 17 November 2022).

In terms of their content creation, Muslim.SG is driven by the Singapore Muslim Identity (SMI) values: Religiously Resilient, Inclusive, Contributive, Adaptive and Progressive (RICAP). During our discussion with the representatives, we found that the primary way they create content would be to do so based on their research on the keywords that tend to be frequently searched online (MUIS representatives, personal communication, 14 March 2022). This research uses software such as Google Trends and Ubersuggest which provide insight and data on search queries. Based on popular keywords, MUIS can glean the themes of importance to Singaporean Muslims, and from there, decide on the content worth creating. Examples of these keywords and themes include *doa* (prayer), mental health, relationships, marriage, and divorce.

This demonstrates a concerted effort by MUIS to participate in surveillance capitalism and datafication, where they collect data about users' behaviours and interests, and subsequently use these data to serve the consumer base better. Although these efforts are not for profit, MUIS's use of data is reflective of its participation in surveillance capitalism, as it allows them to curate content according to their followers' interests, and at the same time, to maintain a strong following. This creates a feedback loop in which users constantly refer to MUIS for its content, and MUIS will always create content that caters to their liking. However, we also acknowledge that while keyword searches may be a useful indicator of the themes which are of concern to Singaporean Muslims, this may not accurately reflect all of their concerns, as there may be questions that they have which they choose to explore through other means or on other platforms.

PERGAS

PERGAS is an NGO which is committed to improving the quality of Islamic education and supporting the welfare of *asatizah* in Singapore. Formed in 1957 by a group of senior religious teachers and prominent members of the Muslim community, PERGAS's activities are split into five pillars: (1) Asatizah Development and Training; (2) Islamic Education; (3) Zakat, Donations and Welfare; (4) Community Dakwah Outreach; and (5) Research Development (PERGAS n.d.). In terms of their online engagement, PERGAS also uses various social media platforms to facilitate its community outreach efforts. For example, they have their own general website on which PERGAS Radio can be found. This online radio service delivers live *azan* (call to prayer) and Qur'anic recitation, lectures by their *asatizah*, and even recipes from the "PERGAS Kitchen" (PERGAS n.d.). There is also a PERGAS Blog, a separate website on which they post articles on themes such as ethics, the arts, contemporary issues, *asatizah* development, and daily Muslim life (PERGAS n.d.). These articles are written in both English and Malay. PERGAS has its own Instagram page where it mainly posts posters of its upcoming events and advertises its PERGAS Radio programmes. They also post videos on their Facebook page and on their YouTube channel, PERGAS TV. These videos are similar to their radio programme in that they are mainly of Qur'anic recitations and lectures by their *asatizah*, the themes of which usually cover rituals, spirituality, and good morals. Finally, they also have a TikTok account, although they only have 37 followers and 15 videos.[2]

During our fieldwork, we spoke to a current member of the Corporate Communications team who has been with PERGAS since 2016. During our conversation, the representative pointed out that PERGAS's target audience tends to be those who have a basic understanding of Islam and who want to know more about Islam. Their social media content is therefore used to pique people's general interests and is not targeted at a specific demographic. However, they also utilize what is referred to in marketing terms as funnelling, or the multi-layered process of attracting the attention of a large number of people and eventually narrowing down this group and achieving the receptivity and loyalty of a smaller sum of people. PERGAS's marketing and outreach strategies thus involve getting their attention on social media first, after which their followers would be "challenged" to deepen their knowledge (PERGAS representative, personal communication, 3 March 2022). The PERGAS representative gave the example of starting with learning the basics of a chapter from the Qur'an, after which some may want to learn more about the mistakes in interpreting or reciting the chapter. After this step, they may be challenged to learn more about other chapters and go through another layer of funnelling. From here, they may be encouraged to eventually attend face-to-face classes.

In addition to advertisements in the local Malay newspaper, PERGAS uses Facebook to garner traffic and maximize their viewership. They also utilize Google's grant for non-profit organizations, so that they will appear in a Google search. While this means that they cannot use Google advertisements, they ensure that their website uses certain keywords so that they will appear in the Google search. Even in editing and publishing articles on their blog, they try to ensure that those articles will appear in a Google search. Based on this, it appears that PERGAS differs from MUIS in its data usage and participation in surveillance capitalism. While MUIS or Muslim.SG in particular is dependent on data analysis to determine the type of content which their consumers want, PERGAS's content creation process is led by their staff, 80 to 90 per cent of whom are under the age of 35. Those who are active in the content creation process are advised by PERGAS board members. PERGAS therefore does not rely on the data of its consumers to determine the type of content that they produce. However, even if this may be so, it is arguable that their use of advertisements still influences the interests of the people who eventually consume their materials and become loyal students of the organization. Furthermore, the top-down centralization of content creation without sensing from the ground might run the risk of being less responsive to the socio-religious needs of the Muslim community.

Addressing Social Problems

Most Muslims in Singapore are Malay by ethnicity, and 99.8 per cent of Malays are Muslims (Lai 2017). The Muslim community is therefore commonly referred to as the Malay/Muslim community. Politicians in Singapore have often spoken about the Malay/Muslim community as an ethno-religious community besieged by various social problems vis-à-vis other communities (Noor Aisha and Azhar 2017). By social problems, we refer to the assertions of grievances and claims regarding conditions alleged to exist regardless of whether they exist objectively. These grievances are constructed based on objective facts or subjective interpretations and are limited and influenced by the social and cultural context in which the social problem is constructed (Hjelm 2009).

Social scientists have substantially analysed and critiqued this narrative over the years. The "Malay Problem", which was a blanket term for an array of social problems faced by the Malay/Muslim community, was first raised by Malay leaders in a 1971 seminar on "Malay Participation in National Development" organized by Majlis Pusat Singapura (Central Council of Malay Cultural Organizations) and the Community Study Centre (Ahmat and Wong 1970). Among the problems highlighted then were educational underachievement, drug abuse, disadvantaged and dysfunctional families, poor socio-economic standing, and low skills of workers. Outside of the seminar, certain religious orientations among Muslims were also viewed as problematic or even impediments to modernization within the community (Alatas 1972). Other recently highlighted problems include high crime rates, job loss, an increase in the number of Malays living in rental flats, and the consequent "possibility of a permanent underclass of two to three generations with multiple family problems" (Heng 2016).

The intersection of Islam and social problems faced by the Malay/Muslim community is highly pertinent. Muslim community leaders and Malay/Muslim Organisations (MMOs) have rallied and committed to addressing the community's myriad social issues (Zaihan 2017; Lim 2018; Syaffiq 2017). There are also ethnic self-help groups set up by the state, allowing members of the respective ethnic groups to take ownership over their community's well-being and progress.[3] Malays/Muslims, as an ethno-religious group, are part of this self-help group system. Mosques and Muslim organizations also provide social services to alleviate social problems faced by the community (Enon and Nur Amali 2008). However, some observers opine that such a setup which is based on racialized or ethnic categorization only serves to exacerbate inequality as unequal resources are allocated to these self-help efforts. More specifically, it has been argued that the Chinese self-help group has more resources than other ethnic self-help groups. For example, Smith et al. (2015) states that:

> While this system was designed to allow each ethnic group to be responsible for its own well-being, some have argued that self-funding may actually be perpetuating inequality among the groups. For example, the Chinese Development Assistance Council (CDAC) has a large number of high-income earners whose CPF contributions are higher than average, and so CDAC ends up with more money and greater resources to help their community than the other ethnic self-help groups. In this sense, it has been argued that the populations who started out in the lead are able to maintain that advantage through the current system.

In Singapore, Muslims are structurally bound to the stipulated laws under the AMLA, which affects areas such as marriage, family matters, and inheritance (Noor Aisha 2004). The religiosity of Muslims and the integral nature of Islam to the Malay Archipelago warrants an investigation into the intersections between religion and social problems among Muslims in Singapore. According to a 2019 study on religion conducted by the Institute of Policy Studies, 88.5 per cent of Muslims in Singapore self-identify as "religious",[4] and the number of Muslims who identify themselves as such come second only to that of Hindus, of whom 88.8 per cent self-identify as religious (Matthews et al. 2019).

The percentages of Muslims who self-identify as "extremely religious" (4.1 per cent) and "very religious" (34.2 per cent) are the highest among the percentages of adherents of other religions who self-identify within the same categories.[5] Additionally, the percentage of Muslims of the ages 18–35 who self-identify as religious (88.7 per cent) is the highest compared to adherents of the same age range of other religions. The percentage of Muslims aged 55 and above who self-identify as "religious" (93.1 per cent) is also the highest compared to other religions. The difference of 4.4 per cent between the former and latter group of Muslims is also the lowest compared to other religious groups. Muslims can thus be considered religious and relatively more religious than adherents of other faiths, and the "decrease" in religiosity from the older to the younger generation is the lowest, indicating a strong continuity of religiosity across generations.

Social Problems Unaddressed under the Social Dimension of Islam

However, despite the high religiosity—even if self-identified—and the acknowledgement of the various struggles faced by the Malay/Muslim community, Muslim religious figures do not address the social dimension of Islam in their discussion of these struggles and challenges. The solutions to individual and societal problems are not addressed as public issues from a structural or systemic angle, but instead are addressed through the angle of personal piety and the importance of religious rituals.

For example, a look through Muslim.SG's website shows that there are several posts on the ritualistic elements of religion, such as supplications for "success in everything" (Muslim.SG 2020b), and guides on how to pray in a congregation at home (Ustaz Fadhlullah Daud 2022). Another theme is that of the implementation of Islamic rulings and concerns over what is halal and haram. These include posts on whether Muslims can use certain outfits or forms of jewellery (Muslim.SG 2020c), and whether it is permissible to celebrate the festivals of other cultural communities (Muslim.SG 2020a). There are also articles on general values as taught by Islam, such as sincerity (Ustaz Muhammad Imran Othman 2022), beauty (Muslim.SG 2022), and sacrifice (Muslim.SG 2021). There is also a reference to an Islamic "Golden Age" (Ayesha Jannah Bharucha 2020) and the end times (Muslim.SG 2021). Additionally, some articles encourage Muslims to do their part to address social issues, such as poverty, and this is done through exhortations to pay zakat to "uplift our community and aid those in need" (Muslim.SG 2021). However, there is little elaboration on Islam's social dimension, which emphasizes public, systemic, and structural solutions to socio-religious problems. Furthermore, much of the content largely caters to the Muslim middle class.

The same can be said about the content that PERGAS produces. A scan through PERGAS Blog reveals articles on similar themes discussed on Muslim.SG. For example, with regard to the emphasis on rulings and the permissibility of certain activities, there are articles on the permissibility of participating in Forex trading (PERGAS Blog 2020), and purchasing bonds (PERGAS Blog 2018). There are also articles which place emphasis on women having to cover their hair (PERGAS Blog 2018b). Similar to Muslim.SG's content on an Islamic "Golden Age", PERGAS Blog also has content on healthy living according to the Prophet and the Qur'an. For example, there are articles on "Healthy Eating According to the Qur'an and Sunnah" (Siti Khadijah 2019), and taking care of one's health according to the lifestyle of the Prophet (PERGAS Blog 2019). Almost all articles above are categorized as "Popular Articles", with views ranging between 2,000 and 4,000. Even with the articles tagged as "Contemporary Issues", the articles tend to deal with topics like the closure of mosques, biomedical and technological ethics, and the relevance of the idea of an "Islamic State" or caliphate, as opposed to social struggles rooted in systemic and structural issues which are specific to Singaporean Muslims and which affect their daily lives.

Thus, it is an orientation that is largely concerned with the ritualistic and legalistic aspects of Islam which dominates in the content produced and/or endorsed by certain platforms created by MUIS and PERGAS. This in turn determines the standard of progress the community holds to. For both these organizations, the themes found on Muslim.SG and PERGAS Blog are consistent across their other new media or social media platforms. While these themes may be of interest to Muslim readers, the predominance of these themes does little to contribute to the alleviation of social problems within the community. Consequently, this might inadvertently contribute to the retention of structural inequalities or systemic barriers in society.

Conclusion: The Need for Functioning Intellectuals

Much of the focus on religious discourse in Singapore has been on how certain religious orientations dominate in Muslim society, and how such orientations are unhelpful in addressing social problems. However, while it is crucial to identify dominant religious orientations and to examine how they can be addressed, it is just as crucial to identify the ideologies or systems which dominate the political economy. As explored above, dataization and surveillance capitalism are what appear to currently dominate the political economy, and it is therefore imperative to acknowledge that a data-driven political economy, alongside surveillance capitalism, will only serve to exacerbate social problems in society and to alienate people from critical consciousness about religion and its social dimension.

In order to address this, there is a necessity for competitive actors in the marketplace of ideas who place emphasis on the public and social dimension of Islam, and whose ideas are rooted in humanism, inclusivity, and equity. These actors should be able to draw upon progressive epistemologies from other traditions that do not conflict with Islam's universal principles and values, and should be rooted in lived realities rather than textualism. Coupled with an active class of functioning intellectuals in Muslim society, all these actors will be more equipped to respond to the changes and challenges brought about by the evolving political economy and other drivers of change.

This contrasts with the current religious actors—in this case, religious organizations—who are complicit in the negative effects of the changing modes of production centred around surveillance capitalism and dataization in the neoliberal political economy. This in turn reinforces certain religious orientations which result in a lack of action in addressing social problems, and which instead focus on rituals and legal technicalities of the religion.

While MUIS is the government authority responsible for managing and addressing religious issues, more can be done by the organization to address the dearth of a class of religious elites who can act as functioning intellectuals to address pertinent social problems. Instead, as evident from their engagement in surveillance capitalism through Muslim.SG, they have adopted the approach of understanding what is popular within the community and producing content in a reactive manner, as opposed to actively guiding the community with fresh content or steering them away from ideas which impede the progress of society. This is also relevant to PERGAS who is often seen as the alternative to MUIS. It is therefore crucial that there is greater initiative among religious organizations to use the tools and influence that they possess in order to spur change in society, instead of viewing the community as mere consumers and products to benefit from in this current political economy.

NOTES

1. MUIS defines millennials as those aged between 18 and 40 years old.
2. As of February 2023.
3. Contributions from the different ethnic groups to their respective self-help group funds are made through deductions from employees' wages, facilitated by the employers, and enforced by the Central Provident Fund.
4. This includes all of those who self-identify as "extremely religious", "very religious", and "somewhat religious".
5. The other religions are Buddhism, Taoism, Hinduism, Catholicism, Christianity, and "No Religion".

REFERENCES

Ahmat, Sharom and James Wong. 1970. *Malay Participation in the National Development of Singapore*. Seminar on Malay Participation in the National Development of Singapore, Singapore.

Alatas, Syed Hussein. 1972. "Religion and Modernization in South-east Asia". In *Modernization and Social Change: Studies in Modernization, Religion, Social Change and Development in South-east Asia*, by Syed Hussein Alatas, pp. 21–52. Sydney: Angus and Robertson.

Amsellem, Audrey. 2022. "Sound and Surveillance: The Making of the Neoliberal Ear". Columbia University. https://doi.org/10.7916/mwsv-3y95.

Ayesha Jannah Bharucha Binte Abdullah. 2020. "4 Muslims Who Made Amazing Discoveries During the Islamic Golden Age". *Muslim.SG*, 3 December 2020. https://www.muslim.sg/articles/4-muslims-who-made-amazing-discoveries-during-the-islamic-golden-age (accessed 22 June 2022).

Azhar Ibrahim. 2008. "Discourses on Islam in Southeast Asia and their Impact on the Singapore Muslim Public". In *Religious Diversity in Singapore*, edited by Lai Ah Eng, pp. 83–115. Singapore: ISEAS – Yusof Ishak Institute.

Enon Mansor and Nur Amali Ibrahim. 2008. "Muslim Organizations and Mosques as Social Service Providers". In *Religious Diversity in Singapore*, edited by Lai Ah Eng, pp. 459–88. Singapore: Institute of Southeast Asian Studies.

Facebook. 2022. "Pergas – Singapore Islamic Scholars and Religious Teachers Association". 4 January 2022. https://www.facebook.com/Pergas.Singapore/photos/a.452274041491748/4884239344961840 (accessed 24 June 2022).

Faris Ridzuan. 2015. "Islam and Social Science: Muslim Senior Undergraduates and their Attitudes Towards Knowledge". Undergraduate Thesis, National University of Singapore.

———. 2022. "Surveillance Capitalism's Social Problems: Progressive Orientation Helps the Most". *The Karyawan*, 15 July 2022. https://karyawan.sg/surveillance-capitalisms-social-problems-progressive-orientation-helps-the-most/ (accessed 20 August 2022).

Heng, Janice. 2016. "More Malay Families Living in Rental Flats". *The Straits Times*, 11 May 2016.

Hjelm, Titus. 2009. "Religion and Social Problems: A New Theoretical Perspective". In *The Oxford Handbook of the Sociology of Religion*, edited by Peter B. Clarke, pp. 924–41. Oxford: Oxford University Press.

Lai Ah Eng. 2017. *Religion*. Singapore: Institute of Policy Studies and Straits Times Press Pte Ltd.

Laidler, John. 2019. "High Tech is Watching You". *The Harvard Gazette*, 4 March 2019. https://news.harvard.edu/gazette/story/2019/03/harvard-professor-says-surveillance-capitalism-is-undermining-democracy/ (accessed 20 June 2019).

Lim, Adrian. 2018. "New Programme Helps Drug Offenders". *The Straits Times*, 17 November 2018.

Majlis Ugama Islam Singapura (MUIS). n.d. "Roles & Functions". https://www.muis.gov.sg/About-MUIS/Roles-Functions (accessed 22 June 2022).

Matthews, Matthew, Leonard Lim, and Shanthini Selvarajan. 2019. "Religion in Singapore: The Private and Public Spheres". *IPS Working Papers* No. 33.

Mohammad Yusri Yubhi Md Yusoff. 2019. "Menjaga Kesihatan Menerusi Amalan Gaya Hidup Nabi" [Taking Care of Health According to the Lifestyle of the Prophet]. *PERGAS Blog*, 6 May 2019. https://blog.pergas.org.sg/menjaga-kesihatan-menerusi-amalan-gaya-hidup-nabi/ (accessed 23 June 2022).

Moustafa, Tamir. 2018. *Constituting Religion: Islam, Liberal Rights, and the Malaysian State*. Cambridge: Cambridge University Press.

Muslim.SG. 2020a. "Can Muslims Touch Dogs? Can Muslims Wish Merry Christmas? Get Your Googled Questions Answered!" 23 September 2020. https://muslim.sg/articles/can-muslims-touch-dogs-can-muslims-wish-merry-christmas-get-your-googled-questions-answered (accessed 22 June).

———. 2020b. "Dua for Success in Everything". 2 October 2020. https://www.muslim.sg/articles/dua-for-success-in-everything (accessed 22 June 2022).

———. 2020c. "Is it Haram to Wear Gold and Other FAQs on Islam and Fashion". 3 December 2020. https://muslim.sg/articles/is-it-haram-to-wear-gold-and-other-faqs-on-islam-and-fashion (accessed 22 June 2022).

_____. 2021. "What Happens When We Pay Zakat?" 30 April 2021. https://www.muslim.sg/articles/what-happens-when-we-pay-zakat (accessed 22 June 2022).

Noor Aisha Abdul Rahman. 2004. "Traditionalism and its Impact on the Administration of Justice: The Case of the Syariah Court of Singapore". *Inter-Asia Cultural Studies* 5, no. 3: 415–32.

_____. 2006. *Colonial Image of Malay Adat Laws: A Critical Appraisal of Studies on Adat Laws in the Malay Peninsula during the Colonial Era and Some Continuities*. Leiden: Brill.

_____. 2008. "The Muslim Religious Elite of Singapore". In *Religious Diversity in Singapore*, edited by Lai Ah Eng, pp. 248–74. Singapore: Institute of Southeast Asian Studies.

Noor Aisha Abdul Rahman and Azhar Ibrahim. 2017. *Malays*. Singapore: Institute of Policy Studies and Straits Times Press Pte Ltd.

Norshahril Saat. 2016. "Rising Conservatism in M'sian Islam Not Just from Arabisation". *Today Online*, 16 July 2016. https://www.todayonline.com/world/asia/rising-conservatism-msianislam-not-just-arabisation (accessed 20 June 2022).

Nur Fadhlin Sakina Bte Ismail. 2021. "Asatizah & Social Media: A Study on Singapore's Prominent Asatizah Influencers". Undergraduate Thesis, National University of Singapore.

PERGAS. n.d. "PERGAS Radio". https://www.pergas.org.sg/radio/ (accessed 22 June 2022).

_____. n.d. "PERGAS Blog". https://blog.pergas.org.sg/ (accessed 22 June 2022).

PERGAS Blog. 2018a. "Women – Aurat and Tabarruj". 15 November 2018. https://blog.pergas.org.sg/women-aurat-and-tabarruj/ (accessed 23 June 2022).

_____. 2018b. "Religious Guidance in the Subscription of Singapore Savings Bonds by Muslims (Part 1)". 16 November 2018. https://blog.pergas.org.sg/religious-guidance-in-the-subscription-of-singapore-savings-bonds-by-muslims-part-1/ (accessed 23 June 2022).

_____. 2020. "Shariah Assessment on Forex Trading: A Guide for the Singapore Muslim Community – Part Two". 16 July 2020. https://blog.pergas.org.sg/shariah-assessment-on-forex-trading-part-two/ (accessed 23 June 2022).

Shaharuddin Maaruf. 1988. *Malay Ideas on Development: From Feudal Lord to Capitalist*. Singapore: Times Books International.

_____. 2002/3. "Some Theoretical Problems Concerning Tradition and Modernization among the Malays of Southeast Asia". Seminar papers, Department of Malay Studies, National University of Singapore.

Siti Khadijah Binte Ali. 2019. "Pemakanan Sihat Mengikut Al-Quran dan Sunnah" [Healthy Eating According to the Quran and Sunnah]. *PERGAS*

Blog, 6 May 2019. https://blog.pergas.org.sg/pemakanan-sihat-mengikut-al-quran-dan-sunnah/ (accessed 23 June 2022).

Smith, Catherine J., John A. Donaldson, Sanushka Mudaliar, Mumtaz Md Kadir, and Yeoh Lam Keong. 2015. *A Handbook on Inequality, Poverty and Unmet Social Needs*. Singapore: Lien Centre for Social Innovation, Singapore Management University.

Steger, Manfred. B. and Ravi K. Roy. 2010. *Neoliberalism: A Very Short Introduction*. New York: Oxford University Press.

Syaffiq, A. 2017. "Malay Groups Roll Out Programme to Give Help". *The Straits Times*, 16 April 2017.

Taufik Abdullah and Sharon Siddique, eds. 1986. *Islam and Society in Southeast Asia*. Singapore: Institute of Southeast Asian Studies.

Teo Youyenn. 2012. "Neoliberal Morality in Singapore: Institutionalising the Logics of Neoliberalism". *ISA Symposium for Sociology*. Singapore: Nanyang Technological University.

Toh Yong Chuan. 2017. "Shanmugam Says Job Loss, Crime and Drug Use Among Key Issues". *The Straits Times*, 2 April 2017.

Towler, Robert. 1984. *The Need for Certainty: A Sociological Study of Conventional Religion*. London: Routledge.

Ustaz Ahmad Nu'man. 2022. "What is Beauty in Islam?" *Muslim.SG*, 17 February 2022. https://muslim.sg/articles/what-is-beauty-in-islam (accessed 22 June 2022).

Ustaz Fadhlullah Daud. 2022. "How to Pray in Congregation at Home". *Muslim.SG*, 22 March 2023. https://www.muslim.sg/articles/how-to-pray-in-congregation-at-home (accessed 22 June 2022).

Ustaz Muhammad Abdul Mateen Bin Hisham. 2021. "Dealing with Recurrent Claims About the End of the World". *Muslim.SG*, 3 December 2021. https://www.muslim.sg/articles/dealing-with-recurrent-claims-about-the-end-of-the-world (accessed 22 June 2022).

Ustaz Muhammad Imran Othman. 2022. "How to Achieve Sincerity in Islam". *Muslim.SG*, 28 March 2022. https://muslim.sg/articles/how-to-achieve-sincerity-in-islam (accessed 22 June 2022).

Ustaz Muhammad Luqman Hakim Bin Roslan. 2021. "The Value of Sacrifice in Islam". *Muslim.SG*, 16 July 2021. https://muslim.sg/articles/the-value-of-sacrifice-in-islam (accessed 22 June 2021).

Zaihan Mohamed Yusof. 2017. "Malay/Muslim Community Leaders Call on Community to Fight Drug Scourge". *The Straits Times*, 30 April 2017.

Zuboff, Shoshana. 2015. "Big Other: Surveillance Capitalism and the Prospects of an Information Civilisation". *Journal of Information Technology* 30, no. 15: 75–89.

7

BEING FUNNY IS TRENDY: *NU GARIS LURUS* VS *NU GARIS LUCU*

A'an Suryana

Internet-based schisms within the most prominent Muslim organization, Nahdlatul Ulama (NU), have been a subject of interest among scholars, particularly between two factions: *NU Garis Lurus* (NU Straight Brigade) (Iqbal 2020) and *NU Garis Lucu* (NU Funny Brigade) (Hoesterey 2021). In the 2015 NU congress held in Jombang, East Java province, these social groups competed for power. NU activists who felt that NU was more liberal, established the NU Garis Lurus and campaigned through conservative social media outlets. Their sympathizers ran for NU's top post, challenging chairman Said Agil Siradj, an NU veteran activist seen to be promoting liberal ideas. Running in the election provided NU Garis Lurus with a platform to increase its influence within the organization. Through the media, they expressed a barrage of criticism that NU leaders had given in to Western ideas of secularism, pluralism, and liberalism (SEPILIS) (Rohman 2020, pp. 269–71).

Alarmed by NU Garis Lurus' influence, the NU liberal camp fought back.[1] Young activists at NU established the NU Garis Lucu, a social media community that "used satire and humour to temper the accusations of NU Garis Lurus and to mobilise social media as a uniting force within Nahdlatul Ulama and Indonesia more broadly" (Hoesterey 2021, p. 85). These youth activists demonstrated that the anti-NU Garis Lurus movement did not represent NU's structure. Hence, the dispute between NU Garis Lurus and NU Garis Lucu is not a social dispute that pits "structural NU" against "cultural NU"; rather, the dispute is an internal schism among the different factions within NU. "Structural NU" refers to a group of NU activists whose members assume formal positions in NU's organizational structure and who are therefore influential among NU members. On the other hand, "cultural NU" refers to a group of NU activists who do not assume formal positions in NU's organizational structure, but they wield considerable influence among NU members due to their expertise in Islam or their exemplary behaviour.

These kinds of discourse contestations among different camps within NU are old contestations that are translated, emphasized, and amplified through new platforms such as social media, in addition to mainstream media. This internal contestation is not novel in NU. Political schisms are not unusual and are most evident during the NU congress which is held every five years. One notable schism occurred ahead of the 1984 congress. At that time, NU was divided between those who supported NU returning to its 1926 original charter, which prevents NU members from being involved in politics, and others who still wished that NU would remain active in politics. In the 2021 congress, the followers of the incumbent chairman, Said Aqil Siradj, pitted against the supporters of his opponent, Yahya Cholil Staquf in their race to chairmanship. The elites were involved in a struggle for power to gain hegemony through discourses conveyed in speeches or lectures in traditional mediums such as classes in *pesantren* (Islamic boarding schools), some formal NU events such as *Bathsul Masail* (discussion forum) or *tabligh akbar* (large religious event).

The advancement of technology and the proliferation of social media make it easier for the NU elite or opinion makers to promote a certain discourse to attain their social, religious, and political objectives. The fact that the discourse contestation between NU Garis Lurus and NU Garis Lucu has gained public attention shows how social media and the Internet have been increasingly important mediums for social groups to attain or maintain social power against their adversaries.

This Internet-based schism within Islamic organizations in Indonesia still receives scant attention from scholars. Among the few scholars who have delved into this topic are Asep M. Iqbal and James Bourk Hoesterey. Asep M. Iqbal (2020) discusses how NU Garis Lurus challenges the hegemony of moderate religious views championed by the NU establishment through the Internet and social media. In contrast, Hoesterey (2021) explains how NU Garis Lucu responds to this challenge, not through tough or cynical statements or condemnations against their rival, but instead, through the use of humorous texts or satirical memes on social media. Existing works also tend to discuss the religious views or social and political agenda advanced by either group (Iqbal 2020; Hoesterey 2021; Erman 2021), or the efforts made by either group to promote their discourse on Twitter (Maria 2020).

This chapter contributes to the scholarship on the Internet and Islam in Indonesia by analysing the Internet-based schism within NU. Drawing on a discourse analysis framework, the chapter argues that the moderate and "funny" religious discourse promoted by NU Garis Lucu appeals to the Indonesian public. The same appeal can also be seen in the efforts of Muhammadiyah Garis Lucu and Catholic Garis Lucu, with whom NU Garis Lucu collaborates. Such a collaboration ensures the dominance of religious moderation discourse in the Indonesian public sphere. Religious moderation here refers to the promotion of more inclusive religious ideas that aim to establish religious harmony among people of different faiths.

Since this research discusses discourse contestation in social media, data for this research was collected through analysing social media and Internet posts by NU Garis Lurus and NU Garis Lucu activists. Analysis of the data involved the interpretation of memes, statements or responses in social media posts by both camps on Twitter, Instagram, or personal blogs. Secondary sources such as survey results, books, journal articles, and media reports were referred to in order to understand the meanings behind their social media posts and to know which ideas had greater reception among NU and the public at large.

This chapter first discusses the social, political, and religious ideas that NU stands for. These have been cultivated and developed since its founding and are considered hegemonic in the minds of NU members and sympathizers. The analysis then moves to the origins of NU Garis Lurus, the narratives of their social media posts, and why their narratives gained attention among NU members. This is followed by a discussion on how NU Garis Lucu activists respond to the narratives of their opponents, promote their agenda, and control public discourse. The fourth part discusses the narratives (be they NU Garis Lurus or NU Garis Lucu narratives) which gained greater reception among NU members and the public at large.

NU's Social, Political, and Religious Ideas

The birth of NU stemmed from the rise of Islamic modernism in the then Netherlands Indies, which threatened the social and religious roles of traditionalist Muslim preachers. The modernist movement in Indonesia was inspired by the parallel Islamic reformist movement introduced by Jamal al-Din Al-Afghani (1839–97) and Muhammad Abduh (1849–1905) in Egypt, which was followed by the rise of Wahhabism in Saudi Arabia (Ismail 2011). Afghani and Abduh introduced Islamic political reforms to challenge Western colonialism that resulted in Muslim backwardness. Meanwhile, Muhammad ibn Abd al-Wahhab preached a puritanical form of Islam, against, among others, superstitions and religious innovations in Islam.

Some Indonesian preachers who went to the Middle East to study Islam were influenced by these reforms. They developed their thoughts, which were wholly or partly influenced by the reforms, and disseminated the thoughts when they returned home. Returning Muslim preachers promoted puritanical forms of Islam in Minangkabau, West Sumatra province, and they challenged local traditional practices being sustained by the nobility and *kaum adat* (local traditional chiefs) that they considered un-Islamic. This resulted in the Padri War that occurred between 1803 and 1837. Returning to Yogyakarta Mecca, Muslim preacher Ahmad Dahlan, who was also an educator and social activist, introduced to Muslims some reformist ideas which were quite similar to Wahhabism. These reforms aimed to challenge traditional religious practices that were considered un-Islamic such as visiting graves and other religious innovations. Besides promoting a puritanical form of Islam, through the Muhammadiyah organization which he founded in 1912, Ahmad Dahlan also campaigned to spur social works in Islam to enhance the welfare of Muslims. Apart from Muhammadiyah, other organizations were established: Sarekat Islam (Islamic Union), Al-Irsyad

(Guidance), and Persatuan Islam (Islam Association) (Ismail 2011). Al-Irsyad and Persatuan Islam fought for similar ideas as Muhammadiyah, namely campaigning for a puritanical form of Islam,[2] but Sarekat Islam was the exception among the Muslim modernists. Sarekat Islam did not support the campaign against traditional religious practices. Instead, it was more concerned with political objectives, namely that it promoted unity among Muslims of different sects or religious orientations in order to enhance their welfare.

The spread of modernist views challenged not only the authority of traditionalist Muslim preachers, but also their social and economic well-being. The modernists were critical of the traditionalist rivals "for their strict adherence to classical law schools….and also the culture of traditionalist Muslims' deference toward their religious leaders" (Fealy and Bush 2014, p. 541). More people following a modernist faith also threatened the source of financial income of traditionalist Muslim preachers because some traders and landowners began to cease their donations to the traditionalist Muslim preachers, and students also began to leave traditional Muslim schools, depriving traditionalist preachers of their income (ibid.).

In the early and mid-1920s, key modernist and traditionalist organizations met through several congresses which were held to defuse tensions. However, for unknown reasons, the modernists excluded the traditionalist *ulama* (religious scholars) from the delegation of Indonesian *ulama* attending the World Islam Congress in Mecca in 1926. This triggered a new crisis in the relationship between the two camps of Islam (Saenong 2021; Fealy and Bush 2014; Ismail 2011). This decision to exclude the traditionalist *ulama* was made in the fifth Indonesian Islamic Congress in Bandung, West Java province, which was held on 6 February 1926.

The decision worried the traditionalists as they feared that in the World Islam Congress, the modernists would persuade the government of Saudi Arabia—in particular Ibn Saud, the King of Saudi Arabia who was promoting Wahhabism—to restrict their access to Islamic historical sites, including the tombs of the Prophet's daughters, and to Saudi Arabia's leading Islamic institutions. The traditionalists also feared that the King would no longer respect the teachings and practices of the four schools of Islamic law that had been taught by many *ulama* across the world, including traditionalist *ulama* who had legitimacy before the King rose to power in 1925. Hence, if the King, who was the guardian of Mecca but also at the same time promoting Wahhabism, no longer respects the practices and teachings of the four schools of Islamic law, traditionalist *ulama* in Indonesia would lose their legitimacy among Muslims in their homeland. This was a serious issue because it is related to the social, political, and economic survival of the traditionalist *ulama*.

To deal with the matter, Abdul Wahab Chasbullah, Hasyim Asyari, and other traditionalist *ulama* held a meeting in Surabaya, the capital of East Java province, on 31 January 1926. The meeting resulted in two outcomes. First, to establish a Hijaz Committee to persuade the King of Saudi Arabia to retain access for Muslims, especially the traditionalists, who wish to visit historical religious sites and eminent institutions of Islam in Saudi Arabia. Two members of Hijaz Committee eventually met the King of Saudi Arabia on 13 June 1928, and they claimed that the King responded positively to their requests, which included the King's continuous respect for the practices and teachings of the four schools of Islamic Law as had been taught by many *ulama* across the world, including the *ulama* in Masjid al-Haram in Mecca and Masjid al-Nabawi in Medina as well as the NU ulama (Ismail 2011).

The second outcome was to establish a Muslim traditionalist organization as an "instrument for traditionalist *ulama* to guide the Islamic community in achieving the glory of Islam and the Muslims" (Ismail 2011, p. 259). This organization, founded in 1926, was to be called Nahdlatul Ulama, or the Revival of Ulama. It is clear that the establishment of this organization was to strengthen the traditionalists' bargaining power to persuade the King, but it also had a long termobjective: to fend off the mounting threat from the growth of the modernist movement and at the same time, to maintain the sustainability of their religious traditions.

NU members or followers, including the traditionalist *ulama* in Indonesia, subscribe to Ahlus Sunnah wal Jama'ah theological orientation (the party of the Sunna). It means that they are the followers of both Prophet Muhammad's traditions and the *ijma* (consensus) of the *ulama* (Mufid 2013). They also follow, among others:

(1) The four schools of Islamic law (Hanafi, Maliki, Syafi'i, Hambali), especially the Syafi'i school;
(2) Theological views of Asy'ariyah-Maturidiyah that are in contrast to the Mu'tazilah view of Islam that put more emphasis on the use of reason in solving human problems and the human pursuit of

truth.³ Instead, Asy'ariyah-Maturidiyah argue that Islamic syariah based on Al-Qur'an, *hadith* and human reason can complement each other in the human pursuit of truth⁴;

(3) Sufi view of Imam al-Ghazali that, among others, argues that human beings need to strive to establish harmony, not only in their relations to God, but also in their relations with other human beings (*hablum minallah and hablum minan nas*).⁵

NU *ulama* have followed the traditions of previous *ulama* who brought Islam to Indonesia for the first time between the seventh and eighth centuries peacefully, especially by respecting and accommodating local culture. This is manifested in the concepts of *fiqh* (Islamic jurisprudence) and *usul al-fiqh* (sources of Islamic jurisprudence).⁶ The proponents of these concepts argue that local customs can be the source of religious laws as stipulated by the Qur'an and *hadith*. As a result, NU "accommodates local cultures and practices as long as they do not harm the fundamental principles of Islam" (Saenong 2021, p. 143). This is manifested, among others, in Muslims' practice of wearing sarongs during prayers. This is in contrast to the modernist, who considered such practices as promoting *takhayul* (superstition), *bid'a* (religious innovation) and *churafat* (superstition) which they consider illegal in Islam.

Since NU follows the Sufi view of Imam al-Ghazali, its *ulama* often proclaim that Islam needs to be *rahmatan lil alamin*, or a blessing to the universe. It means that Islam, in the eyes of NU, should bring benefit not only to Muslims, but also to people of different faiths. To attain this objective, NU *ulama* encourage their followers to show or to implement two main characters, namely *tawasuth* (moderate character) and *i'tidal* (fair character) (Ulum 2017). *Tawasuth* means that the people of NU are willing to take middle path when they meet two extreme ideological choices. They are encouraged to promote the moderate and contextual version of Islam, which means that the interpretation of Islamic tenets, such as Qur'anic verses, need to take into account the context in which the verses were created. *I'tidal* means that they need to treat other people fairly even if they dislike them.⁷

These two characters are reflected in the attitude of NU's members: *tasamuh* (tolerance), balance in the use of syariah and reason in solving human problems or in seeking the truth (*tawazun*), and the promotion of dialogue or discussion instead of unilateral action (*musyawarah*) (Ulum 2017). To sum up, NU had already adopted inclusive and accommodative approaches towards other social and religious ideas—including local folk religion—in its early development. These approaches are reflected in their approaches to dealing with contemporary problems, among others, interfaith relations. In the next two sections, this chapter will discuss religious orientations and discourses that NU Garis Lurus and NU Garis Lucu have been promoting. In doing so, it will demonstrate how NU Garis Lurus' social, political, and religious ideas have deviated from NU's original ideas.

NU Garis Lurus: Challenging NU Establishment's Hegemony

NU Garis Lurus began gaining attention in the run up to the 2015 NU Congress in Jombang, East Java province. It was not a formal group at the time and was suggested by a journalist with *Alkisah* Magazine.[8] Referring to a loose grouping of several NU figures who regularly expressed their conservative and anti-NU establishment views, the group consists of individuals like Luthfi Bashori, Yahya Zainul Ma'arif (Buya Yahya), Muhammad Idrus Ramli, and Muhammad Najih Maimoen. Some of these people were already openly critical before this group emerged in public. In 2009, Luthfi Bashori established a website (www.pejuangislam.com) on which he and his staff or followers often expressed their opposition to the NU establishment, and also explained their conservative views of Islam. In 2012, Muhammad Najih Maimoen published a book that accused some NU figures of supporting liberal views stemming from Western civilization.

However, this loose group of young and senior NU scholars began to steal public attention in 2015 after they supported the NU chairmanship candidacy of one of their own, Idrus Ramli. This support came in the form of interviews in mainstream media, and more importantly, followers of the NU Garis Lurus movement established social media accounts that promoted NU Garis Lurus' views and support for Idrus Ramli's candidacy. These accounts were on Twitter, Instagram, Facebook, and the NU Garis Lurus' website (www.garislurus.com; it no longer exists).

Their support for Idrus Ramli generated public attention for various reasons. Firstly, it is quite rare for younger individuals to run for NU chairmanship. NU Garis Lurus' support for Idrus Ramli, who was still in his 40s, therefore attracted public attention. Secondly, they courted controversy as they appeared to have highlighted an anti-NU establishment campaign while publishing their support for Idrus Ramli. For example, they highlighted accusations that some of the elites in NU's top positions received money from certain parties in Saudi Arabia and Iran in return for their support for the spread of Wahhabism and Shi'ism in Indonesia.[9]

Those responsible for this are mostly younger members who claim to be the graduates of NU's *pesantren*, and who choose to be anonymous as they fear backlash from the NU establishment. However, there is also suspicion that they are not part of NU, but are outsiders who "attempt to divide NU".[10] They have refuted this accusation, arguing that all of their posts and statements on social media have not violated the social and religious guidance (*Qanun Asasi*; lit. constitution) as formulated by NU's founder, and which every NU members must heed.[11]

In contrast, older members of NU Garis Lurus have been fearless in socially and politically challenging the NU establishment. There are at least four well-known senior proponents of NU Garis Lurus, namely Luthfi Bashori, Yahya Zainul Ma'arif, Idrus Ramli, and Muhammad Najih Maimoen. All of them are graduates of Islamic boarding schools and have been active in teaching and even running Islamic boarding schools that are affiliated with NU. Luthfi Bashori and Muhammad Idrus Ramli in particular have been active in NU's executive committee. While NU Garis Lurus does not have headquarters or an organizational structure, it is clear that its members work with one another to achieve their social and political objectives. For example, efforts were made to support Prabowo Subianto and Sandiaga Uno, the presidential and vice-presidential candidates in the run up to the 2019 presidential election. Luthfi Bashori, Idrus Ramli, and other NU Garis Lurus activists reportedly met on 10 February 2019 in Surabaya to pursue their cause to support the candidates.[12]

At the level of discourse, their conservative and anti-NU establishment voices are expressed through various outlets. For example, Luthfi Bashori promotes his religious, social, and political views on his website (www.pejuangislam.com), where numerous articles have been published since 2009. Most of the articles are made for easy reading and are only about 300 words, while some articles are more than

10,000 words. While Luthfi is the author of most of the articles, a good number of articles are written by other conservative Muslim figures such as Irfan S. Awwas, who is an activist with Majelis Mujahidin, an organization that aims to implement *syariah* law. The articles written by Luthfi tend to promote sentiments against secularism, the west, minority religious groups, and "liberal" Muslims, He also writes about his support for the formalization of the *syariah* in Indonesian law, and once expressed his objection against an NU elite who did not hesitate to give a speech to a Christian congregation in a church in Surabaya. He argued that it was an embodiment of a liberal attitude.[13] As a whole, the articles on this website tend to deviate from the issues which NU activists typically discuss in public. While NU activists promote a more moderate version of Islam, NU Garis Lurus members promote a more conservative approach. Thus, there are articles on the website which other members of NU Garis Lurus share Luthfi's views. For example, in 2021, Muhammad Idrus Ramli criticized Said Aqil Siradj, former chairman of NU (2010 and 2021), for "his leaning to liberal and Shi'ism thinking".[14] On 28 February 2022, Muhammad Najih, an influential Muslim cleric, also rebuked NU and its elite whom he accused of "having a habit of receiving illicit money, and that this habit has been done since the chairmanship of Abdurrahman Wahid".[15] Muhamad Najih, one of the executives at Al Anwar Islamic boarding school in Rembang regency, Central Java province, even asked people to fight against NU elite to stop this habit. His rant, which appeared in one of NU Garis Lurus' YouTube videos, went viral and was picked up by mainstream media.[16]

NU Garis Lucu: Sustaining the Hegemony of Religious Moderation in a Fun Way

Due to the rise of NU Garis Lurus' popularity among the public, several NU cadres established NU Garis Lucu social media accounts to challenge the narratives that NU Garis Lurus have been propagating. While top NU executives have denied that the social media accounts with the name NU Garis Lucu officially represent the organization (Hidayatullah and Darmaningrum 2019), it is clear from the narratives that these accounts are in line with the social and political views of the NU establishment.

Panggabean, Alam, and Ali-Fauzi (2010, pp. 246–47) have developed categories of religious issues that can contribute to the occurrence of religious conflicts. While they mainly discuss religious conflicts in offline environments, these categories are useful to make sense of the religious issues that NU Garis Lucu promotes. These categories are broad; they address physical conflict and also address verbal expressions conveyed during street protests about religious issues or conflicts. The authors posit that there are six religious issues which are prone to religious conflict. These are: (1) moral issues such as those related to gambling, prostitution, pornography, and the consumption of alcoholic beverages; (2) sectarian issues, which include any dispute on interpretations of Islam that could result in schisms, such as in the case of Lia Eden and the Ahmadiyya community, or any dispute that concerns leadership status, for example, the leadership dispute in the Huria Kristen Batak Protestan (HKBP) community; (3) communal issues which are related to social disputes or hostility between different religious communities, such as between Muslim and Christian communities, or between Sunni and Shi'a communities; (4) terrorism issues related to acts of terror, such as against members or properties that belong to other religious groups; (5) issues concerning sentiments against western ideology and culture; and (6) other issues that include, for example, affairs related to black magic.

Based on this framework, it can be observed that NU Garis Lucu—in their bid to promote their moderate and inclusive version of Islam—discusses some of these issues on their social media accounts. Most of their posts are related to sectarian and communal issues. These posts express the social, political, and religious views of the members in a satirical and humorous manner, in contrast to NU Garis Lurus who tend to be more rigid and divisive in their tone and perspective.

For example, an Instagram post by NU Garis Lucu (see Figure 7.1) illustrates the importance that they accord to building good relations with people, and not solely emphasizing on religious dogma which demands one's complete submission to God. In English, the content of the post translates to "If there are two people who hate each other; the best among them is not the one that is close to God, but the one who greets the other person first". It is therefore an indirect rebuke against Muslim conservatives who tend to prioritize piety over complete submission to God above all else. Ultimately, the post stems

FIGURE 7.1
NU Garis Lucu Instagram post, dated 3 May 2022

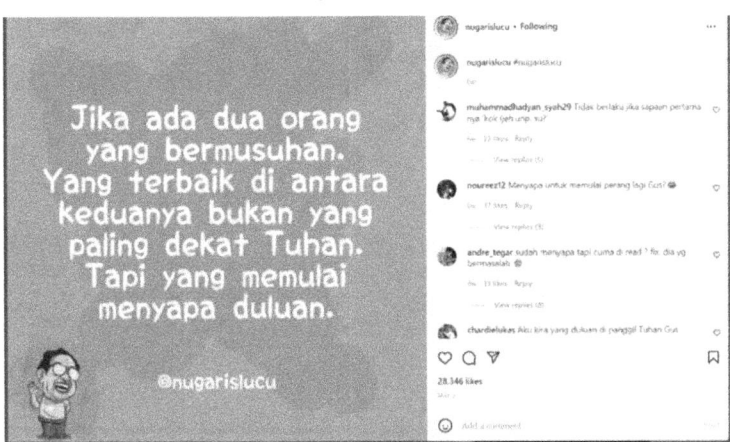

from a concern that in some cases, overzealous worship could result in religious tribalism that would be detrimental to inter-religious harmony. Religious tribalism would boost social tension, which can often lead to violence. The post therefore implies that people should find common ground instead of highlighting differences or assuming a position of superiority. This sort of narrative, illustrative of religious moderation, is ubiquitous on NU Garis Lucu's Twittter and Instagram posts.

Another theme that stands out on NU Garis Lucu's social media accounts is religious inclusivity. For example, one of their Twitter posts (see Figure 7.2) illustrates their attempt to build cordial relations with other religious communities. The content of the post was in response to an earlier post by the Catholic Community's Garis Lucu (Komunitas Katolik Garis Lucu) account, in which the latter coolly remarked that students in the Catholic seminary are often sleepy during class even though they are given time to nap in the afternoons. NU Garis Lucu humorously responded and said, "In Islamic boarding schools, if students are sleepy, they are ordered to slurp salt". The post is therefore an attempt to share Muslim students' experiences and to draw similarities between the two by illustrating how students in boarding schools undergo the same sense of exhaustion or even boredom. Ultimately, it is a post which promotes religious tolerance.

FIGURE 7.2
NU Garis Lucu Twitter post, dated 15 June 2022

> **NU Garis Lucu**
> 53,5K Tweets
>
> **Tweets**   Tweets & replies   Media   Likes
>
> Show more
>
> **NU Garis Lucu** @NUgarislucu · 21h
> Di pesantren kalau ngantuk suruh ngemut garam 😂
>
> > **Komunitas Katolik Garis...** · 21h
> > Di Seminari, para siswa juga ada tidur siang. Meski begitu, anak Seminari tetap aja ngantukan. Belajar di kelas atau Misa pagi di kapel, beberapa dari mereka pasti ada yang merem. ...
>
> 💬 15   🔁 6   ♡ 127   ⬆

This is in contrast to the firm and rigid approach by Muslim conservatives, such as those in NU Garis Lurus who discourage Muslims from inter-religious interactions. For example, some writers from NU Garis Lurus once published a commentary discouraging Muslims from expressing Christmas greetings to Christians, as doing so would cause the former to lose their faith.[17]

These findings support earlier research on the topic which discuss how NU Garis Lucu's social media accounts promote peaceful coexistence among people of different faiths as part of their wider aim to encourage religious moderation. Ery Erman (2021, p. 58) explains that the accounts "present crisp humours in that they educate people to enhance their religious tolerance toward others". Hidayatullah and Darmaningrum (2019) found that NU Garis Lucu's campaign for religious moderation and inclusivity is targeted at three categories of people: internal NU members, Muslim non-NU members, and non-Muslims. The examples above are illustrative of this. There are also cases in which NU Garis Lucu interacts with other religious communities just for the sake of humour, and not necessarily with the specific intention to draw inter-religious similarities. These interactions tend to revolve around basic religious themes or figures, or certain events in society.

For example, when the Komunitas Katolik Garis Lucu's account posted a tweet asking "why is Jesus not smiling or laughing in most pictures of him?" (see Figure 7.3), NU Garis Lucu responded as such: "because all these pictures were taken when he was still single [laughing emoji]".

Another example is when Deddy Corbuzier—a former magician-turned-social media celebrity with millions of followers social media (YouTube: 18.9 million; Twitter: 4.3 million; Instagram: 11.3 million

FIGURE 7.3
Komunitas Katolik Garis Lucu Twitter post, dated 18 July 2018

as of 14 July 2022)—left the Catholic faith and converted to Islam on 21 June 2019. News of his conversion went viral, and the Komunitas Katolik Garis Lucu and NU Garis Lucu Twitter accounts posted humorous tweets about the event. The former first tweeted:

> Hari ini kami serahkan @corbuzier ke @Nugarislucu untuk selanjutnya silahkan disunat dan diarahkan....
> [Today, we hand over @corbuzier to @Nugarislucu for him to be circumcised and to get religious guidance...] (Hidayatullah and Darmaningrum 2019, p. 194).

The tweet illustrates how Komunitas Katolik Garis Lucu did not see Corbuzier's conversion as a problem, but instead humorously asked NU Garis Lucu to ensure his circumcision (a mandatory practice for Muslim males, and which is normally part of the conversion process) and to provide him with religious guidance. NU Garis Lucu then re-tweeted the post and included their response:

> Siap, ndan. Ajaran-ajaran baik dari sampean tetap kami pertahankan.
> [We are ready, Buddy. We will sustain your good (Catholic) religious tenets] (Hidayatullah and Darmaningrum, 2019, p. 194).

Their post was in marked contrast to Muslims who more often than not would regard a conversion as a victory for Muslims since Islam gets another follower, while Catholicism loses one. Consequently, they would be arrogant and disrespectful towards the Catholics. NU Garis Lucu was the opposite. They demonstrated humility, and even said they would encourage Corbuzier to maintain good Catholic practices despite his conversion.

Apart from the Catholics, NU Garis Lucu's social media presence has inspired other religious groups to follow in their footsteps by influencing public discourse through humorous posts on their own accounts. These groups are, among others, Muhammadiyah (Muhammadiyah Garis Lucu), and the Buddhists (Buddhist Garis Lucu). However, these accounts are not the official accounts of their respective religious organizations, the same way NU Garis Lucu is not the official account of the NU organization. These accounts were created solely out of concerns about the rise of conservatism in their respective communities. For example, one of the founders of Muhammadiyah Garis Lucu said that he created Muhammadiyah Garis Lucu Facebook and Twitter accounts in 2018 "to make more moderate" the growing number of

Muhammadiyah followers who were shifting their religious outlook further to the right along the religious spectrum.[18]

Dominating Narratives in the Public Sphere

The contestation of discourses between NU Garis Lucu and NU Garis Lurus as presented above, borrowing a term used by Norman Fairclough, is a social event that has a textual character (Fairclough 2003, p. 21). Through text, their activists disseminate messages which are mediated by their respective social media accounts. The text can be analysed by using Fairclough's types of text meaning: action, representation, and identification (ibid., p. 27). Action implies social relations in that through their messages in the form of texts on social media, NU Garis Lurus and NU Garis Lucu activists inform, advise, promise, and warn their readers on a particular issue or several issues. Representation means that NU Garis Lucu and NU Garis Lurus represent two different entities, especially in the form of their social and religious outlooks. In terms of identification, the activists express their commitments, judgments, and undertakings via messages on their social media accounts.

Parts of or the whole texts produced by the NU Garis Lurus and NU Garis Lucu activists embody a part of or the whole triad of action, representation, and/or identification. All these elements of action, representation, and identification are reflected in, among others, NU Garis Lucu's response to Komunitas Katolik Garis Lucu's Twitter post on Deddy Corbuzier's conversion. Through their response, NU Garis Lucu activists informed and assured [action] their Catholic counterparts that they would guide Corbuzier to keep practising Catholicism's religious tenets. Their response is also illustrative of NU Garis Lucu's moderate religious ideological outlook [representation], which is different from other more conservative social groups, including NU Garis Lurus. Finally, their response also expresses NU Garis Lucu's commitment to inter-religious harmony and religious moderation [identification].

The elements of action, representation, and identification can also be found in the titles and content of some articles published on NU Garis Lurus' website. Take for example, the following paragraph from an article titled "Dialog Tokoh-Tokoh Islam Seputar Ucapan Selamat

Natal" ("Dialogue Between Islamic Figures Concerning Christmas Greetings"):[19]

> In my opinion, once it is forbidden in Islam, it will be forbidden all the time. It is forbidden in all forms. It is forbidden to be done by any Muslims. Indeed, Prophet Muhammad once prayed that Jews obtained blessings, health and all goodness in profane life. But it (such as greeting good morning or extending Christmas greetings) does not apply in the matter of salvation, because non-Muslims will never get salvation. Imam Nawawi has explained in detail how extending Christmas greetings to non-Muslims is unlawful in Islam...Probably, not many Muslim figures have read [Nawawi's] works, including Prof. Din Syamsuddin. They need to read books written by Salafi figures, so that they can maintain the implementation of right Islamic Law, hence they will not be contaminated with non-Islamic outlooks such as liberalism.[20]

The article is written in the form of a dialogue between Muslim figures, including a key figure from NU Garis Lurus, Lutthfi Bashori. The paragraph above is a quote from Bashori himself and was circulated to other Muslim figures via short-messaging system (SMS) in 2016. His statement warns and persuades Muslims not to extend Christmas greetings to Christians [action], and is illustrative of their conservative approach to Islam [representation]. It also shows Bashori's commitment to the stricter implementation of Islamic law [identification].

It is therefore evident that these are competing discourses in the public sphere as a result of the differences in approach between NU Garis Lurus and NU Garis Lucu. While the former is more conservative, the latter is more moderate. This is evident from their approaches to issues such as inter-religious relations, the implementation of Islamic law, as well as other issues relating to religion and the state. However, these competing discourses beg the question: which narrative is more dominant?

Teun van Dijk (1993, p. 255) argues that "power and dominance are usually organized and institutionalized". This idea is important in distinguishing institutionalized power from the one-time use of power, for example, in the case of sexual harassment that occurs on the street. In the case of the former, there are some elites in society who have capacity to organize and institutionalize power to attain social dominance, especially at the level of discourse. These elites will get more social power if they are capable of controlling access to discourse.

NU Garis Lucu and NU Garis Lurus are both socially powerful due to their control on social media. They get legitimacy as opinion leaders due to the ideological views that they represent: NU Garis Lucu is perceived to represent NU's progressive strand and the organization as a whole, while NU Garis Lurus is thought to represent the conservative strand of NU. Their prolific social media and Internet posts appeal to respective audiences, and these viewers become their captive markets.

Ahead of the NU congress in 2015, NU Garis Lurus was at the peak of its popularity. One of its websites (www.nugarislurus.com) attracted much public attention as a result of its anti-NU establishment content. While it is unclear when the website was created, the website's administrator claimed in 2015 that it once ranked among the 300 most visited websites in Indonesia.[21] In December 2016, the website ceased to exist for three days after it "attacked" President Joko Widodo.[22] The website eventually completely stopped operating, although it is unclear when this happened. Nevertheless, they continued to propagate their views through their YouTube channel, NU Garis Lurus Media, which still exists as of 4 July 2022. At least two videos on this channel have gone viral. The first is a video from 12 March 2022 which criticizes a Christian priest—who happens to be a supporter of the Minister of Religious Affairs, Yaqut Cholil Qoumas—for proposing to remove 300 verses from the Qur'an.[23] The second video, from 28 February 2022, accuses NU executives of earning illicit money for years.[24] The virality of the videos thus shows how influential the channel is among the public. It also has 29,700 subscribers, which is a large number.

However, despite the public attention which NU Garis Lurus receives, it is evident that NU Garis Lucu dominates the public sphere. Set up in March 2015, NU Garis Lucu's Twitter account had 884,200 followers as of 4 July 2022. They also had 829,000 followers on Instagram. Furthermore, as mentioned earlier, NU Garis Lucu's popularity spurred other religious groups to create similar accounts, thus demonstrating their popularity. The same could not be said about NU Garis Lurus. Additionally, NU Garis Lucu often initiates interactions with these other accounts, which hence facilitates their greater presence on social media. Their inclusive ideas on religion therefore become more dominant online. Finally, a basic Google search also shows that NU Garis Lucu is more popular than NU Garis Lurus. A search of the former's name generated 61,000 results on 4 July 2022, while a search of the latter's name only generated 14,900 results in comparison.

Conclusion

This chapter has discussed discourse contestation between NU Garis Lurus and NU Garis Lucu. Through the messages that they post on the Internet and social media, it is evident that NU Garis Lurus promotes a conservative brand of Islam and is anti-NU establishment, while NU Garis Lucu promotes a more inclusive and moderate brand of Islam. As a result of their light-hearted and often humorous posts, in addition to the inter-religious interactions which they engage in, NU Garis Lucu dominates the social narrative online. Furthermore, the fact that they have encouraged other religious groups to establish similar accounts of their own provides the opportunity for them to sustain and expand their inclusive discourse online. This is in contrast to NU Garis Lurus whose posts do not garner as much attention. NU Garis Lucu has thus set a trend in approaching Islam and issues relating to religion.

The chapter thus explains how the Internet and social media serve as a crucial medium in propagating the ideological views of religious organizations, and consequently attracting the attention of the public. Future research on the Internet and Islam in Indonesia would do well to delve further into this topic and to conduct quantitative studies to find out why people are interested in the genre of NU Garis Lucu's posts. Future research could also expand on the schisms in other big Islamic organizations, such as Muhammadiyah, so as to have a deeper understanding of the diversity of Islamic thought and how it plays out on the Internet.

NOTES

1   A senior official at one of NU's biggest chapters considers the NU Garis Lurus movement "a joke" and maintained that NU members "will remain loyal to *kiai* [respected religious figures] in NU". See Pipit Maulidiya, "Tanggapan PWNU Jatim Soal Kemunculan NU Garis Lurus: 'Anggap

Lelucon Saja Lah'", *Surya Tribun News*, 11 February 2019, https://surabaya.tribunnews.com/2019/02/11/tanggapan-pwnu-jatim-soal-kemunculan-nu-garis-lurus-anggap-lelucon-saja-lah (accessed 4 July 2022).

2 Aqwam Fiazmi Hanifan, "Cap Wahabi dan Dinamika yang Tidak Hitam Putih", *Tirto*, 6 March 2017, https://tirto.id/cap-wahabi-dan-dinamika-yang-tidak-hitam-putih-ckg6 (accessed 4 July 2022).

3 Abdul Hadi, "Sejarah Mu'tazilah: Tokoh Aliran, Pemikiran, dan Doktrin Ajarannya", *Tirto*, 14 August 2021, https://tirto.id/sejarah-mutazilah-tokoh-aliran-pemikiran-dan-doktrin-ajarannya-gixq (accessed 4 July 2022).

4 Syamsul Dwi Maarif, "Sejarah Aliran Asy'ariyah, Pokok Pemikiran, dan Tokoh Pendirinya", *Tirto*, 20 August 2021, https://tirto.id/sejarah-aliran-asyariyah-pokok-pemikiran-dan-tokoh-pendirinya-gidU (accessed 4 July 2022). See also Abdul Hadi, "Sejarah Aliran Maturidiyah, Tokoh, Pemikiran dan Doktrin Ajarannya", *Tirto*, 26 July 2021, https://tirto.id/sejarah-aliran-maturidiyah-tokoh-pemikiran-dan-doktrin-ajarannya-gh2q (accessed 4 July 2022).

5 Alhafiz Kurniawan, "Penjelasan Imam Al-Ghazali tentang Tasawuf dan Sufi", *NU Online*, 16 September 2019, https://islam.nu.or.id/tasawuf-akhlak/penjelasan-imam-al-ghazali-tentang-tasawuf-dan-sufi-WAUd3 (accessed 4 July 2022).

6 *Al-'ada* or *al-'urf muhakkama*. It literally refers to the sources of Islamic law and the discipline dedicated to elucidating them and their relationship to the substantive rulings of the law. See "Uṣūl al-fiqh", *Encyclopedia Britannica*, 2 April 2018, https://www.britannica.com/topic/usul-al-fiqh (accessed 14 July 2022).

7 See "Pengertian Aswaja dan Karakter Tawassuth, Tawazun, I'tidal", *PCNU Jember*, 3 December 2021, https://pcnujember.or.id/2021/12/03/pengertian-aswaja-dan-karakter-tawassuth-tawazun-dan-itidal/ (accessed 14 July 2022).

8 See "Ulama Garis Lurus Meluruskan Tuduhan Fungsionaris PBNU", *Portal Berita Politik Jatim*, 14 November 2019, https://www.rmoljatim.id/2019/11/14/ulama-garis-lurus-meluruskan-tuduhan-fungsionaris-pbnu (accessed 4 July 2022).

9 Panji Islam, "NU Garis Lurus: 'Lebih Baik Sok Lurus, daripada Sok Sesat!'", *Hidayatullah*, 14 August 2015, https://hidayatullah.com/berita/wawancara/read/2015/08/14/75800/nu-garis-lurus-lebih-baik-sok-lurus-daripada-sok-sesat.html (accessed 4 July 2022).

10 Muhammad Saad, "KH. Hasyim Asyari dan Fenomena 'NU Garis Lurus' [1]", *Hidayatullah*, 21 April 2015, https://hidayatullah.com/artikel/ghazwul-fikr/read/2015/04/21/68524/kh-hasyim-asyari-dan-fenomena-nu-garis-lurus-1.html (accessed 4 July 2022).

11 Panji Islam, "NU Garis Lurus: 'Lebih Baik Sok Lurus, daripada Sok Sesat!'".

12 "NU Garis Lurus Deklarasikan Dukungannya Ke Prabowo-Sandi", *Kabar Today*, 10 February 2019, https://www.kabartoday.co.id/nu-garis-lurus-deklarasikan-dukungannya-ke-prabowo-sandi/ (accessed 4 July 2022).
13 Luthfi Bashori, "Konsep NU & Krisis Penegakan Syariat", *Pejuang Islam*, 3 October 2016, https://www.pejuangislam.com/main.php?prm=karya&var=detail&id=6 (accessed 4 July 2022).
14 Resty, "Sebut Pemikiran Said Aqil Siradj Banyak Menyimpang, Idrus Ramli: Condong Syiah dan Liberal", *Makassar Terkini*, 22 September 2021, https://makassar.terkini.id/sebut-pemikiran-said-aqil-siradj-banyak-menyimpang-idrus-ramli-condong-syiah-dan-liberal/ (accessed 4 July 2022).
15 NU Garis Lurus Media, "PBNU Sudah Kebanyakan Makan Uang Haram Sejak Gus Dur", YouTube, 28 February 2022, https://www.youtube.com/watch?v=8OseyRy3cWc (accessed 10 July 2022).
16 Ibid.
17 Tim AMAL (Aswaja Menangkal Aliran Liberal), "Halal Bihalal Lintas Iman Ala Menag, Pendangkalan Aqidah Berbungkus Toleran", *Pejuang Islam*, 21 May 2021, https://www.pejuangislam.com/main.php?prm=berita&var=detail&id=1626 (accessed 10 July 2022).
18 "Dakwah Garis Lucu NU-Muhammadiyah", *Kumparan News*, 11 January 2019, https://kumparan.com/kumparannews/dakwah-garis-lucu-nu-muhammadiyah-1547175616360531881/full (accessed 10 July 2022).
19 Ustadz Luthfi Bashori, "Dialog Tokoh-Tokoh Islam Seputar Ucapan Selamat Natal", *Pejuang Islam*, 20 August 2016, https://www.pejuangislam.com/main.php?prm=karya&var=detail&id=8 (accessed 10 July 2022).
20 In the original Bahasa Indonesia: "Menurut saya, yang haram selamanya haram, sekalipun dikemas dalam bentuk apapun, oleh siapapun, berapapun jumlah pelakunya. Memang Nabi SAW pernah mendo`akan orang Yahudi agar mendapat hidayah, kesehatan, dan kebagusan duniawi. Tapi tidak untuk keselamatan (semisal selamat pagi - selamat natal) karena selama-lamanya orang kafir itu tidak bakal selamat. Imam Nawawi telah menerangkan dengan detail masalah haramnya mengucapkan selamat Natal pada kaum kafir, dalam kitab beliau al-Adzkar dengan dalil hadits-hadits Nabi. Barangkali tidak banyak tokoh Islam yang membacanya termasuk juga Prof. Din Syamsuddin. Mereka perlu baca kitab-kitab Ulama Salaf agar lebih konsisten memegang Syari'ah yang benar, tidak terkontaminasi oleh paham-paham dari luar Islam semisal Liberalisme, Afwan wa syukran, Wassalam. (Tembusan kepada Pengurus MUI Pusat Bpk. Ikhwan Sam, KH. Ma'ruf Amin dan KH. Kholil Ridwan, Prof. Din Syamsuddin)". See link above.
21 Panji Islam, "NU Garis Lurus: 'Lebih Baik Sok Lurus, daripada Sok Sesat!'"

22 Duta Islam #01, "Simalakama Cyber Aswaja Mengatasi Anak Nakal NU Garis Lurik (NUGL)", *Duta Islam*, 20 December 2016, https://www.dutaislam.com/2016/12/simalakama-cyber-aswaja-mengatasi-anak-nakal-nu-garis-lurik.html (accessed 10 July 2022).
23 NU Garis Lurus Media, "Pendeta Kurangajar Pendukung Menag Ini Usulkan 300 Ayat Al Quran Dihapus", YouTube, 12 March 2022, https://www.youtube.com/watch?v=FKsT6s-8wkI (accessed 10 July 2022).
24 NU Garis Lurus Media, "PBNU Sudah Kebanyakan Makan Uang Haram Sejak Gus Dur", YouTube, 28 February 2022, https://www.youtube.com/watch?v=8OseyRy3cWc (accessed 10 July 2022).

REFERENCES

Erman, Ery. 2021. "Ruang Publik Keagamaan: Intoleransi dan Narasi Human NU Garis Lucu". *Fikri: Jurnal Agama Sosial dan Budaya* 6, no. 1: 50–63.
Fairclough, Norman. 2003. *Analysing Discourse: Textual Analysis for Social Research*. London; New York: Routledge.
Fealy, Greg and Robin Bush. 2014. "The Political Decline of Traditional Ulama in Indonesia". *Asian Journal of Social Science* 42: 536–60.
Hidayatullah, Ahmad and Khaerunnisa Tri Darmaningrum. 2019. "Inklusifitas Dakwah Akun @NUgarislucu di Media Sosial". *Islamic Communication Journal* 4, no. 2: 183–96.
Hoesterey, James Bourk. 2021. "Nadhlatul Ulama's 'Funny Brigade': Piety, Satire, and Indonesian Online Divides". *CyberOrient* 15, no. 1: 85–118.
Husein, Fatimah and Martin Slama. 2018. "Online Piety and Its Discontent: Revisiting Islamic Anxieties on Indonesian Social Media". *Indonesia and the Malay World* 46, no. 134: 80–93.
Iqbal, Asep. 2020. "Challenging Moderate Islam in Indonesia: NU Garis Lurus and Its Construction of the 'Authentic' NU Online". In *Rising Islamic Conservatism in Indonesia: Islamic Groups and Identity Politics*, edited by Leonard Sebastian, Syafiq Hasyim and Alexander Arifianto, pp. 95–115. New York: Routledge.
Ismail, Faisal. 2011. "The Nadhlatul Ulama: Its Early History and Contribution to the Establishment of Indonesia State". *Journal of Indonesia Islam* 5, no. 2: 247–82.
Maimoen, Muhammad Najih. 2012. *Membuka Kedok Tokoh-Tokoh Liberal Dalam Tubuh NU*. Rembang: Toko Kitab Al-Anwar.
Maria, Chelsea Sivana Sofie. 2020. "Pesan Dakwah Akun Twitter NU Garis Lucu: Analisis Semiotik Roland Barthes". Undergraduate Thesis, UIN Sunan Ampel Surabaya.

Mufid, Ahmad Syafi'i. 2013. "Paham Ahlu Sunnah Wal Jama'ah dan Tantangan Kontemporer dalam Pemikiran dan Gerakan Islam di Indonesia". *Harmoni: Jurnal Multikultural & Multireligius* 12, no. 3: 8–18.

Nisa, Eva F. 2018. "Social Media and the Birth of an Islamic Social Movement: ODOJ (One Day One Juz) in Contemporary Indonesia". *Indonesia and the Malay World* 46, no. 134: 24–43.

Panggabean, Samsu Rizal, Rudi Harisyah Alam and Ihsan Ali-Fauzi. 2010. "The Patterns of Religious Conflict in Indonesia (1990–2008)". *Studia Islamika: Indonesian Journal for Islamic Studies* 17, no. 2: 233–98.

Rohman, M. Saifullah. 2020. "Intoleransi dan Radikalisme di Jawa Timur: Studi tentang Dinamika di NU dan Pembangunan Narasi Positif di Grassroot NU". In *Intoleransi dan Pollitik Identitas Kontemporer di Indonesia*, edited by Cahyo Pamungkas and Yogi Setya Permana, pp. 261–98. Jakarta: Lembaga Ilmu Pengetahuan Indonesia (LIPI).

Saenong, Farid. 2021. "Nadhlatul Ulama (NU): A Grassroots Movement Advocating Moderate Islam". In *Handbook of Islamic Sects and Movements*, edited by Muhammad Afzal Upal and Carole Cusack, pp. 129–50. Boston: Brill.

Ulum, Miftahul. 2017. "Tradisi Dakwah Nadhlatul Ulama (NU) in Indonesia". *Al-Iman: Jurnal Keislaman dan Pemasyarakatan* 1, no. 1: 139–69.

Van Dijk, Teun A. 1993. "Principles of Critical Discourse Analysis". *Discourse & Society* 4, no. 2: 249–83.

Yang Hui, Jennifer. 2010. "The Internet in Indonesia: Development and Impact of Radical Websites". *Studies in Conflict and Terrorism* 33, no. 2: 171–91.

PART III

Influencers Driving Trends

8

AMAR MAKRUF DAN NAHI MUNGKAR: MORAL POLICING OF FEMALE MUSLIM CELEBRITIES AND INFLUENCERS IN BRUNEI, MALAYSIA, AND INDONESIA

Sharifah Nurul Huda Alkaff

Introduction

According to Fox (2010, p. 355), "Recent years have seen a growing interest, both scholarly and otherwise, in the intersection of religion and media. Much of the commentary has been organised around the idea that, as media have taken on the role of a public religion, contemporary religious life has become suffused with sensibilities that derive from television, popular films, and the Internet". In maritime Southeast Asia, particularly the Muslim-majority societies, popular culture has become part of everyday lived Islam. Sounds and images about Islam abound in contemporary popular culture in the form of films, music, television, radio, comics, fashion, magazines, and social media. However, along with the development of modern and increasingly accessible modes of communication come broad implications for what gets articulated in the public sphere. Eickelman and Anderson (1999, p. 14), for instance, describe how as the role of the media has increased, the gatekeeper role of nation-states has decreased, and as a result, more people have gained access to redefining Muslim thought.

The most potent entity of this expanded mediascape is the Internet and social media. Bunt (2009, p. 1) states that many Muslims, in both majority and minority contexts, are relying on the Internet as the primary source of news, information, and communication about Islam. He uses the term "cyber-Islamic environment" (CIE) to describe this digital space that represents the diversity of "varied Muslim worldviews within the House of Islam". He also notes that the new media culture that emerged recently has led to the creation of new concepts such as "e-jihad" ("Electronic Jihad"), which presents itself in myriad forms such as promoting militaristic activities or coordinating peaceful protests.

Similarly, on the role of social media, Ibahrine (2014, p. 37) argues that the impact of social media on "religious behaviours of individuals and communities in environments characterized by conservatism and traditionalism, will be even more profound than in environments characterized by liberalism and openness". He notes that many Islamic scholars today are highly enthusiastic about using social media to spread their messages as they recognize the power of these platforms to engage with a bigger audience. In fact, proselytization on social media is not limited to religious leaders but is also done by ordinary Muslims who often post Qur'anic verses and *hadith* (sayings of the Prophet Muhammad) on their social media accounts. In response to this new trend, Ibrahine (ibid., p. 738) believes that the "continuous digitization of Islam and the Islamization of the digital world represents both a blessing and challenge to the religion of Islam in the 21st century". Interpretations of the Qur'an and *hadith* that used to be exclusive domains of religious scholars have now been usurped by non-scholars who utilize social media sites to disseminate their versions of sacred interpretations. As a result, Ibahrine (ibid., p. 740) states that "the traditional concept of religious authority has come under attack, and has been shaken in many forms…consequently, religious authority has become a contested domain". Mandaville (2001) also made similar observations about the Internet being a double-edged sword for Islam. While the Internet has provided opportunities for more people to engage in discussions about Islam, he argues that it has also become a site of friction where Muslim netizens can engage in criticizing and condemning other Muslims whom they perceive as possessing values that are not aligned with their viewpoints.

In relation to this, this chapter investigates the responses of the Muslim public in Brunei, Indonesia, and Malaysia towards local female Muslim celebrities and social media influencers' (henceforth SMIs) choice of dressing. It also examines the prevailing discourses on social media, particularly within the comments section of these personalities' Instagram (IG) posts, to understand the beliefs and mindsets of contemporary Muslims in these societies. It can be observed that although both male and female Muslim personalities are increasingly expected to conform to strict Islamic moral codes, women are subjected to more intense scrutiny due to their perceived subjugated position in Muslim societies. Furthermore, this policing comes not from the state but from the public. Thus, this chapter analyses how the public projects its moral policing onto these personalities under the guise of *amar makruf dan nahi mungkar*. This concept is based on a Qur'anic verse which commands Muslims to become the best of the *umma* (people) in this world by encouraging acts of virtue (*makruf*) and removing all kinds of vices (*munkar*).

According to Cook (2000) in his monograph, "Commanding Right and Forbidding Wrong in Islamic Thought", Islamic jurists and scholars from the medieval period struggled to come to a consensus as to who holds the authority to correct alleged wrongdoings or how this duty should be performed. Accordingly, without a clear consensus, this principle has been interpreted differently throughout the different phases of Islamic history. Ismail (2017, p. 3), for example, reveals that the writings of early Muslim scholars implied that the said concept "started as regulators for market surveillance to avoid fraud and unjust transactions between traders and consumers in conducting business, (but) had developed into the wider sphere of the activities from public morality". Nonetheless, despite differing interpretations, the notion of collective effort by both the people and state to uphold good values and correct wrongdoings is generally agreed upon by most Muslims.

However, the extent of the public's involvement in correcting wrongdoings is yet another point of contention. While there are those who may baulk at the thought of policing personal matters, others may perceive this to be part of their religious obligation. With the advent of social media, which has allowed once private matters to be made public, many Muslims now perceive their online activities as part of their pious endeavours and as "practising Islam through social media" to improve their religiosity (Slama 2018, p. 3). As such, the current situation regarding the public policing of social media in contemporary Muslim societies of Southeast Asia has inspired this current research.

Background

Islam in Southeast Asia is often referred to as "Islam with a smiling face", where Islam and secularism can co-exist and accommodate one another (Osman 1985; Weintraub 2011). Indonesia and Malaysia in particular have been described as nation-states characterized by "moderate Islam" where flexible interpretations of "religious and legal sources regarding scripture, law, gender, and democracy that respond to the contemporary needs of Muslims" exist (Weintraub 2011, p. 20). Southeast Asia's reputation of "moderate Islam" is not surprising as historians such as Aljunied (2019) attest that women in the Malay world always had agency unlike women in other regions such as South Asia and the Middle East. He cites various examples of Muslim women in the Malay world who helmed kingdoms and were entrusted with great power prior to the advent of colonization by Western powers in the nineteenth century.

However, these scholars also note that from the 1980s onwards, there was a gradual conservative turn in Southeast Asia. In Indonesia, following Suharto's New Order which saw rapid improvements to the economic conditions of the Muslim population (Weintraub 2011), Indonesian Muslims, with their new-found affluence, could afford to perform the Haj pilgrimage in Mecca and study either in Europe, Australia or the Middle East to deepen their religious knowledge. Furthermore, mosques and Islamic schools in Indonesia started to grow in ever-increasing numbers while stores selling Muslim attire and merchandise mushroomed. Similarly, in Malaysia, Aljunied (2019) observes "gradualist Islamization" from the 1980s onwards, evident by a marked increase in the number of Islamic educational establishments and the adoption of Islamic modest clothing by both men and women, amongst other signs of increased religiosity in Malaysian society.

Alongside Indonesia and Malaysia, Brunei too experienced a conservative turn in the 1980s. The end of Brunei's status as a British protectorate nation in 1984 marked the beginning of a new era when Sultan Hassanal Bolkiah proclaimed that Brunei "shall be forever a sovereign, democratic and independent Malay, Muslim Monarchy upon the teachings of (Sunni) Islam". A new official national ideology was promulgated: *Melayu Islam Beraja* (Malay Islamic Monarchy, MIB), whereby the Malay race (M), Islam (I), and the monarchy (B) were enshrined as the core elements of national identity. In addition to holding the post of Prime Minister and several Ministerial appointments, the Sultan was also proclaimed as "Allah's vice-regent on earth" (*khalifah*) and the "leader of believers" (*ulil amri*). Thus began the country's passionate engagement in "Islamist mobilization" (Muller 2018). Like Indonesia and Malaysia, visible signs of Islamic identity also dominated the social landscape in Brunei. However, Brunei went a few steps further to cement an Islamic blueprint in the nation's ethos by enacting numerous religious rulings such as banning the sale of alcohol in 1990, enforcing strict segregation laws in establishments such as hair salons, and implementing strict halal certification requirements for supermarket products. Furthermore, it was promulgated that all businesses in Brunei must close for two hours during Friday prayers and that during the holy month of Ramadan, all eating establishments must close for dining in during daylight hours. In 2014, the country made international headlines when it became the first country in Southeast Asia to formally introduce syariah law in its legal framework.

Consequently, this resurgence of Islamic values and beliefs in the Muslim World has cast the spotlight on women's bodies and their appearance. Kugle (2007, p. 9) describes that "Muslim women's bodies have emerged as the site of contention and the gauge of change, whether as the object of the colonial gaze, the goal of secularist reforms, the concern of the traditionalist reaction, or the target of fundamentalist resurgence". In particular, the most visible and potent symbol of this renewed Islamic awakening is the wearing of headscarves among women. In Southeast Asia, Aljunied (2017, p. 131) posits that "the donning of the hijab is a relatively new phenomenon that can be traced back to the end of the 1970s when the headscarf gained prominence during the height of the Iranian Revolution in 1979".

Decades after the watershed event in contemporary Islamic history, the majority of Muslim women in Southeast Asia began adopting the headscarf as part of their daily attire. It is important to note that in all three Muslim-majority countries of Southeast Asia, wearing the headscarf is not made mandatory by the authorities, unlike in Iran and Afghanistan. Only in ultra-conservative Muslim-majority provinces such as Aceh in Indonesia and Kelantan in Malaysia are Muslim women required to cover their hair. In Brunei, despite its image as a strict Islamic country, it is only mandatory for girls enrolled in government secondary schools. Though the exact figures are not available, scholars and casual observers alike can agree that the streets of villages, towns, and cities in these countries are filled with women covering their hair, suggesting that that it has become the norm for women of all social classes, including the elites who were thought to be more resistant to embracing an outward display of Islamic identity given their more Westernized background.

Subsequently, the popularity of the headscarf has ushered in the rise of a multi-million-dollar industry for Muslim women's clothing and set forth a *hijabista* sub-culture where young Muslim women actively adapt the latest Western fashion trends to conform to their perceptions of Muslim-friendly dressing. This "hijab revolution" has also been spurred by an increasing number of Muslim female celebrities in Malaysia and Indonesia. Recent years have seen female Muslim celebrities abandoning their liberal lifestyles in favour of Islamic ones, and their new-found piety is often widely shared with their fans and followers. However, amidst the increasing displays of religiosity, new tensions have emerged between those who choose to wear the headscarf and those who have not or have yet to do so. Bullock (2002, p. 25) observes that "the hijab is often obsessed over as if it's the thing that makes a woman a Muslim or not".

Generally, these disputes, which often arise due to differing opinions regarding Muslim women's choice of dressing, are most visible on the social media accounts of female Muslim celebrities and SMIs from Indonesia, Malaysia, and Brunei. However, despite the visibility of these tensions, relatively little research has been done on this topic. Instead, most studies on online religiosity in these societies are focused on analysing the content and performance of online sites that explicitly promote Islamic *da'wa* (proselytization), either by religious preachers or religious activists (Beta 2019; Hew 2018; Nisa 2018). Thus, filling this gap in the current literature, this study, which analyses the performance of Islamic piety on sites that focus on *duniawi* (earthly) matters, such as the IG accounts included in this chapter, can provide a deeper understanding of the prevailing beliefs and thoughts of contemporary Muslims in these societies. In addition, the findings of this study will reveal greater insights into how social media, religion, and the everyday intersect in these societies. It will be seen that the concept of *amar makruf dan nahi mungkar* is, perhaps, best demonstrated when it operates in secular, non-religious spaces. Subsequently, the chapter will reveal the underlying tensions and conflicts that inevitably follow the imposition of a moral code that may not be shared by all users on a particular social media platform.

Research Methodology

Data for this research was taken from the official IG accounts and fan accounts of six Muslim female personalities (two in each context). All six female personalities do not wear the *hijab* and are well-known in their respective countries, as evidenced by their large number of followers. In the case of Indonesia, data was collected from the official IG account of Bunga Citra Lestari (@bclsinclair), and a fan account called (@bungaciitrallestarii). Data was also collected from another Indonesian celebrity, Raline Shah (@ralineshah). In the case of Malaysia, two female actresses were selected for this study. They are Emma Maembong (@emma_maembongofficial) and Intan Najuwa (@intannajuwa). Data was also gathered from an entertainment portal, Rotikaya (@rotikaya). In the case of Brunei, the female personalities chosen are Liyana Yus (@liyanayus), an actress, and Malai Batrisyia Kameela (@malaibatrisyia), an SMI.

Given that this study focuses on the visual images of Muslim female personalities, IG is preferred as it is essentially an image-based social media platform. Furthermore, IG is one of the most popular social media networks worldwide. In 2019, there were almost

815 million users who accessed IG on a monthly basis. In 2023, this figure is projected to reach nearly 1.2 billion users. Notably, Indonesia is the fourth leading country in the world in terms of IG audience size (Statista 2022a). Malaysia, a country with a population of approximately 32 million people, had an estimated 13.8 million IG users as of March 2021. Meanwhile, Brunei is listed as the leading country globally for IG audience reach, with 92 per cent of the population using the platform (Statista 2022b).

The IG posts selected for this study consist of still photos, and the comments function under each post are fully enabled. However, it is worth noting that although the ability to post comments has not been restricted, it is possible that some of the comments have been deleted by either the personalities themselves or the administrators of their accounts. Hence, a decision was made to include posts from fan accounts or an entertainment portal, in the case of Malaysia, so as to collect a more diverse response for analysis. In addition, as this study aims to investigate the public's response towards Muslim women who do not adhere to the Islamic norms of dressing, the posts collected for this study depict all six female personalities wearing western-style attire without any head coverings.

A total of twelve posts were collected from the above-mentioned IG accounts. In terms of the number of comments, the Indonesian posts received between 70 to more than a thousand comments while the Malaysian posts garnered between 70 to more than 600 comments. The Bruneian posts, given Brunei's small population, gathered less than 20 comments. The data collected were then coded and organized into themes or "categories of interest" (Gill 2000, p. 179). According to Merriam (2009, p. 15), "in discourse analysis, the researcher is the primary instrument for data collection and analysis and therefore has to decide on the number or size of data to be gathered as a corpus for the study. The guiding principle should be the concept of saturation which is the point at which there are fewer surprises and there are no more emergent patterns in the data". Based on this reasoning, I declare that the data accumulated is sufficient to highlight the prevailing discourses within the comments section of the selected posts and that it is adequate in showing how social media policing is primarily practised by netizens.

Data obtained from the various IG accounts was then analysed using discourse analysis. As stated by Gill, "discourse does not occur in a social vacuum" (ibid., p. 175). It is shaped by social and cultural contexts in which the discourse is embedded and it, in turn, has an impact on these same contexts. Establishing the dialectical relationship between discourse and social-cultural contexts would then allow the researcher to identify the connections between language, religious identity, and culture in this study.

The findings of this study will be presented separately according to the different contexts starting with Malaysia, Indonesia, and lastly Brunei. By presenting the findings separately, it is easier to identify the most dominant discourses on local Muslim female celebrities and SMIs in Malaysia, Indonesia, and Brunei, respectively.

Malaysian IG Accounts

To examine responses towards Muslim women who do not adhere to the Islamic norms of dressing in Malaysia, a total of four IG posts were collected, of which two posts feature Emma Maembong, a Pan-Asian actress. Three years ago, prior to her marriage, Emma courted huge controversy when she abandoned her *hijab*. The other two IG posts feature Intan Najuwa, a young, single, rising star in the world of Malaysian TV dramas. Out of the four selected posts, three were taken from the official IG accounts of these personalities while one, a photo of Emma and her family in Dubai, was from Rotikaya's IG account. The latter had uploaded a photo from Emma's own IG account which has since been deleted. While some of the comments on the selected posts displayed admiration and love for these personalities based on their looks, personality, and talent, most of the comments, especially those on Rotikaya's post (which have not been filtered), were critical of their "un-Islamic" choice of dressing. Below are some of the dominant discourses that can be observed in the Malaysian data.

Discourse of Outrage

In response to Emma's official IG post which featured the actress wearing short pants and black stockings in Dubai, many commenters expressed shock and outrage at her choice of dressing. Most of these comments came from Rotikaya's account which appears to be unfiltered. Although Emma's own IG post had similar comments, they only make up a minority of the comments. Similarly, Intan's IG post also triggered a number of comments from netizens, many of whom expressed their outrage at Intan's choice of outfits, by invoking Islamic phrases such as *Allahuakbar* (Allah is the greatest), *Nauzubillah* (we seek refuge with Allah), *Astagfirullahalazim* (I seek forgiveness from Allah) and *Subhanallah* (glory be to Allah). Though these phrases, in the literal sense, mean seeking forgiveness and protection from Allah, they are often used in popular culture when Muslims see something wrong or shameful. Table 8.1 shows some other examples of how Muslims in Malaysia express their views upon seeing such a "sinful" act being publicly displayed.

TABLE 8.1
Comments Made by Malaysian IG Users on Rotikaya's and Intan Najuwa's IG Accounts

Comments	Translated
"*Allahuakbar...klau saya kesana tengok kebesaran allah swt...tapi ni tak takut ke...kamu ngan aurat ditayang...*"	"*Allahuakbar*...if I am there I will look at the wonders (created by) Allah... but are you not afraid of showing your *aurat*..."
"*Yg post niii pun nk join berdosa juga ke post gambar org camtuu... Astagfirullahalazim*"	"The one who posted this wants to join in sinning by posting this photo... *Astagfirullahalazim*"
"*Subhanallah*"	"Glory be to God"
"*Terdedah sangat, siapa yg nak tanggung dosa nanti*"	"Too revealing, who will bear the burden of the sin"
"*Nauzubilah*"	"We seek refuge with Allah"
"*Pasangan yg bijak bg pakai mcm tu... ALLAHUAKBAR*"	"A smart couple wearing clothes like that...*ALLAHUAKBAR*"

Discourse of Advice

Apart from expressing outrage, many commenters advised and reminded the two Malaysian personalities to observe the teachings of Islam regarding female modesty or face punishment in the hereafter. Noticeably, some of these comments were expressed in the form of hedging such as "you are beautiful" or "pretty" and accompanied by emojis expressing love. Some also tried to tone down their comments by asking these personalities not to take offence at their sincere advice. Table 8.2 shows some of the comments.

TABLE 8.2
Comments Made by Malaysian IG Users on Emma Maembong's and Intan Najuwa's Official IG Accounts

Comments	Translated
"Cover your *aurat* pretty"	
"*Kak jaga aurat*...You're beautiful... *Semoga mendapat hidayah*"	"*Kak* (older sister) cover your *aurat*... You're beautiful...May you be given guidance"
"*Jangan marah ye sis. delete lebih baik sis drpada jadi tatapan org ramai. sama2 kita berubah ke arah yg lebih baik*"	"Please don't be angry, sis, to delete [this] is better than to expose this to the public. May both of us be given guidance to a better way of life"

However, most Malaysian netizens were less gentle in dispensing their advice and their comments were often accompanied by emojis depicting fire and angry faces, which were invoked to show their displeasure (see Table 8.3).

TABLE 8.3
Comments Made by Malaysian IG Users on Intan Najuwa's IG Post

Comments	Translated
"*Jaga aurat wey*"	"Take care of your *aurat*"
"*Kak intan tak pandai jaga aurat ehh...kita orang Islam kene jaga aurat tak tahu malu ke. Tak takut dosa ke*"	"*Kak* (older sister), you don't know how to take care of your *aurat*...We are Muslims. We have to take care of our *aurat*. Are you not ashamed? Are you not afraid of committing sin?"
"*neraka tu panas...kira lepas la mata aku dah nasihat ko ya*"	"Hell is hot...I have done my duty in advising you"

Unlike the previous discourse, this form of discourse often led to heated debates in the comments section due to differing opinions regarding the concept of *amar makruf dan nahi mungkar*. While there are those who feel that it is their duty as Muslims to adhere to the concept of *amar makruf dan nahi mungkar*, some take the view that personal matters should be left to the individual (see Table 8.4).

TABLE 8.4
Comments Made by Malaysian IG Users on Emma Maembong's IG Post

Comments	Translated
"*Ini yang dia pilih biarlah. Kita baiki diri kita masing2*"	"This is what she has chosen. Let it be. We work on improving ourselves"
(In response) "*Amar maaruf nahi mungkar itu wajib, puan*"	"*Amar maaruf nahi mungkar* is compulsory, *maam*"
(In response) "*Ya. Tp kita boleh nasihat… sbg org muslim…spya tutup aurat dgn sempurna*"	"Yes. But we can offer advice…as Muslims… so they will cover their *aurat* completely"

While many netizens alluded to the principles of *amar makruf dan nahi mungkar* to justify their involvement, only one commenter posted specific verses of the Qur'an to remind the personalities of the teachings of Islam regarding female modesty. This user, in fact, submitted several comments which include the Malay and English translations of the Qur'an (see Table 8.5).

TABLE 8.5
A Comment Made by a Malaysian IG User on Emma Maembong's IG Post

Comment	Translated
"O Prophet! Tell your wives, and your daughters, and the women of the believers, to lengthen their garments. That is more proper, so they will be recognized and not harassed. Allah is Forgiving and Merciful. Quran Al Ahzab verse 59. *Sayangilah Orang yg tanggung dosa kita. Selamatkanlah mereka dari azab api neraka…aamiin*"	"O Prophet! Tell your wives, and your daughters, and the women of the believers, to lengthen their garments. That is more proper, so they will be recognized and not harassed. Allah is Forgiving and Merciful. Quran Al Ahzab verse 59. Love the people who bear our sins. Save them from the torment of hellfire…*aamiin*"

Discourse of Collective Sin

According to the Qur'an and *hadith*, a man's responsibility of taking care of his family is a comprehensive one. He is not just responsible to provide for them, but he is also enjoined to order his spouse and children to abide by the teachings of Islam in all aspects of their lives. This includes ordering women in the family to abide by Islamic dress codes. If a husband fails to perform this duty, he would then be committing a sin for not ensuring that the women cover their *aurat*. However, if the women refuse to abide by the teachings of Islam even after being ordered or reminded by their husbands or fathers, the sins that they are deemed to have committed will be borne by the women themselves. As shown in Table 8.6, many commenters under Emma's IG account referred to this concept.

TABLE 8.6
Comments Made by Malaysian IG Users on Emma Maembong's IG Post

Comments	Translated
"*Dosa isteri d tanggung suami...*"	"The sins of a wife are borne by the husband..."
"*Kesian suami dpt dosa free isteri bagi...tp klu suami dh tegur...lps dari api neraka...Semoga mendapat hidayah...Allah dan nabi sedih tgk umat nabi jadi mcm ni...Susah nabi nak pertahankan Islam kita buat main2...*"	"Pity the husband for being given a free (gift) of a sin by the wife...but if the husband has reminded her... [he] is free from the fires of hell... May you be given guidance. Allah and His prophet are sad to watch the *umma* like this. Our Prophet has gone through great challenges to uphold Islam [but] you take this [matter] lightly..."
"*Dosa free dpt laki dia*"	"The husband got a free (gift) of a sin"

A few commenters also criticized Emma's husband as a *dayus*, for knowingly allowing his wife to act or behave in an unchaste manner, as evidenced in the comments in Table 8.7.

TABLE 8.7
Comments Made by Malaysian IG Users on Emma Maembong's IG Post

Comments	Translated
"*Dayus sorg lelaki yg membiarkan isterinye memdedahkan aurat nya... moga diberi hidayah. wallah hualam*"	"*Dayus* is a man who lets his wife expose her *aurat*...may you be given guidance. Allah knows best"
"*ELOK LAA JADI LAKI DAYUS BODOH KELDAI*"	"THAT'S GOOD, [YOU'RE] A *DAYUS* HUSBAND, STUPID DONKEY"

The term *dayus* is often used against husbands who have failed in their duty to enjoin their wives to behave in a chaste manner. It is akin to accusing a husband of being a cuckold and is thus viewed as an inflammatory remark.

For Intan Najuwa, as she is unmarried, most of the commenters blamed her parents for not enjoining her to adhere to the proper Islamic dress code. Despite not knowing Intan personally, they appear confident that her parents have not taught her well (see Table 8.8).

TABLE 8.8
Comments Made by Malaysian IG Users on Intan Najuwa's IG Post

Comments	Translated
"*Mak bapak ajar agama kecik2 dlu ni ke hasil dia*"	"Your parents taught you the religion when you were a child, this is the result?"
"*Sebab mak bapak tak ajar agama jd macam ni la*"	"Because your parents didn't teach you the religion that's why you are like this"

Discourse of Ridicule

Apart from the discourse of outrage and advice, some commenters also used vulgar and abusive remarks to express their anger at these personalities for flouting the teachings of Islam, especially for not covering their *aurat* fully (see Table 8.9).

TABLE 8.9
Comments Made by Malaysian IG Users on Emma Maembong's and Intan Najuwa's IG Accounts

Comments	Translated
"*Tua2 pun bodo*"	"Even though you are old, you are still stupid"
"*tu bkn stylo...tu haram jadah namanya*"	"That's not style...that's what we call a bastard"
"*Persis pelacur*"	"Like a prostitute"
"*Cam pondan muka kaki belalang*"	"Like a transvestite with face and legs like an insect"

Indonesian IG Accounts

For the Indonesian data, four posts were collected for analysis, of which two posts were taken from the official IG account of Raline Shah, who is unmarried and a famous actress and media personality from a prominent Muslim family. The other two posts were from the official IG account of Bunga Citra Lestari (henceforth known as BCL) and a fan account. BCL is a well-known successful singer, actress, and entrepreneur whose husband, Ashraf Sinclair, a former Malaysian celebrity, passed away suddenly in February 2020. In terms of following, both women have garnered millions of followers on their IG accounts.

Unlike the Malaysian data, most of the comments on the Indonesian personalities' official IG accounts expressed great admiration and love for them. BCL's IG account, in particular, received only positive comments, reflecting a carefully curated account. A post of BCL wearing tight-fitting exercise attire in a gym, for instance, generated more than a thousand positive comments. Almost all of them, except for a few comments, were highly complimentary. However, comments under BCL's fan account, in which posts were presumed to be unfiltered, revealed many negative sentiments directed towards her choice of outfit. Comments of this nature, which focus on the perceived un-Islamic images of both women, were analysed to examine the prevailing discourses present in Indonesia. Below are the findings.

Discourse of Collective Sin

Most of the Indonesian data came from a post on BCL's fan account which displayed BCL in a revealing gown at one of her concerts. This post has generated more than 1,200 comments to date and most of these remarks allude to her current status as a widow. The commenters advised BCL to cover her *aurat* as a sign of respect to her late husband. I categorize these comments under "discourse of collective sin" rather than "discourse of advice" as they specifically express pity for her late husband for having to bear the burden of his wife's sins in the hereafter, as shown in the excerpts in Table 8.10.

TABLE 8.10
Comments Made by Indonesian IG Users on Bunga Citra Lestari's IG Post

Comments	Translated
"*Kesian suami kamu dalam kuburan*"	"Pity your husband in [his] grave"
"*Kasihan almarhum suaminya, di alam kubur kebagian dosanya istrinya yg ngumbar aurot. Nauudzubillah*"	"Pity your late husband, in his grave, part of his sin is his wife showing her *aurat*. We seek refuge with Allah"
"*Mbba bcl mas asraf dan ayahnda mu lagi di asab di siksa di akherat setiap istrinya seperti ini...Astagfirullah...Berpakaian tpi telanjang*"	"Big sister bcl brother asraf and your father will be punished in the hereafter for the wife [behaving] like this...*Astagfirullah*...Wearing clothes but naked"

Notably, this discourse generated heated discussions among the commenters. Some disagreed with the notion of BCL's late husband having to bear sins in the hereafter for his wife's lack of modesty, as shown in Table 8.11.

The ensuing debate was resolved when a commenter, appearing to be knowledgeable on the issue, posted a detailed comment explaining that a husband is only responsible for his wife's sin if he did not urge his wife to cover her *aurat* during his lifetime. Subsequently, once the husband has passed on, he is no longer responsible for the

TABLE 8.11
Comments Made by Indonesian IG Users on Bunga Citra Lestari's IG Post

Comments	Translated
"*astagafirulazim...semoga di beri hidayah tuk menutup aurat...kesian kt awrah suami dia...*"	"*astagafirulazim*...may [you] be given guidance to cover [you] *aurat*...pity her late husband..."
(In response) "*Dosa tu ga diturunkan! Yg berbuat istrinya koq suami yg udah meninggal disiksa?*"	"The sin is not inherited! The one committing the sin is the wife, why is [it] her husband who has passed away will be punished?"
(In response) "*Ada ayat nya ga di Alqu'ran? Islam ga mengenal dosa warisan...*"	"Is there a verse in the Al Qur'an? Islam does not recognize inherited sin..."
(In response) "*Anda Islam bukan bu? Kalo anda Islam mesti dipertanyakan ke Islaman anda*"	"Are you not a Muslim? If you are a Muslim, your [knowledge] of Islam should be questioned"

sins committed by his wife that he has left behind in this world. Table 8.12 shows an excerpt of this very lengthy post.

TABLE 8.12
A Comment from an Indonesian IG User on Bunga Citra Lestari's IG Post

Comment	Translated
"*Jika membangkang ya sdh menjadi dosa pribadi yg msh hidup, yg meninggal sdh tdk berdosa dan sdh berlepas diri karena sdh tdk ada kuasa dia mendidik lagi. Segala amal perbuatan dan kewajibannya sdh terputus Ketika mereka meninggal*"	"If the husband does not enjoin his wife to cover her *aurat*, that is his personal sin committed while he is alive, those [husbands] who have passed away are no longer responsible for [the wife's] sins as he is no longer able to educate her. All [his] deeds and responsibilities have ended upon his death"

Discourse of Advice

Like the Malaysian data, another prominent discourse observed in the Indonesian data is the discourse of advice, though there appear to be fewer comments compared to the former. Below are some examples of posts exhibiting this type of discourse on the Indonesian IG accounts (see Table 8.13).

TABLE 8.13
Comments from Indonesian IG Users on Bunga Citra Lestari's and Raline Shah's IG Accounts

Comments	Translated
"*Udah jaman nya berhijab mba Bcl... artis udah banyak yg hijrah semoga cepet nyusul nutup aurat*"	"The time has come for [you] to wear the hijab big sister BCL...many artistes have migrated may you soon follow and cover your *aurat*"
"*Bu Raline udah kepala 3, mestinya bs mnutup. Klo ga bisa sekaligus, minimal dikit2 lah*"	"Maam Raline you are in your 30s, [you] must cover up. If you are not able to do so all at once, cover a little at a time"
"*Ingat Tuhan dosa Paksi pakaian yang gitu*"	"Remember God [it is] a sin to wear clothes like that"

Discourse of Outrage

Similarly, compared to the Malaysian data, the Indonesian data reveal fewer comments engaged in the discourse of outrage, suggesting that both discourses of advice and outrage are less prevalent in the Indonesian data. Interestingly, some comments that expressed outrage at BCL's outfits were posted by Malaysian netizens as the language used reflected colloquial Malay rather than Bahasa Indonesia, as in the first example in Table 8.14. The word *minah*, for instance, is a slang word used by Singaporean and Malaysian Malays to refer to a young woman or girl. It is sometimes used in a derogatory way as well (see Table 8.14).

TABLE 8.14
Comments from Malaysian and Indonesian IG Users on Bunga Citra Lestari's IG Post

Comments	Translated
"*Makin teruk minah CL ni lps suami meninggal*"	"This *minah* [girl] CL is getting worse since her husband passed away"
"*Astaghfirullah...Busananya itu, kok jelek banget skrg*"	"*Astaghfirullah*...Her outfits, why so disgusting now"
"*KECEWA PAKAIANMU BCL*"	"DISSAPOINTED IN YOUR CLOTHES BCL"

Discourse of Ridicule

Another type of discourse that can be observed under the comments section of the selected posts is the discourse of ridicule. Likewise, there were fewer instances of this discourse in the Indonesian data compared to the Malaysian data. However, as BCL is well-known to be the wife of a Malaysian celebrity, some of the comments regarding her non-Islamic appearance came from Malaysian netizens. In the first example in Table 8.15, the phrase *balu gersang* (promiscuous widow) is a Malay slang word while in Bahasa Indonesia, the term would be *janda terangsang*. Furthermore, some of the comments directed to BCL referred to her physique and even body-shamed the celebrity as shown in Table 8.15.

TABLE 8.15
Comments from Indonesian IG Users on Bunga Citra Lestari's IG Post

Comments	Translated
"*Balu gersang*"	"Promiscuous widow"
"*Gemukan ya*"	"Getting fat ya"
"*Yang mau dperlihatkan juga body yg bgmna...udah pada kendur semua...apa gak malu*"	"What kind of body are you trying to show...everything is saggy now...are you not ashamed"

Bruneian IG Accounts

Moving to the Brunei data, data was taken from the IG accounts of Liyana Yus (@liyanayus), a well-known actress and SMI, and Batrisya Kameela (@malaibatrisya), an SMI. Liyana Yus is one of the most established actresses in the Bruneian film industry. She is known for her lead role in the popular local film *Yasmine* (2014), which was only the third feature film made in the country then. She is also married and has one child. Batrisya, on the other hand, is a young SMI with one of the highest numbers of followers among female SMIs in the country. She is currently a student at a private university in Kuala Lumpur, Malaysia. Two posts, each from their official IG accounts, were referred to for this study. For context purposes, as Brunei is a small country with a small-scale entertainment industry, most of the top IG accounts based in Brunei belong to SMIs rather than actors and singers. Furthermore, given Brunei's small population, it is natural that the selected IG posts garnered fewer comments compared to those selected from Malaysia and Indonesia. In fact, each post had less than 20 comments. In addition, it is also important to highlight that both personalities do not wear the *hijab*. However, they do occasionally post photos of them wearing the *hijab* for special events.

Interestingly, the findings from the Bruneian data reveal a different scenario compared to the Indonesian and Malaysian data. Although Liyana's IG account contains photos of her with and without the *hijab*, she did not receive any negative comments on her account for her inconsistent *hijab*-wearing practices. Conversely, Emma Maembong, the Malaysian actress included in this study, faced backlash from the Malaysian public for the same action. While this could be due to the careful filtering of comments carried out by Liyana and her team, this could also be due to a more tolerant attitude towards the *hijab* in Brunei where it is quite common for young girls and women to wear the *hijab* only on some occasions such as weddings, Eid celebrations or to work/school. In fact, it is a norm for Bruneian women to go out and post photos on their social media accounts without the *hijab*.

Generally, Liyana's posts were filled with praise despite the actress not wearing the *hijab* in most of her posts. Most of her posts, in fact, indicate that she normally dresses modestly. The only post of her wearing a slightly revealing outfit was in January 2020 when she attended a film premiere and dressed in a suit that revealed her midriff. This post, however, did not garner any criticism from her followers regarding her attire. On the other hand, Batrisya, who is younger and unmarried, often posts images of herself in more revealing outfits. Yet, no comments were made based on her attire. The only comment that focuses on her *aurat* is from a user, shown below, who has made similar comments in many of Batrisya's posts. Given that these comments have not been deleted, this may suggest that the user is an acquaintance of Batrisya whose comments are simply treated as friendly banter (see Table 8.16).

TABLE 8.16
Comments from A Bruneian IG User on Batrisya Kameela's IG Account

Comments	Translated
"*Aurat aurat*"	
"*Aurat nampak*"	"[Your] *aurat* can be seen"

The only dissenting opinion that can be found on Batrisya's IG account is a comment from a user who questioned her "un-Islamic" dressing style and accused her of deleting "unfavourable" comments, as shown in Table 8.17.

TABLE 8.17
A Comment from a Bruneian IG User on Batrisya Kameela's IG Account

Comment
"Saw someone comment about you being Muslim yet dress like that a while ago then you seem to delete the comment instead of deleting this pic"

Discussion

The findings of this study demonstrate that social media is a fertile ground for what is described by Haji Mohamad (2017, p. 1) as the "performance of religiosity in the forms of preaching to others, constant self-reminders, prayers, and exhibiting religious self". This phenomenon has been labelled as "soft *da'wa*" (Islamic propagation) by Nisa (2018, p. 71) who states that "Instagram has become a platform for female Indonesian Muslim youth, who hold a firm belief that "a picture is worth a thousand words", to educating one another in being virtuous Muslims". She sees that women create the majority of *da'wa* IG accounts in Indonesia and they form the majority of followers of these accounts. Given that statistically, more women access Instagram regularly compared to men (Statista 2022c), it is not surprising that most of the commenters in this study are women. They are also found to be responsible for some of the most vitriolic comments in the study. In light of this situation, Herring (2011) mentions that women are more drawn to social media sites compared to men as they allow women to have more control of public discourse as compared to face-to-face communication where men tend to dominate. This point is illustrated perfectly by Beta (2019) who shares that despite their loud voices on social media and online *da'wa* activities, Muslim women activists in her study still conformed to traditional patriarchal norms when sharing a physical space with their male counterparts during their activist engagements.

Hence, the freedom afforded to women on social media has resulted in more opportunities to morally police others in ways that are often left unchallenged. As noted by Baulch and Pramiyanti (2018) in their study of Indonesian *hijabis* on IG, these women often style themselves as religious authorities and offer Islamic advice by quoting the Qur'an and *hadith*. The authors argue that this act has been made possible through the "fragmentation of Muslim authority that affords new roles for Muslim women in public Islam". In another study carried out by Nisa (2018, p. 72), she notes that unlike the past where "the mediation of religious knowledge was performed and 'monopolized' by graduates of traditional Islamic boarding schools and Islamic universities", the diverse *da'wa* landscape in contemporary Indonesia has resulted in a plethora of new "preachers" who did not graduate from Islamic studies. This "democratization" of Islamic religious knowledge has been the most visible on social media platforms, as this study has demonstrated.

In relation to this development, it is not surprising that the most dominant discourse found in both the Malaysian and Indonesian data is the discourse of advice, followed by the discourse of collective sin, which can also be seen as a form of advice that focuses on the alleged sin(s) committed by men on account of their wives/daughters not adhering to Islamic female modesty standards. While many commenters expressed their opinions using Islamic terminology and frames, a closer analysis of these comments reveals a lack of knowledge of basic Islamic concepts. For instance, it is imperative for Muslims to preserve the dignity of a person when giving advice to them. They should not expose their *aib* (flaws) in public and should use gentle language to demonstrate compassion and sincerity (Islamweb.net 2019); most commenters, as shown above, clearly did not adhere to these basic principles. Another interesting finding from this study is the lack of understanding among some commenters regarding a man's responsibility over his wife's/daughters' dressing. In particular, the case of BCL reveals the level of ignorance some commenters have on this issue, not knowing that according to Islamic teachings, a man's responsibility over his wife/daughter is confined to his life only and is not "carried over" to his death.

Although some commonalities can be found across all three contexts, Mohamad (2021, p. 2) emphasizes that "it is imperative to be cognizant of their diversities". The Malaysian data, in particular, contain among the most vitriolic comments, with many of them bordering on cyberbullying. In fact, a recent international report placed Malaysia as the second country in Asia for cyberbullying, indicating that this problem is particularly acute in the country (The Star 2022). The Malaysian data also reveal considerable misogyny within society. While there have been several cases of Malaysian male celebrities having their raunchy private photos exposed online, they generally face minimal backlash for their behaviour. Conversely, Malaysian female celebrities like Emma Maembong suffered serious repercussions in both her personal and professional life for shedding her *hijab* image.

On the other hand, the Bruneian data display no instances of this behaviour among the commenters, although it is acknowledged that the data from this context is very limited. This could be due to a few reasons. Firstly, it can be said that the populace, including the youth, is generally aware of the negative repercussions of such public displays of opinions. Notably, Mohamad (2021, pp. 3–4) mentions that "Brunei's collectivistic culture where cultural sensitivity and self-censorship are prevalent" means that only a few cases of blatant "transgressions" on the display of *aurat* occur. Thus, only a few commenters can be found berating the Bruneian personalities for their perceived lack of modesty. However, it must be acknowledged yet again that the IG accounts of the Bruneian personalities seem to be carefully curated as negative comments have been deleted, as revealed by at least one comment found in the Bruneian data.

Secondly, the tight controls imposed by the state on Bruneian society mean that there are fewer opportunities and avenues for diverse views to be expressed, unlike in Malaysia and Indonesia, where there are relatively fewer controls imposed by the authorities. Indonesia, in particular, following the post-Suharto period, has embarked on a more open and less centralized direction.

Thirdly, Mohamad (ibid.) also observes that despite Brunei's image as a conservative Muslim nation, young Bruneians on social media are more interested in being lifestyle influencers rather than religious influencers. This does not mean that Bruneians are not interested in religious and spiritual matters. Visiting Malaysian celebrity preachers such as Datuk Ustaz Kazim Elias (DUKE) and Ustaz Don Doniyal, in fact, attracted large crowds when they visited Brunei for talks. However, to be a religious influencer in Brunei is challenging since matters pertaining to Islam are tightly controlled by the state, presumably to prevent ideologies that are not compatible with the teachings espoused by the authorities to take root and spread in the country. This is largely why Bruneian preachers do not have similar mass appeal akin to the names cited above.

As the reach of the Internet and social media become increasingly dominant in everyday life, the findings of this study can offer useful insights for policymakers in the region. Given that most social media users are in the younger age brackets, this chapter is crucial for those studying the future trajectory of ideas and attitudes in these three Muslim-majority countries of Southeast Asia. The findings from the Malaysian data, as revealed in this study, are especially concerning as there appears to be a lack of tolerance among Malaysian social media users regarding the divergent expressions of Muslim identity. However, this may not necessarily be a sign of growing religious extremism in Malaysia as these commenters do not form the majority of social media users there. Rather, they may just be part of the "noisy minority", who thrive on fostering negativity online while the silent majority simply looks away if they disagree with any content that goes against their personal beliefs.

Furthermore, Mcclain (2021) reports that most social media users never or rarely post or share about political or social issues online. In fact, those with relatively moderate views are more reluctant to participate in online discussions, suggesting that online platforms are becoming increasingly polarized with extreme views on either side gaining more prominence. However, given that the "noisy minority" are currently the loudest voices on social media, they may eventually influence public perception by normalizing intolerance and hostility towards people who are perceived to be different from them. This is concerning as according to a 2020 Pew Research Centre study, it was found that an increasing number of social media users, especially younger people, are being influenced to change their views on political and social issues based on what they view online (Perrin 2020). Although these studies cited above are conducted in the United States, it is possible that their findings are highly applicable to the three contexts in this study, given the very high social media penetration rate in these countries. In January 2022, Malaysia and Indonesia scored above average for social media penetration rate worldwide with the former ranked second place worldwide in active social network penetration (Statista 2022a).

Conclusion

This study has demonstrated that although the concept of *amar makruf dan nahi mungkar* is often a contentious one with various interpretations circulating in Muslim societies past and present, in contemporary Muslim societies of Southeast Asia, the prevailing notion pertaining to this concept revolves around the policing of personal morality. In particular, the wearing of the *hijab* by Muslim women has been singled out as among the most prominent markers of this phenomenon. This form of social control is most visible on social media, particularly on IG. As the IG accounts in this study are selected for their non-religious content, they provide a particularly vivid description of ordinary Muslims displaying their performance of personal piety in the form of moral vigilantism.

In an age where social media engagement is increasingly seen as a barometer of a society's attitudes, beliefs, and aspirations, it is thus imperative that policymakers place greater attention on what is being created, shared, and commented on in the digital world. In view of the pervasive influence of social media, especially among the young, policymakers and authorities should attempt to establish some level of control on the type of discourses being produced and circulated online. However, this should not be achieved by censorship as firstly, it may prove to be ineffective and counterproductive, and secondly, technological advances may render these attempts impossible. Rather, there should be a greater concerted effort to educate social media users on the importance of being sensitive to the feelings of others and not forcing their ideals upon everyone else. Given social media's impact on a variety of fronts, including on mental health and extreme ideology, efforts to steer online content and narrative to reflect more moderate views should be prioritized.

REFERENCES

Aljunied, Khairudin. 2017. *Muslim Cosmopolitanism: Southeast Asian Islam in Comparative Perspective*. Edinburgh: Edinburgh University Press.

———. 2019. *Islam in Malaysia: An Entwined History*. New York: Oxford University Press.

Baulch, Emma and Alila Pramiyanti. 2018. "Hijabers on Instagram: Using Visual Social Media to Construct the Ideal Muslim Woman". *Social Media + Society* 4, no. 4.

Beta, Annisa. 2019. "Commerce, Piety and Politics: Indonesian Young Muslim Women's Groups as Religious Influencers". *New Media & Society* 12, no. 10: 1–20.

Bullock, Katherine. 2002. *Rethinking Muslim Women and the Veil: Challenging Historical and Modern Stereotypes*. London: International Institute of Islamic Thought.

Bunt, Gary. 2009. *iMuslims: Rewiring the House of Islam*. Chapel Hill: University of North Carolina Press.

Cook, Michael. 2000. *Commanding Right and Forbidding Wrong in Islamic Thought*. Cambridge: Cambridge University Press.

Eickelman, Dale and Jon Anderson. 1999. "Redefining Muslim Publics". In *New Media in the Muslim World: The Emerging Public Sphere*, edited by Dale Eickelman and Jon Anderson, pp. 1–18. Bloomington: Indiana University Press.

Fox, Richard. 2010. "Why Media Matter: Critical Reflections on Religion and the Recent History of 'the Balinese'". *History of Religions* 49, no. 4: 354–92.

Gill, Rosalind. 2000. "Discourse Analysis". In *Qualitative Researching with Text, Image and Sound*, edited by Martin Bauer and George Gaskell, pp. 172–90. London: Sage.

Herring, Susan. 2011. "Communication Styles Make a Difference". *The New York Times*, 4 February 2011. https://www.nytimes.com/roomfordebate/2011/02/02/where-are-the-women-in-wikipedia/communication-styles-make-a-difference (accessed 15 June 2022).

Hew Wai Weng. 2018. "The Art of *Dakwah*: Social Media, Visual Persuasion and the Islamist Propagation of Felix Siauw". *Indonesia and the Malay World* 46, no. 134: 61–79.

Ibahrine, Mohammed. 2014. "Islam and Social Media". In *Encyclopedia of Social Media and Politics*, edited by Kerric Harvey, pp. 737–41. Los Angeles: SAGE Reference.

Islamweb.net. 2019. *Giving Sincere Advice*. https://www.islamweb.net/en/article/183709/giving-sincere-advice (accessed 15 June 2022).

Ismail, Siti Zubaidah. 2017. *Amr Makruf Nahi Mungkar and Social Order: How Far Should Moral Policing Be Allowed in Modern Society?* In 4th International Conference Islamic Economics and Finance Congress (IIEFC 2017), 15–16 July 2017, Istanbul Sabahattin Zaim University, Istanbul, Turkey.

Kugle, Scott. 2007. *Sufis and Saints' Bodies: Mysticism, Corporeality and Sacred Power in Islam*. Chapel Hill: University of North Carolina Press.

Mandaville, Peter. 2001. "Reimagining Islam in Diaspora: The Politics of Mediated Community". *International Communication Gazette* 63, nos. 2–3: 169–86.

Mcclain, Colleen. 2021. "70% of U.S. Social Media Users Never or Rarely Post or Share About Political, Social Issues". Pew Research Centre, 4 May 2021. https://www.pewresearch.org/fact-tank/2021/05/04/70-of-u-s-social-media-users-never-or-rarely-post-or-share-about-political-social-issues/ (accessed 15 June 2022).

Merriam, Sharan B. 2009. *Qualitative Research: A Guide to Design and Implementation*. 2nd ed. San Francisco: Wiley.

Mohamad, Siti Mazidah. 2017. "Performance of Religiosity on a 'Techno-Religious' Space". *Advanced Science Letters* 23, no. 5: 4918–21.

⸻. 2021. "Micro-celebrities' Practices in Muslim-Majority States in Southeast Asia". *Popular Communication* 19, no. 3: 235–49.

Müller, Dominik. 2018. "Islamic Authority and the State in Brunei Darussalam". *Kyoto Review of Southeast Asia*, no. 23. https://kyotoreview.org/issue-23/islamic-authority-and-the-state-in-brunei-darussalam/ (accessed 15 June 2022).

Nisa, Eva F. 2018. "Creative and Lucrative *Da'wa*: The Visual Culture of Instagram Amongst Female Muslim Youth in Indonesia". *Asiascape: Digital Asia* 5, nos. 1–2: 68–99.

Osman, Mohd Taib. 1985. "Islamization of the Malays: A Transformation of Culture". In *Readings on Islam in Southeast Asia*, edited by Ahmad Ibrahim, Sharon Siddique and Yasmin Hussain, pp. 44–47. Singapore: Institute of Southeast Asian Studies.

Perrin, Andrew. 2020. "23% of Users in U.S. Say Social Media Led Them to Change Views on an Issue; Some Cite Black Lives Matter". Pew Research Center, 15 October 2020. https://www.pewresearch.org/fact-tank/2020/10/15/23-of-users-in-us-say-social-media-led-them-to-change-views-on-issue-some-cite-black-lives-matter/ (accessed 15 June 2022).

Slama, Martin. 2018. "Practising Islam through Social Media in Indonesia". *Indonesia and the Malay World* 46, no. 134: 1–4.

The Star. 2022. "Malaysia is 2nd in Asia for Youth Cyberbullying". 14 January 2022. https://www.thestar.com.my/news/nation/2022/01/14/malaysia-is-2nd-in-asia-for-youth-cyberbullying/ (accessed 15 June 2022).

Statista. 2022a. "Active Social Network Penetration in Selected Countries and Territories as of January 2022", 27 July 2022. https://www.statista.com/statistics/282846/regular-social-networking-usage-penetration-worldwide-by-country/ (accessed 3 February 2023).

———. 2022b. "Number of Instagram Users Worldwide from 2019 to 2023", 23 May 2022. https://www.statista.com/statistics/183585/instagram-number-of-global-users/ (accessed 3 February 2023).

———. 2022c. "Distribution of Instagram Users in the United States as of March 2022, by Gender", 31 January 2023. https://www.statista.com/statistics/530498/instagram-users-in-the-us-by-gender/ (accessed 3 February 2023).

Weintraub, Andrew. 2011. *Islam and Popular Culture in Indonesia and Malaysia*. London & New York: Routledge.

9

YOUTUBE ISLAMIC WEB SERIES AND MEDIATIZED PIETY AMONG URBAN MUSLIMS IN INDONESIA

Andina Dwifatma

Introduction

Muslim identity has become a discursive battleground in contemporary Indonesia. With over 229 million Muslims—that is, approximately 87 per cent of its total population, Indonesia is home to the world's largest Muslim population. One of the most prevalent practices among Indonesian Muslims today, particularly those from urban areas, is to display their religious activities and traits on social media (Slama 2018; Weng 2018; Nisa 2018). In her study on the role of commercial television in mainstreaming Islam in Indonesia, Rakhmani (2017) posits that urban Muslims are experiencing a "spiritual anxiety"—that is, the desire to adopt a more Islamic way of life and behaviour, and seeking moral guidance through media content such as television shows. Notably, in today's digital era, urban Muslims rely on social media for religious content such as watching YouTube sermons, following Instagram religious study groups, and streaming movies with Islamic values as they are easily accessible and offer audio-visual message delivery. Furthermore, more Muslims are utilizing social media as the technological and interactive capabilities of social media enable personal expressions and discussions of Islam, fostering a more individualized form of piety. To explain this new phenomenon, Bunt (2018, p. 1), in his book *#Hashtag Islam*, notes that contemporary expressions of Islam are increasingly relying heavily on digital media in which "faith, command, and control are manifest across complex systems of Muslim beliefs".

According to Hefner (2010), the Islamic resurgence in Indonesia is part of a much larger religious resurgence in contemporary Asia. This spans from Catholic Filipinos converting to Pentecostal Christianity, the proliferation of meditation movements in Vietnam, to the increasing number of Buddhists in China despite the country's secular Marxist-Leninist ideology. Interestingly, in all three cases, social media plays a crucial role, serving as a platform for individuals to display their piety, interact and exert influence on one another. A similar trend can also be observed in the Arab world where a group of young, middle-class, pious urban Muslims known as GUMmies (Global Urban Muslims) demonstrate how to live a modern, global lifestyle in an Islamic manner on Instagram (Zaid et al. 2022).

With the rise of digital Islam in the post-Suharto era, van Bruinessen (2013) speculates a conservative turn transpiring in Indonesia's mainstream Islam. In this context, "conservative" refers to religious views that conform to existing dogmas and societal structures. I argue that the use of social media by urban Indonesian Muslims, particularly for the "cultivation of piety" in their social circles, is one of the key mechanisms in idealizing Muslimhood. Here, "cultivation of piety" is a term from Saba Mahmood's work on the women's piety movement in Cairo. To study the ritual of *salat* (praying), Mahmood (2001) conducted an ethnographic observation of women's Islamic study groups in mosques in Cairo and discovered that *salat* is not only an embodied ritual that is learned through a series of disciplinary acts, but it also fosters self-empowered pragmatic actions such as patience, kindness, and feeling at peace. Mahmood (p. 830, original emphasis) termed this concept "cultivation of piety", with piety meaning "being close to

God: a manner of *being* and *acting* that suffused all of one's acts, both religious and worldly in character". Schielke (2010), however, criticized Mahmood's work for narrowly focusing on religious study groups. To Schielke, rather than observing committed Muslims in consciously pious settings, more focus should be placed on regular Muslims who are not always pious and spend most of their time outside religious settings. Employing both Mahmood's and Schielke's arguments, I aim to further this debate by suggesting that Mahmood's concept of "cultivation of piety" can in fact be observed in regular Muslims' everyday lives, particularly in Indonesia where piety is increasingly becoming mediatized.

This chapter aims to investigate the significance of social media as a platform to encourage piety among urban Muslims. I first begin by examining the trajectory of Islamic representations in Indonesian media before the age of social media. This is followed by a discussion on what distinguishes web series from other media platforms in cultivating Muslimhood, and an analysis of *Cinta Subuh* (Love at Dawn), one of the most-watched Islamic web series in Indonesia. The chapter then concludes with an examination of netizens' comments on *Cinta Subuh* and what they imply for the audience's shared mediatized piety.

Islamic Representation in Indonesian Media

Representations of Islam have always been prominent in the Indonesian media. Frederick (1982) highlights that the earliest representation of Islam in the Indonesian entertainment industry was done through *dangdut*, a popular music genre with populist and Islamist messages that was well-known in the early years of New Order era (1975–81). One of the most famous *dangdut* superstars in Indonesia at the time was Rhoma Irama. He popularized Islamic *da'wa* (preaching) through songs and movies. Frederick referred to Rhoma's feature film, *Perjuangan dan Do'a* (Struggle and Prayer, 1980) as "the world's first Islamic rock musical motion picture…with its heavily *da'wa* message" (119). It was estimated that at least 15 million people watched Rhoma's films during the years 1978–79—which represented approximately a tenth of the total population of Indonesia at that time.

Apart from films and songs, prior to the advent of the Internet, mediums such as the radio, television, and fiction novels were also utilized to spread Islamic *da'wa* in Indonesia (Farihah 2013; Sasono 2010; Wahid and Makruf 2017). Interestingly, today, even after the emergence of the Internet, these platforms continue to be employed to disseminate Islamic *da'wa*. For instance, Islamic communities in smaller towns and institutions in Indonesia still use local radio to reach their audiences. Apart from radio, novels are also another popular medium to spread Islamic *da'wa*. Best-selling Indonesian novels such as *Ayat-Ayat Cinta* (Verses of Love) and *Ketika Cinta Bertasbih* (When Love Glorifies God) attracted such high readership that they were adapted into blockbuster films in 2008 and 2009 respectively. In addition, television shows, particularly Islamic soap operas (locally known as *sinetron*), are always in demand every Ramadan (the holy month of fasting). Nevertheless, nothing surpasses the technological affordances of social media which allows users to consume religious content based on their own preferences.

During the Suharto era (1967–98), however, Islamic representations in the Indonesian media were rather limited. Heryanto (2011) argues that during this period, Islam experienced political repression, economic exclusion, and cultural humiliation. For almost three decades, Muslims were forced by the government to suppress their identity as a way of preventing Islam from growing into a massive political threat. Similar circumstances also occurred in the national broadcasting industry. During Sukarno's era (1945–67), the state-owned public television network, Televisi Republik Indonesia (TVRI), depicted all religions in Indonesia as the nation's unifier. The emphasis was not on the distinctiveness of each religion, but on the fact that despite the existence of diverse religions in the country, they are all a part of one Indonesia. Hence, at the time, Indonesia's state ideology was centred on the linkages between nationalism, religion, and communism. To illustrate, films during the New Order era were mostly concerned with social and political issues. For instance, Sasono (2010, p. 50) argues that Muslims were often portrayed as heroes who "fight the Dutch colonialists, helping the poor, supporting Nationalism, and bringing rational thinking and modernism to the general public".

The emergence of private televisions (TV) in 1989–90 was a game-changer for Islamic representation in Indonesia, particularly with the establishment of Rajawali Citra Televisi Indonesia (RCTI) and Surya Citra Televisi Indonesia (SCTV) in 1989 and 1990 respectively.

President Suharto was in power at the time, and his son, Bambang Trihatmodjo, owned RCTI, while his cousin, Sudwikatmono, owned SCTV. Rakhmani (2013) argues that from 1989 onwards, representations of Islam transformed dramatically as television networks became more commercialized. Unlike public TV stations, the new private TV stations did not want their shows to appear too secular but instead wanted to create shows that appeal to the wider Muslim audience. For this reason, Islamic sermons and talk shows began to appear on TV. From the 1990s onwards, production houses also started producing Islamic-themed soap operas for Ramadan. One of the earliest and arguably most popular Islamic soap operas in Indonesia then was *Doaku Harapanku* (My Prayers, My Hopes, 1998) which centres around the life of a Muslim female protagonist who lives in a heteropatriarchal society in which heterosexual males have control over females and other gender identities. The soap opera delves into the female protagonist's infertility and her relationship with her authoritative but loving husband and hostile mother-in-law. Following its release, the film became an instant hit in Indonesia and eventually paved the way for greater Islamic representation in entertainment formats in the broadcasting industry. Thus, as a result of Islam's commercial and political value as a media commodity, there has been greater mainstreaming of Islam in Indonesia (Rakhmani 2017). Muslims are increasingly seeing their identities and daily lives being portrayed on screen, not just on television but also on large theatre screens.

The resignation of President Suharto in 1998 (also known as the "Reform Era" or *Era Reformasi*) after 32 years of undisputed power also led to significant changes in Indonesian media as it ushered in a new generation of urban-based, highly-educated Muslims. Heryanto (2014) asserts that the new generation of urban Muslims juggle three roles—being devoted Muslims, honoured citizens, and members of the global producers and consumers community. Unlike the older generation, they use their capital to engage in cultural and aesthetic activities which allow them to express their identities, aspirations, political and economic positions. Consequently, Sasono (2010) argues that following the Reform Era, most Islamic movies began to centre around personal themes, such as finding soulmates and educational and career success. For instance, male protagonists in popular Islamic films such as *Ayat-Ayat Cinta* and *Ketika Cinta Bertasbi* were portrayed to be from low-income families who through Islamic education, were able to uplift their socioeconomic status. Both received scholarships to study at Al-Azhar University, Egypt's oldest Islamic university, and later married women from wealthy, well-known families. Their successes in their career, education, and marriage were portrayed as a reward for their piety.

Islamic Web Series

Islamic web series are online film series, typically uploaded weekly to video-sharing platforms like YouTube and TikTok, produced by young, urban Muslim communities. It is important to study the recent emergence and popularity of Islamic web series as the control of cultural production has now been shifted from major studios and cable networks to social media content creators. These web series are particularly attractive compared to other traditional forms of media, as apart from them being free and accessible at any time, the audience can also discuss their watching experiences with other viewers in the comments section. Unsurprisingly, such technological capability has led to the formation of numerous fan-based audience groups. Keluarga Film Maker Muslim (KFMM) is said to be the largest web series fan community in Indonesia, with over a thousand members in 34 cities.[1] Established in 2017 by Film Maker Muslim (FMM) Studios—a pioneering Islamic online series channel established in 2012—KFMM promotes FMM's web series and participates actively, both in online and offline spaces, through activities such as maintaining social media channels and hosting film screenings and seminars. Another prominent web series fan community is *Sisterlillah Community* (the phrase "Sisterlillah" translates to "we are sisters because of Allah"), which was originally a fan community for Teladan Cinema—a YouTube channel which produces Islamic content. Since its establishment, the *Sisterlillah Community* has evolved into an independent community of young Muslim women from 14 cities with 1,500 members who wish to remain religious while being modern, active, and empowered.[2] The *Sisterlillah Academy*, for instance, organizes seminars to teach practical life skills such as public speaking, creative writing, and entrepreneurship to young Muslim women. Since the COVID-19 pandemic, their academy has moved online.

The success of Islamic web series is partly due to the fact that they provide precisely what urban Muslims require—a spectacle that entertains and teaches them how to be "true" Muslims. Targeted at urban Muslim youth, the underlying themes of these web series demonstrate Islamic orientations that privilege ritualism and symbolism and focus on individual's goals such as finding a life partner, marriage, family, and career achievements. For instance, in most episodes, female characters were portrayed as a "reward" to motivate the male characters to cultivate their piety. In addition, female characters in most Islamic web series embraced their *kodrat* (God-given differences) as homemakers and disciplined their bodies through clothing and career choices. The popularity of these web series indicate that the characteristics listed above are expressions of piety for young urban Muslim women today. Preparing to be good wives and mothers as portrayed in the web series may not necessarily constitute oppression or subordination, but rather elements of their, quoting Mahmood (2011), "pious self-cultivation". Interestingly, Islamic web series creators and viewers also actively participate in the interpretation and reinterpretation of the concept of piety, and their interactions with one another enrich the discourse of urban Muslims' piety on social media.

Despite YouTube's current cultural impact, Burgess and Green (2018) argue that its initial goal was always technological. The platform was founded in 2005 by three ex-PayPal employees to provide a platform for non-expert users to upload their videos online. In their investment pitch to Sequioa Capital in 2005, YouTube's founders stated that their mission was "to become the primary outlet for user-generated content on the Internet, and to enable anyone to upload, share, and view this content" (ibid., p. 16). Its major success can be attributed to these key technological affordances and its community-formation function which allows YouTube to become not only a video-sharing platform but also a social media platform (ibid.). Its user-generated content (UGC) feature, in particular, is significant to the concept of social media as it enables individuals to broadcast their ideas and establish social relationships through interactions on the platform, without the intervention of broadcasting networks. Waldron (2013) notes that UGC is a term that media researchers use to describe digital content that is created by ordinary people (as opposed to large television networks), uploaded to the Internet, and freely accessible to all.

This study focuses on one of the most prominent forms of UGC: web series, defined as "short, screen-based episodic series made for online delivery and made freely available by its creators to their audiences" (Taylor 2021). Web series differ from television series and on-demand streaming services in that viewers do not have to pay to view them, and network executives do not solicit, licence, or produce them. According to Ellingsen (2012), web series have the potential to become an emerging entertainment platform due to the use of less expensive production tools, rapidly expanding bandwidth, and a rapidly growing global audience. Web series are also part of what Craig and Cunningham (2019, p. 5) refer to as social media entertainment, which is an "emerging proto-industry fuelled by professionalising, previously amateur content creators using new entertainment and communicative formats, including vlogging, gameplay, and do-it-yourself (DIY), to develop potentially sustainable businesses based on significant followings that can extend across multiple platforms". From an industrial perspective, web series are not only about participatory culture, but also an emerging business ecosystem that empowers individuals financially. In fact, many Islamic web series creators grow into small-scale production houses as they create web series for various companies, not only Islamic businesses such as Muslim fashions, schools, and charity boards, but also regular products such as kitchen appliances.

Current research on web series focuses primarily on "Audience Reception" through social media. Krüger and Rustad (2019), for instance, highlight that the Norwegian teen web series *Skam* is a potential space for their audience to learn how to navigate a media-saturated society. The authors note that the predominantly adolescent *Skam* viewers not only discuss the show on WhatsApp and Messenger groups but also apply the plot to their own media consumption. On the other hand, Ng and Li (2020) observe that the fandom of *Guardian*, a Chinese queer web series, responds to government censorship by establishing fan groups to actively promote trending hashtags on *Weibo* (China's most popular microblogging platform) and circulating memes, fan videos, fan art, and fan fiction.

Research on web series in Indonesia, however, tends to focus on the role of web series as a marketing tool for companies. Recently, it can be observed that many companies from various industries are investing in web series instead of direct advertising to soft sell their brands. As a result of these efforts to create engaging stories, it has been found that the audience are generally more persuaded to buy their products (Cokki et al. 2019). In addition, existing research on Islamic web series in Indonesia is primarily conducted by scholars of Islamic studies, focusing specifically on how web series has become one of the emerging preaching platforms (*media da'wa*) for representing Islamic values and moral ethics (Prita 2020; Karim and Erwhintiana 2020; Langga et al. 2019). This research aims to continue the conversation by analysing YouTube comments to investigate how the audience interpret and make meaning of the web series narratives.

This chapter analyses *Cinta Subuh*, arguably one of the pioneers of Islamic online episodes with more than three million views on YouTube. The episode was created by FMM and had approximately 80 million views and 700,000 subscribers at the time of writing in June 2022. The plot is very straightforward: a Muslim woman (Ratih) breaks up with her boyfriend (Angga) because he did not attend morning prayers. Following the breakup, Angga proceeded to cultivate a new habit of rising before sunrise, and his life improved drastically. At the end of the episode, Angga was able to obtain employment and eventually proposed to the girl. Similar personal stories can be found among the 2,000 comments under the video, all of which encouraged other Muslims to pray on time as it is said to be significantly correlated with one's success in life. Overall, the total number of comments under *Cinta Subuh's* page at the time of writing was 2,654, and I extracted these comments for qualitative analysis.

The Mediatized Piety: Analysing User Comments

Three main themes can be observed following a thorough analysis of the comments section. The first theme is the belief that piety is a part of *self-development*. Like the narratives propagated by the web series, the audience sees piety as a means of achieving personal objectives such as having good careers or pious wives and husbands. Some users even shared similar experiences comparable to those of Ratih and Angga.

> [a1] *A highly inspiring series. I remember when I neglected my duty for Fajr prayer, how reckless I was. After watching this movie, I feel encouraged to pray in the mosque especially Fajr. And thank God, now Allah makes it easy for me to achieve all my goals.*

[a2] *Three years ago this video became a motivation for me to pray regularly in mosque, especially Fajr. At that time, I was hoping that I could get a job soon. Thank God (alhamdulillah)...Allah granted my wish.*

[a3] *Pray for Allah and Allah only, if we can pray regularly then Allah will make our lives better, including giving the best life partners for us.*

From these comments, the audience regards piety as a necessary trait for self-improvement and the betterment of their lives. Piety is not seen as something that must be attained out of fear of punishment for disobedience, but because there are benefits being religious, as portrayed by the characters. Hence, the viewers are more motivated to become pious and to be rewarded and incentivized for their growing compliance.

The second theme is piety as *symbolism-ritualism*. In this section, viewers pay close attention to how the web series present their characters, particularly in terms of their physical appearance. For instance, there are numerous negative comments regarding a scene in which the male lead was filmed wearing shorts in his bedroom; in Islam, legs are considered *awrah* (parts of the body that should be covered) for men. Other viewers protested over a scene in which a man was wearing a T-shirt depicting a metal music band while praying at a mosque, and a scene that showed a minion doll with one eye as it resembled *dajjal* (an evil figure in Islam similar to the Antichrist).

[b1] *The series is good, but it would be better if Angga did not show his awrah by using short pants. I think it is not proper. I mean, I know it is just a movie and you guys are acting but do not deviate from Islamic law.*

[b2] *The film is highly inspiring, but it would be better if Angga wear something to cover his awrah in the bedroom scene.*

[b3] *In 8:30 there is a talent using my favorite band t-shirt, Machine 56. But how can you do that? It is not proper to use metal band t-shirt to go pray at mosque. Anyway, it is just my opinion.*

[b4] *Maybe next time you can change the doll* (in Ratih's room-author). *It is a one-eyed doll, minion symbol* (similar to *dajjal*-author)

Other comments emphasized the ritual aspect of the story: the act of praying. Here, praying is viewed as a means of displaying the glory of the Islamic community (*umma*), particularly the morning prayer, as it is frequently regarded as the most demanding form of piety. Some viewers stated that a full mosque during morning prayers is an indication of an Islamic revival.

> [b5] *The mosques in Indonesia should be full of worshipers, especially at dawn. That would make the world seem more "fresh"!*
>
> [b6] *One sign of the progress of the Islamic* umma *is the number of people who attend morning prayers at the mosque.*
>
> [b7] *Where would we find a mosque that is full of young people just like in this movie? Mosques now are full with old men, you know...I think if they could sell mosques, they would.*

The third theme is piety manifested in *halal* relationships. Comments under this theme are mostly critical of the relationship between the male and female lead of the web series. For instance, there are strong objections to the story plot as Ratih and Angga are portrayed as a couple who frequent motorbike dates. Some viewers expressed concern that the web series advocates for "Islamic dating" and that it might inspire young Muslims to engage in the same behaviour. Other users, on the other hand, questioned the motivation behind the male lead's transition to becoming more religious—was it to please God, or to regain the girl's affection?

> [c1] *This episode sort of inspires young Muslims to do sinful relationships. Why are they dating and even riding motorcycle together? Our religion does not condone this behaviour. You can say the creator of the series mean well, but still, they do it the wrong way.*
>
> [c2] *My first impression of this episode is "you have to do morning prayer so that your girl does not break up with you..."*
>
> [c3] *I don't like the female lead character. She seems to be aggressively chasing the boy. I think the creator should change that so the movie would be better.*

The analysis presented above shows that Islamic web series tend to adopt similar narratives to Islamic blockbuster films, such as *Ayat-Ayat Cinta*, with both emphasizing piety and personal success in terms of career and relationships in their storylines (Sasono 2010). The question is: why do urban Muslims find these topics appealing? According to van Bruinessen (2013), there are two possible explanations for this.

First, after the New Order era, support for liberal and progressive Islamic thought, which had previously come from Muslim intellectual figures such as Munawir Sjadzali, Nurcholish Madjid, and Abdurrahman Wahid virtually decreased, giving space to "other Muslim discourses" which had been repressed under the New Order period. This led to the emergence of the theme of "purification of Islamic identity", whose primary objective was to distinguish Islam from other religions in Indonesia. In some web series, for instance, this is reflected in the plot and characters—Muslim youth do not date, do not display their *awrah*, collectively perform morning prayer in mosques, marry young, and do not work in banks to avoid the risk of *riba* (usury).

Second, the chaos and violence that occurred throughout Indonesia's transition to democracy have led urban Muslims to favour "soul-healing" topics. Spiritual therapy like meditation and mental training seminars are preferred to political Islamic discourses. The technological and interactive capabilities of social media platforms have also encouraged greater personal expression and discussion of Islam, fostering a more individualized understanding of piety.

Conclusion

Targeted at urban Muslim youths, the underlying themes of most Islamic web series on YouTube demonstrate that contemporary Islamic orientations privilege ritualism and symbolism over social and political values. Following the narratives of classic Indonesian Islamic films such as *Ayat-Ayat Cinta*, mediatized piety is typically perceived by urban Muslim youth to be beneficial for their self-development and for the achievement of individual objectives, such as having a better career and a life partner.

Since Islamic web series are based on a free-to-use social media platform, there have been contestations between various content creators regarding the narratives they choose to present. Islamidotco, for instance, published an Islamic web episode about religious tolerance in Indonesia. The page discussed the difficulties faced by religious minorities to access basic rights such as housing. In another episode, the page narrated the story of a Muslim man who refused to accept *kue keranjang* (Chinese New Year specialty cake) from his Tionghoa neighbours. However, in terms of viewership, Islamidotco continues to lag behind its counterparts. Its most popular episode only achieved hundreds of thousands of viewership while *Cinta Subuh* has gained more than three million views at the time of writing and is currently being adapted to the big screen.

Overall, Islamic web series have shown that they have the capability of inspiring young Muslims to focus on self-developmental aspects such as becoming more pious and successful in their careers, businesses, relationships, and so on. With many advantages such as low-cost production tools and a growing global audience, coupled with the technological affordances of social media which encourage religious sociability within the audience, it will be interesting to see the societal changes that Islamic web series can bring about if they delve into non-traditional topics such as social injustice, education, and religious minorities. From these Islamic web series, it is evident that crucial issues in the Islamic world can be presented in an engaging manner to Muslim youth and spark meaningful discussions about public Islam.

NOTES

1 Personal interview with FMM Studios' co-founder Ali Ghifari, 24 August 2021.
2 Personal interview with Sisterlillah Community's co-founder Fira Nuraini, 22 April 2022.

REFERENCES

Bunt, Gary R. 2018. *Hashtag Islam: How Cyber-Islamic Environments Are Transforming Religious Authority*. Chapel Hill: University of North Carolina Press.

Burgess, Jean and Joshua Green. 2018. *YouTube: Online Video and Participatory Culture*. Cambridge; Metford: Polity Press.

Cokki, Lydiawati Soelaiman and Ida Puspitowati. 2019. "Transformasi Digital Merek-Merek Indonesia dalam Bentuk Penempatan Produk Pada Web Series di Situs Web YouTube". *DeReMa Jurnal Manajemen* 14, no. 1: 155–70.

Craig, David and Stuart Cunningham. 2019. *Social Media Entertainment: The New Intersection of Hollywood and Silicon Valley*. New York: NYU Press.

Ellingsen, S. 2012. "Web Series, Independent Media and Emerging Online Markets: Then and Now". In *Crossmedia Innovations: Texts, Markets,*

Institutions, edited by Indrek Ibrus and Carlos Scolari, pp. 199–215. Berlin: Peter Lang.

Farihah, Irzum. 2013. "Media Dakwah Pop". AT-TABSYIR; Jurnal Komunikasi Penyiaran Islam 1, no. 2: 25–45.

Frederick, William. 1982. "Rhoma Irama and the *Dangdut* Style: Aspects of Contemporary Indonesian Popular Culture". *Indonesia*, no. 34: 103–30.

Hefner, Robert. 2010. "Religious Resurgence in Contemporary Asia: Southeast Asian Perspectives on Capitalism, the State, and the New Piety". *Journal of Asian Studies* 69, no. 4: 103–47.

Heryanto, Ariel. 2011. "Upgraded Piety and Pleasure: The New Middle Class and Islam in Indonesian Popular Culture". In *Islam and Popular Culture in Indonesia and Malaysia*, edited by Andrew Weintraub, pp. 76–98. Abingdon; New York: Routledge.

———. 2014. *Identity and Pleasure: The Politics of Indonesian Screen Culture*. Singapore: NUS Press.

Karim, Muhdie Amir and Ifi Erwhintiana. 2020. "Pola Tutur Perlokusi Dalam Web Series Di Balik Hati: Sebuah Tnjauan Pragmatik Perspektif Leech". *Pujangga: Jurnal Bahasa Dan Sastra* 6, no. 2: 177–95.

Krüger, Steffen and Gry Rustad. 2019. "Coping with Shame in a Media-Saturated Society: Norwegian Web-Series Skam as Transitional Object". *Television & New Media* 20, no. 1: 72–95.

Langga, Fathin Hanifah, Hafiz Aziz Ahmad and Alvanov Zpalanzani Mansoor. 2019. "Web Series Animasi Nussa Sebagai Media Pendidikan Islami Pada Anak". *Wimba: Jurnal Komunikasi Visual* 10, no. 1: 57–69.

Mahmood, Saba. 2001. "Rehearsed Spontaneity and the Conventionality of Ritual: Disciplines of Şalat". *American Ethnologist* 28, no. 4: 827–53.

———. 2011. *Politics of Piety: The Islamic Revival and the Feminist Subject*. Princeton: Princeton University Press.

Ng, Eve and Xiaomeng Li. 2020. "A Queer 'Socialist Brotherhood': The Guardian Web Series, Boys' Love Fandom, and the Chinese State". *Feminist Media Studies* 20, no. 4: 479–95.

Nisa, Eva. 2018. "Social Media and the Birth of an Islamic Social Movement: ODOJ (One Day One Juz) in Contemporary Indonesia". *Indonesia and the Malay World* 46, no. 134: 24–43.

Prita, Rahayu. 2020. "Pesan Akhlak Dalam Web Series Di Balik Hati Karya Film Maker Muslim (Analisis Semiotika Roland Barthes)". Undergraduate Thesis, Institut Agama Islam Negeri Ponorogo.

Rakhmani, Inaya. 2013. "Regime and Representation: Islam in Indonesian Television, 1962 to 1998". *RIMA: Review of Indonesian and Malaysian Affairs* 47, no. 1: 61–88.

———. 2017. *Mainstreaming Islam in Indonesia: Television, Identity, and the Middle Class*. New York: Palgrave Macmillan US.

Sasono, Eric. 2010. "Islamic-Themed Films in Contemporary Indonesia: Commodified Religion or Islamization?" *Asian Cinema* 21, no. 2: 48–68.

Schielke, Samuli. 2010. "Second Thoughts about the Anthropology of Islam, or How to Make Sense of Grand Schemes in Everyday Life". *ZMO Working Papers*, no. 2: 1–16.

Slama, Martin. 2018. "Practising Islam through Social Media in Indonesia". *Indonesia and the Malay World* 46, no. 134: 1–4.

Taylor, Stayci. 2021. "'Just Ask "What If?" And Go from There': The Role of Mainstream Story Structures in Women's Web Series Script Development". *Studies in Australasian Cinema* 15, nos. 1–2: 48–64.

Van Bruinessen, Martin. 2013. *Contemporary Developments in Indonesian Islam: Explaining the "Conservative Turn"*. Singapore: Institute of Southeast Asian Studies.

Wahid, Din and Jamhari Makruf. 2017. *Suara Salafisme Radio Dakwah Di Indonesia*. Jakarta: Kencana.

Waldron, Janice. 2013. "User-Generated Content, YouTube and Participatory Culture on the Web: Music Learning and Teaching in Two Contrasting Online Communities". *Music Education Research* 15, no. 3: 257–74.

Weng, Hew Wai. 2018. "On-Offline Dakwah: Social Media and Islamic Preaching in Malaysia and Indonesia". In *Mediatized Religion in Asia*, edited by Kerstin Radde-Antweiler and Xenia Zeiler, pp. 89–104. Boca Raton: Routledge.

Zaid, Bouziane, Jana Fedtke, Don Donghee Shin, Abdelmalek El Kadoussi and Mohammed Ibahrine. 2022. "Digital Islam and Muslim Millennials: How Social Media Influencers Reimagine Religious Authority and Islamic Practices". *Religions* 13, no. 4: 335.

10

BEING SPIRITUAL AND TRENDY: SINGAPORE'S ISLAMIC AUTHORITY IN THE AGE OF CAPITALISM AND POPULISM

Norshahril Saat

Introduction

Islam is closely tied to the cultural identity of Singapore Malays. Based on the 2021 census report, the Malays constitute 15.1 per cent of Singapore's 5.5 million population ("Population in Brief 2021" 2021), of which 98.0 per cent profess Islam. The religious elite—the *ulama* (Islamic religious scholars), religious teachers, and preachers—wield significant influence on the religious community regarding spiritual matters. However, their authority has been somewhat challenged in the new media and digitization age. What does this mean for their future and the quality of religious discourse in Singapore? This chapter focuses on the movers and shakers of the Singapore Malay/Muslim community's religious discourse and outlook.

As the religious elite ride on new digital mediums of instruction, they easily migrate from the traditional print, radio, and television platforms to the new digital ones. They utilize the Internet and have become social media savvy. Consequently, the local religious elites must venture beyond conventional ways of preaching and compete with preachers from different parts of the world as religious learning is no longer confined to the mosques and madrasahs. The pressure to apply new forms of preaching does not apply to Islamic elites only. According to Naim (2013), the rise of new Pentecostal and charismatic churches has also redefined religious authority in Christianity.[1] He also argues that while the arrival of these micropowers does not undermine traditional authority, the "big players" can no longer take their power for granted (ibid., pp. 196–97).

However, I contend that the religious elite's digital ventures are not necessarily accompanied by shifts in their thinking. The dominant religious orientation continues to manifest traditionalism. This orientation is now ushered by capitalism and populism, presented and repackaged with sophistication via the new media, and sustained by the growth of the Muslim middle class. The middle class riding on Islamic symbolic commodities and reaping financial incentives to raise their social positions (Muzakki 2008, p. 205) further complicates any possibility of reform. Significant changes in the discursive arena are further slowed by state policies that accord the *asatizah* (religious teachers) the sole authority to speak on Islamic matters. Through occupational licensing, this legitimacy given to the theologians resulted from the state's attempt to tackle radicalism through the religious lens.[2] Yet, moderate Islam discourse ignores attention to other aspects of modernization and development: tackling irrationalism and addressing inequality.

This chapter builds on existing works from the sociology of religion, discussing the nexus between social media, digitization, and religious authority. The growing interest in the subject originates from the 1970s when new modes of communication and technology started to ease previously inaccessible and distant discourses closer to where consumers live. Stolow (2016, p. 548) explains, "the growing, and increasingly globalised public visibility of religious actors, religious actions, and religious modes of discourse. This expanding visibility is centrally, deeply, and inextricably tied to the technological, symbolic, and economic shifts that have given rise to the modern global media landscape".

The chapter first highlights the different modes of orientation—traditionalism and progressivism.[3] This will be followed by a section discussing Islamic religious authority in Singapore before the age of social media, where I examine four religious elites who garnered society's recognition without the use of digital tools. This will be followed by an explication of globalization's impact on religious discourse, and how occupational licensing has been used to safeguard the Singapore religious elite's authority and quality of ideas. Though this method has somewhat curbed radicalism or terrorism in Singapore—which is the policy's original intent—I argue that it neither tackles traditionalism, excessive capitalism nor irrationalism but further legitimizes it. The last section discusses the changing nature of religious authority and discourse in the age of social media.

Modes of Thinking

The September 2001 terrorist attacks in New York (commonly known as 9/11) transformed global discourses about Islam and Muslims. While negative images of Muslims preceded the attacks as attested by Said's seminal work *Orientalism*, the events of 9/11 cast the spotlight on Muslims further. Islamophobia became widespread in the United States and Europe where Muslims constitute a small minority (El Fadl 2022). In Singapore, following 9/11, Muslims' behaviour was scrutinized. Government leaders urged community leaders to stand against terrorism and promote religious harmony.[4] It followed that a few months after 9/11, the Singapore security agencies detained several Malay/Muslims who were plotting to attack key installations in the country. They were found to be staunch followers of the regionally based terrorist group Jemaah Islamiah (JI). This discovery gave rise to further doubt that a segment within the Malay/Muslim community was not integrating with the mainstream, predominantly non-Muslims and non-Malays.

Consequently, the religious elite responded by reaching out to non-Muslims and initiating inter-religious dialogues with other faith leaders.[5] Yet, discussions on Singapore Muslims became highly securitized. The community was urged to define what constitutes "moderate" Islam; with the state encouraging the "progressives" to speak up against radicalism and fundamentalism. Responses towards terrorism then became the primary determinant of whether one is moderate or extreme. Those who publicly condemn terrorist acts, perpetrators of violence, or engage in rehabilitating terrorists, are characterized as "moderates", arguably setting the bar to become moderates. In a way, conservatives who remain uncommitted towards gender equality (Noor Aisha 2007) or display exclusivist attitudes towards religious minorities (such as the Shi'as and Ahmadiyyahs) or cast doubts about Singapore's secular ideology in favour of Islamic governance (Noor Aisha 2020) are regarded as moderates as long as they publicly condemn terrorism. While in other parts of the world the definition of violence has been stretched to include hate speech or conservative attitudes that have the effect of fanning hatred towards others—blurring the line between violent extremism and non-violent extremism—this was not the case in post-9/11 Singapore.

The dominance of the security lens also relegates previous sociological interest in studying religious orientations and its impact (Azra 2004; Alatas 1973; Shaharuddin 2002, 2006). Conversely, the post-9/11 discourse began conflating religious views and culture with religious values and ideas, a phenomenon Roy describes as culturalism (Roy 2004, pp. 10–12). As a result, there has been a failure to distinguish Islam as a set of fixed principles and values from how communities express them, the latter which I describe as orientations which are conditioned by space, time, socialization, politics, and context. To fully understand the mode of thinking of Muslim trendsetters in Singapore and the impact of their ideas and attitudes, this chapter illustrates how sociologists have sought to understand religious orientation. This will enable one to discern whether trends hamper or encourage the progress of the community. In the following, traditionalist orientation is distinguished from the progressive based on how one approaches religious traditions and texts. This does not mean that the behaviour of Muslims (and our concern in this chapter, religious trendsetters) is shaped solely by text or religion. To avoid being culturalist, it is incorrect to assume that religious doctrines determine one's behaviour given that social class, socialization, place, and spatial factors also shape one's orientation.

Generally, traditionalism is a form of religious orientation that is resistant to change. It is an attitude that clings to the past and feels the need to maintain the status quo (Towler 1986). Its attitude towards new forms of knowledge is a closed one, and apart from being relatively dismissive of innovations, it often quotes verses or hymns to justify the attitude of resisting innovations.⁶ It is worth noting that traditionalism is not opposed to all change, but it is relatively slower at embracing it compared to its progressive counterpart. Even if traditionalists embrace change, they do so reluctantly or pragmatically rather than understanding the merits of the change.

On the other hand, the progressives constantly re-evaluate traditions to meet the current needs. In the context of Islam, they would determine religious traditions based on the Qur'an and *hadith* (narrations of the Prophet Muhammad) and the larger corpus of knowledge within them. Though the traditionalists often label their progressive counterparts "un-Islamic" or "disrespectful" of Islamic texts, most progressives are committed to the Islamic traditions and corpus, believe in the merits of reading and re-reading Islamic texts for social change, and are practising Muslims. Still, the main disagreement with the traditionalists is that Islamic traditions are more extensive than restricted to the Islamic golden age 1,400 years ago when the Prophet Muhammad and the three generations after him lived.

As I have outlined, the distinction between the progressive and traditionalist orientations can also be applied to other religions (and secular life). However, since this chapter is concerned with Islam and Muslims, how do these orientations feature in Sufism, Wahhabi-Salafism, and liberal modes of thinking that have been used—albeit loosely—when discussing Singapore Muslims? Departing from the conventional view in Singapore that considers Sufism "progressive", Wahhabi-Salafism "puritan", and liberalism "deviant", I propose that traditionalism and progressivism can exist in these three modes of religious life depending on the issues they discuss.⁷

I wish to highlight another relevant influence to the Muslim religious life: capitalism. These are further intertwined with existing orientations: traditionalism and progressivism. Capitalism means business, and the causes can be either noble and cunning, honest and deceptive, or humane and exploitative. Muslims often remark that the Prophet Muhammad was a businessman and are encouraged to do business. However, there can be progressive or traditionalist interpretations of this. The progressive would argue that Muslims can engage in all types of business, not necessarily restricted to barter trade like the Prophet.

Progressives could also expand the tradition to mean that the Prophet encourages work and effort. Traditionalists, however, would have a restrictive view of this to represent all other forms of work that do not constitute the *Sunnah*. According to the traditionalists, barter trade represents the most noble form of work.

This chapter is not interested in labels, or whether one is traditionalist, progressive, capitalist, or humanist. The concepts mentioned above are not restricted to Muslims in Singapore and are also not specific to the study of religion. The chapter is interested in evaluating whether the so-called "moderate" religious trendsetters live up to their name beyond security matters. It is not engaging with the conclusions made in other studies that have considered Islamists and revivalists as containing reformist elements (Anjum 2017, p. 305).[8] I am also not delving into the debate of whether Singapore Islamists have now moved towards the post-Islamist phase, defined as a breakaway from Islamists by emphasizing rights and inclusivity over exclusivity and being duty-centred (Bayat 2010, p. 307).

Religious Elites in Singapore: Before the Age of Social Media

Traditionally, the religious elite refers to a group of Muslim leaders that provides theological guidance for the community. This group possesses the authority and legitimacy to shape religious discourse, and these are not necessarily achieved through being "trendy". They are generally not what Mills (1956) described as the super-rich, celebrities, or the corporate rich in his *The Power Elite*.[9] The *ulama*, widely regarded as *waratsatul anbiya* (heirs of the Prophet), constitute an important group within the Islamic religious elite. Educational background and the institutions the religious elite occupies determine whether he is authoritative. They are trained in religious sciences such as theology, *hadith*, *fiqh* (Islamic jurisprudence), Qur'anic interpretation, and philosophy, among others.[10] Today, the definition of the *ulama* (plural for *alim*) prioritizes authority in the religious sphere and is restricted to those who receive formal training in the madrasahs, Islamic universities, or private institutions in the religious sciences.

In Singapore, the term used to describe individuals who possess the authority to speak on religious matters and trained in religious sciences is the *asatizah*. A typical *asatizah* would have to undergo elementary and secondary education training in one of the local madrasahs. There are currently six madrasahs in Singapore, some focusing on primary education, some secondary and post-secondary, and some both. Upon graduating from a madrasah, a handful will pursue degrees in Islamic studies at a university in the Middle East, and some in neighbouring Indonesia and Malaysia. Many of them pursuing a degree in the Middle East would enrol in courses at the prestigious Al-Azhar University, the so-called "Harvard" of Islamic Studies (Norshahril, Azhar, and Noor Aisha 2021; Norshahril 2018).

Beyond the religious training requirement, religious authority today is also tied to the charisma of the teacher or preacher. Those who receive informal religious training but have a strong appeal can be considered *asatizah* or *ulama*. These older generations of *asatizah* can be popular preachers, leaders of *tariqah* (Sufi orders), or Qur'anic teachers. Those who receive training in national/secular schools but learn religion part-time can also be part of the religious authority. There are prominent religious figures in Singapore today who wield a significant following from the community despite never having attended a full-time madrasah.

The following are examples of the Singapore religious elite who obtained legitimacy through various means. Some are government-appointed, others are charismatic, and the rest are a mix of different sources. They are the elites who emerged before the age of social media. One prominent Islamic scholar in Singapore was Ahmad Sonhadji Muhamad (b.1922–d.2010). Trained in Madrasah Aljunied, he learned Islamic studies through the Islamic boarding school system. He authored thirty chapters of Qur'anic exegesis, though they were primarily written recordings of his lectures on local radio. Ahmad Sonhadji then became an *imam* at the Muhajirin Mosque and was a religious teacher and principal at the madrasah. He was also the teacher of the two prominent *asatizah*, Syed Isa Semait and Syed Abdillah Aljufri. His student, Syed Isa Semait (b.1933), received formal religious training—he studied at the local madrasah, and later graduated from the Al-Azhar University in Cairo (Syed Zakir 2012). As a student, he was a strong activist and founded the Singapore student association at Al-Azhar University (Perkemas). While Syed Isa did not author any major scholarly contribution in the form of Qur'anic exegesis or books, he was appointed the Mufti of Singapore (the highest authority of religious scholars) between 1972 and 2010. Although Syed Isa could claim authority and legitimacy because of his function as a state appointee, he regularly led prayers in mosques.

Syed Isa's contemporary Syed Abdillah Aljufri (b.1938–d.2003) also had a stint at the Islamic Religious Council of Singapore (also known as Majlis Ugama Islam Singapura or MUIS), but the community regarded him as an independent scholar. However, unlike Syed Isa, Syed Abdillah never graduated from any Islamic university. Syed Abdillah began writing his Qur'anic exegesis but did not live long enough to complete the thirty chapters like his mentor Ahmad Sonhadji. Still, he regularly contributed his opinion to the local newspaper, *Berita Harian*. In addition, Syed Abdillah also headed a non-governmental organization (NGO) called the Singapore Islamic Scholars and Religious Teachers Association (Persatuan Ulama dan Guru-Guru Agama Islam Singapura, PERGAS). Given these efforts, Syed Abdillah may be considered a trendsetter of the 1980s and 1990s: his voice regularly aired on the radio, his columns were published weekly in the newspapers, and he had a significant following in mosques. His funeral was attended by about 3,000 congregants at the Sultan Mosque, exceeding the capacity of the largest mosque in Singapore. Another prominent teacher Habib Syed Hassan Al-Attas (b.1950) may not have graduated from prominent Islamic universities such as Al-Azhar University, Medina University, or the International Islamic University of Malaysia. Yet, in terms of scholarly contributions, the Sufi master at Ba'alwie Mosque is well-read and understands the different theological positions of different schools of thought. The government recognized his involvement in interfaith work, and he has received numerous awards for his role in the religious scene. His training is informal: from his father and personal meetings with scholars.

The *asatizah* mentioned above were trendsetters from the 1970s to 1990s. They used radio, print media, madrasahs, and mosques to disseminate their ideas. Some received formal training and contributed to scholarly debates. Generally, most of their views touched on spirituality, and most of their peers upheld a traditionalist orientation. More importantly, they had a strong following without the need for any form of certification or licensing from any accredited body. That was the situation before 9/11.

Regulating Authority Through Licensing and its Limitations

Many scholars disagree with the high level of authority that the religious elite holds today. While Zaman (2002) opines that the *ulama* can ride the wave of new media to remain relevant in the religious domain, Saeed (2004) contends that the *ulama* have already been weakened if not replaced by public intellectuals. I posit that both Zaman and Saeed are correct. Challenges to traditional and institutional authority have triggered some from this group to migrate to new platforms and mediums, taking the social media and populist route. Since the arrival of new media, the preachers' landscape has also evolved from relying on Friday sermons from mosque pulpits to the era of televangelism (Muzakki 2008, p. 214)—what we refer to today as the digital era. Signs of producing religious content into digestible versions were already happening during the televangelist era between the late 1990s and early 2000s, but in this digital age, content has been further reduced to bite-sized portions.

While the transmission medium has evolved significantly, the state's concern regarding Islamic discourse continues to centre on contextualization and countering radicalism. This is undeniably the outcome of post-9/11. Fearing that religious education is not facilitating Muslims to be part of the mainstream, the state implemented the Asatizah Recognition Scheme (ARS) (Mohammad Hannan and Irwan Mohd Hadi 2018). The introduction of the ARS is one way to mediate the religious discourse in Singapore's current context. The scheme permits only licensed religious elites to teach and preach about Islam. The purpose is noble: it seeks to weed out radical ideas derailing Islam's teachings. A panel of senior religious elites will determine whether a religious teacher is qualified to teach or preach in mosques or homes, and the scheme is extended to include Qur'an teachers. The scheme ensures that only specific individuals who meet the criteria can speak about religion, and the basis for this recognition is the institutions they study, the types of discipline they undertake, and whether they pass the qualifying interview (ibid.). Overall, the ARS scheme aims to ensure Singapore Muslims receive proper guidance that will not lead to violent conduct or deviant teachings.

However, the ARS is also a form of occupational licensing that prevents non-*asatizah* from speaking on religious matters. Lindsey and

Teles' *The Captured Economy* provides a useful comparison regarding the merits and demerits of occupational licensing (Lindsey and Teles 2017). While the book deals with the effects of market forces in the United States and how it generates inequality, their arguments on occupational licensing can also be applied to study the nature of religious knowledge and transmission in Singapore, and the effectiveness of the ARS scheme. According to Lindsey and Teles, occupational licensing is meant to protect consumers. "By setting minimum qualifications to play a particular trade", the authors opine, "the government can weed out the incompetent and unethical to ensure that consumers aren't ripped off or physically harmed" (ibid., p. 92). However, Lindsey and Teles warn that licensing only benefits some consumers and penalizes the rest. Furthermore, they assert that "licensing regimes and requirements they impose are all too often highly arbitrary" (ibid., p. 93). Occupational licencing may also create the perception of occupational protectionism into the profession, which means that the cost would be passed to consumers. Clearly, it defeats the primary objective of religion: to be practised by the masses.

Considering this, the ARS is also limited by the nature of religious/Islamic studies. Firstly, there are instances in which those who were not trained in the madrasahs or who did not receive any formal religious education were still inducted into the ARS scheme. Moreover, a preuniversity diploma in Islamic studies is sufficient to qualify as a *asatizah* under the scheme (Norshahril, Azhar, and Noor Aisha 2021). Degrees and diplomas from private institutions merely increase the supply of *asatizah*. There is also no proper evaluation of the quality of religious studies even in prominent Islamic universities, which arguably, remains short of standards compared to modern-day universities (ibid.). There remains an emphasis on rote learning and memorization rather than critical thinking. Furthermore, the ARS prevents progressive and critical voices from speaking in religious forums and mosque settings, where the pious constituents congregate.[11]

On top of that, occupational licencing in the form of the ARS has not prevented excessive capitalistic, anti-intellectual, and traditionalist orientations. Instead, it may have the unintended effect of reaffirming it. On one level, the ARS endorses *asatizah* on the basis of the institutions they graduated from. On the second level, it weeds out elements of radicalism and terrorism, and any views that break Singapore's multicultural and multireligious fabric. Nevertheless, it is not concerned about magical orientation or highly marketized religion. This problem is exacerbated by unlimited Internet and social media access which makes the ARS futile since Singapore Muslims can seek religious knowledge privately from popular, online preachers. As a result, local *asatizah* are forced to compete with Malaysian and Indonesian popular preachers, and the contest is less determined by the quality of scholarship but rather, by popularity or trendy.[12]

Capitalism and the Rise of Malay Middle Class

Not to mention with economic development, a segment of the Singapore Malay/Muslim community has experienced an increase in income, and the rise of the middle class. With this, consumption habits have changed, and this is not limited to a move towards materialism but has driven some to participate in humanitarian causes. For the former, this includes spending unnecessarily on luxury items and hobbies; for the latter, middle-class Muslims are donating their wealth not only to the underprivileged in Singapore but also constantly seeking to contribute to overseas causes. Despite their divergence on how wealth is spent, the dominance of the traditionalist orientation means that Islam factors in their considerations. To illustrate, most of the spending is restricted to halal goods and services, syariah-compliant products, and for causes that uplift the global Muslim *umma*. Some would be attracted to join halal cruises or syariah-oriented hotels but shun others. Some would only consider donating to Muslim orphanages locally or overseas but not to other forms of charities that touch on culture, heritage, or entertainment. Additionally, Muslims tend to donate to Muslim countries struck by natural disasters (like the massive earthquakes that hit Turkey and Syria in February 2023) but turn a blind eye when similar disasters hit non-Muslims. Singapore Muslims are more concerned about the Palestine-Israel conflict or the Rohingya crisis in Myanmar since these affect Muslims, but less inclined to discuss about the Russian invasion of Ukraine. While one should not be overly critical of such behaviour, since every person is entitled to spend their wealth in ways they deem fit, from a critical standpoint, this was shaped by and continues to promote exclusivism. While Islam champions care for humanity—which traditionalist

Muslims also agree with—these actions demonstrate the prioritization of Muslims over humankind.

Notably, the changing nature of consumption patterns also impacts Islamic preaching and learning (Hoesterey 2016; Friedman 2021). Consumers of religion have their taste adjusted, and the suppliers, the *asatizah*, either adjust to this development to meet their growing needs, or are forced to tag along with the market economy due to a lack of opportunities in their traditional domains of mosques, madrasahs, and preaching. In the past, topics in religious classes mainly dealt with faith, jurisprudence, ethics, and rituals. While these subjects continue to dominate contemporary religious courses, the medium of instruction is no longer restricted to the physical, face-to-face interactions in mosque or classroom settings, especially following COVID-19, which for a certain period, pushed these physical classes online. It is now common for classes to be held online via Zoom or Skype. Some preachers even utilize Facebook or Twitter. However, it is important to note that even before the COVID-19 pandemic, the community was already witnessing some changes to religious mediums. Classes conducted on cruises and five-star hotels were attracting patrons among the Malay professionals and middle class, some for charitable causes. Meals during these classes would include fine dining, in contrast with ordinary religious classes in the past where congregants sat cross-legged on the floor and had communal meals. Some of these halal cruises are held during the school holidays, targeting middle-class families. A three days and two nights halal cruise package averages around $400 per person, and the programme includes completing the recitation of the thirty chapters of the Qur'an and congregational prayers.

Along with the rise of the middle class also come new trends such as halal tourism. Halal tourism is no longer restricted to visiting holy places such as Mecca, Medina, Jerusalem, or Turkey, which are the traditional countries that offer Islamic history, artefacts, and lifestyle but is extended to Western countries that offer halal-based programmes and activities as well. This is a recent development as in the past, Muslim-owned tour agencies organized trips solely to Saudi Arabia for the annual hajj season or mini-pilgrimage (*umrah*). While this continues to be the mode of business by Islamic tour agencies—because of the religious rituals that require guidance—hajj and *umrah* packages offered now have also changed with the rise in the economic status of Singaporeans. Now, Singaporeans accept no less than five-star accommodation when they travel to Mecca and Medina for pilgrimage. Furthermore, Islamic tour packages are also riding on the trend to extend syariah-compliant tours to Japan, Korea, China, and Europe. Such tours are no different from other profit-making tour agencies, except that they cater halal food, allocate prayer times, and accommodate prayer spaces. This also ties in with the halal certification market for food and restaurants as some consumers demand that the restaurants or food outlets they patronize carry halal certificates from accreditation bodies.

Trendy Muslim Preachers in the New Media Age

Discussions in the previous paragraphs all point to the creation of a new phenomenon in current times: trendy Muslims. As mentioned earlier, although occupational licensing has been successful in countering radicalism, it has its limitations when curbing non-intellectual and even regressive magical discourse. Consumers continue to access alternative modes of religious transmission, namely through social media and the Internet and prioritize forms of preaching rather than the substance. Moreover, changes in halal consumption patterns mean that the religious elites are driving themselves towards lucrative business, and in return, venture into areas that do not require top-notch Islamic training. This happens when consumables are reduced to permissible and non-permissible (halal or haram).

The Singapore religious market is currently witnessing the rise of religious influencers. Without discounting their knowledge and years of religious training, the content of the sermons delivered by these influencers caters mainly to the young and those who patronize social media. These religious influencers also tend to limit in-depth discussions of texts, or the large corpus of religion, since Islam is reduced to bite-sized sermons. Focusing on this mode of religious transmission does not necessarily mean reducing Islam to sensationalism; it is a matter of choice for both the suppliers and consumers of knowledge. Religious influencers often upload short videos on social media to deliver their sermons, and it is clear their target audience is the youth. It follows that the content of sermons touches on issues that deal with spirituality.

Within Singapore, three young *asatizah* stood out from the rest as far as social media outreach is concerned. Although their following varies on different social media platforms: Instagram, Twitter, and Facebook, they are known to have a large following. The first is Zahid Zin, who has attracted thousands of youths on social media. As of June 2022, Zahid has 37,100 followers on Instagram, 6,381 followers on Twitter, and 12,028 followers on Facebook. His short yet captivating messages on Instagram have made him popular among the youth and attracted them to his online and offline religious classes. Where it concerns religious training, Zahid studied in Syria but his presence has allowed him to collaborate with community leaders who are also grappling with youth-related issues and the perceived growing religiosity among them. His contemporary is Tarmizi Wahid or Mizi Wahid (how he is identified in his publications). Mizi's followership on Instagram is three times more than Zahid's (132,000 as of June 2022), while his Twitter and Facebook following are 67,000 and 8,192 respectively. He too has classes online and has been attracting Muslim youth to attend these sessions. While he has written several books, as will be discussed shortly, they are often concerned with spirituality unlike his predecessors Syed Abdillah Aljufri and Ahmad Sonhadji, who engage in Qur'anic exegesis. The following are some excerpts from his books, which showcase the objectives of his writings:

> For the last ten years, I am blessed to have gotten the chance to meet with people from all walks of life. Beautiful people, with interesting stories, sometimes tragic, but always inspiring. Their struggles have taught me many lessons about life. Most prominently, the events that happen to us don't get to decide when our story is over. God does... Thanks to the nature of my profession, I have been "thrown into the deep waters" very early in my career, to handle issues and cases relating to matters that were way beyond my years (Mizi 2021a, p. 7).

Mizi's mission is akin to a self-help guru. In the preface of his book *You Are Loved*, Mizi states, "My hope for this book is that it becomes the go-to book for those interested to start believing in themselves again. If this is you, I hope it will help you believe in a better tomorrow" (Mizi 2021b, p. 18).

Mizi's social media outreach can be considered extensive by any *asatizah* standards. Community leaders also solicited his religious views and tapped into his online presence. Mizi, who currently sits on MUIS' *fatwa* council, also has a podcast channel. His classes, as evident from the advertisements promoted on his social media accounts, touch mainly on prayers, self-help, and Qur'anic studies. His popularity extends beyond Singapore shores, and his books have obtained best-seller status in Malaysia, which signifies his growing popularity outside of Singapore.

One religious teacher who stands out among females is Liyana Musfirah. Liyana started out by organizing roadshows mainly catering to women's needs and struggles. Her following on Instagram is 84,300, and her Twitter has 7,100 followers. She has been less active on Facebook since March 2022. Liyana is popular among female youth and her sermons touch on the challenges of young mothers. Advertisements of Liyana's products show that her talks centre on motherhood, Islamic parenting, divorce, and family relationships. Liyana is popular on Instagram and runs her own consultancy company, known as *Liyana Musfirah Network* (LiyanaMusfirah.com). The website clearly states the objective of the network: "This is a network for you, where we care as you navigate your religiosity, your spirituality, and your relationship". Other consultancies are also part of Liyana's network, including the Hayaa' Network, which provides services targeting the well-being of families such as couple assessment packages and family nucleus assessment packages, including psychological assessment.

Although there are many other *asatizah* who are active on social media, the three above-mentioned *asatizah* dominate the already saturated field. As the COVID-19 pandemic left the religious elites with no choice but to utilize the Internet to conduct sermons and classes, this resulted in a surge of online religious activities. Mosques and physical classes were forced to shut down during the early stages of the pandemic, and all classes migrated online. Even established senior preachers had to move their classes online. Undoubtedly, the younger preachers, such as the three mentioned above, are savvier, as one would expect, but their online presence serves as an added challenge to the other religious teachers in Singapore. The Singapore religious elite, already large in numbers, face competition from Malaysian and Indonesian preachers, especially those who are more charismatic. Furthermore, some Singapore preachers who attained good grades in Islamic universities are already facing the brunt of competing with their more charismatic counterparts such as Zahid, Mizi, and Liyana.

TABLE 10.1
Social Media Following of Liyana Musfirah, Zahid Zin, and Tarmizi Wahid, as of June 2022

	Instagram	Twitter	Facebook
Liyana Musfirah	84.3k Followers (@liyanamusfira)	7,161 Followers (@liyana_musfira) *Inactive. Last posted on 20th April 2021	Unknown *Inactive. Last posted on 2nd March 2022. Post only garnered 48 likes.
Zahid Zin	37.1k Followers (@zahidzin)	6,381 Followers (@mdzahidzin) *Inactive. Last posted on 20th January 2022	12,028 Followers (Zahid Zin)
Tarmizi Wahid	132k Followers (@miziwahid)	67k Followers (@mizi_wahid)	8,192k Followers (Mizi Wahid))

Facing competition from preachers from Singapore's neighbours—who can converse in Malay and English—is the last expectation in their minds. Moreover, with English now being a language of religious instruction, Singapore Muslims, especially the middle class, are now patronizing preachers from the Middle East, the United States, and Europe. In this aspect, occupational licensing through the ARS has its limitations.

In addition, trendy scholars are also challenging the role of mosques and institutions. There are perceptions that religious teachers who are part of official platforms do not have independence of religious thought. At times, the number of viewers for mosque-run classes online and offline is relatively low, unless they invite the charismatic and spiritual preachers, which have a large audience and following.

Clearly, sources of religious authority today have adopted a neoliberal turn (Weber 1930; Friedman 2021). Authority is now measured in terms of social media following and "likes". Some of these popular preachers are even promoted by political elites, functioning as patrons.

Some have been sponsored by corporate figures to speak in mass rallies, or to publish their books. The religious elites too have redefined themselves to garner higher engagement. They promote themselves on social media as successful entrepreneurs, allowing the public to scrutinize activities in their private life, and their association with "high culture". Their outreach often goes beyond Singapore shores, and their publications are read by Malaysians. Several religious preachers are also in the business of halal cruises, and the programmes include reciting and completing recitations of the Qur'an on cruises. Thus, trendy preachers are now part of the Islamic economy, an ecosystem that includes "production, trade, regulation, consumption, entrepreneurship, and science", which has gained interest not only from the religious followers but also from states/governments, civil society, businesses, and the education sector (Fischer and Jammes 2020, p. 1).

Moreover, the prevalence of social media also means that the religiously trained elites no longer have a monopoly on the religious discourse in the public sphere. There are instances in which they become figureheads when speaking on issues such as halal banking and halal certification, even while this falls outside their domain. Banking and finance professionals interested in syariah-compliant wills, syariah economics, halal insurance, halal cosmetics, and halal fashion often work with the *asatizah* to provide the rubber stamp. Hence, these capitalists mainly use the religious elites to gain legitimacy, whose role is akin to any social media influencer.

However, these ventures, though purely capitalistic, may have negative implications of promoting an exclusivist mindset of Islam versus the secular, and the religious elite are mainly the face of these capitalistic ventures. Some became "fashion" models for Islamic fashion, some were hired to promote books, and some endorsed shariah-compliant businesses.

In the long run, the emphasis on being popular and trendy may weaken the community's intellectual or scholastic approach towards religion. It is known that most of the popular preachers' publications and sermons are on spirituality, which is the least controversial topic. The positive is that their teachings resonate with common problems: divorce, jobs, employment, and family and the solutions often revolve around theological ones and self-help. There are also moments when the discourse becomes anti-intellectual (Shaharuddin 2022). Discussions on provocative topics (those deemed taboo) remain swept under the carpet: for example, the rights of religious minorities, LGBTQ+, women's leadership, and the impact of laws on Muslims and non-Muslims. There is also very little interest in ground-up approaches to understanding problems, one that applies social science methods.

Therefore, online and trending preachers and occupational licensing do not guarantee progressive or moderate religious discourse. Today, Islamic medicine, or *ru'yah* is becoming popular. Liyana Sulaiman, in her study of religious orientations among Singapore Malay/Muslims, argues that magical orientations persist despite economic progress (Liyana 2018). There is the belief that Islam has the alternative cure for illnesses such as cancer and other aspects of social and community life such as "love, family, school and work life, social relations, health, and illnesses" (ibid., p. 2). As the concept of mental well-being is foreign to Islamic medicine, the diagnosis of these afflictions is often attributed to *rasuk* or being possessed. Furthermore, young *asatizah*, who are facing competition from fellow *asatizah*, social media influencers, and capitalistic-oriented professionals, are now conducting courses on *ru'yah* and Islamic healing, and venturing into "house cleansing" (from evil spirits). Some *asatizah* are also in the business of ghostbusting. It is important to note that these preachers who promote Islamic healing are not excluded from the ARS, since they are not a security threat. However, this is concerning as these individuals are given the licence to speak on Islamic matters, which the intellectuals, who are neither madrasah-trained nor graduates of Islamic universities, are not. In the long run, this may drag the community away from embracing modern scientific knowledge based on rationalism.

Conclusion

The concept of religious authority in Singapore has significantly changed in today's context where populism, globalization, and capitalism dominate. While religious elites have been able to reinvent themselves by riding on the wave of technological advancement, this may have the reverse effect of increasing competition within the sector and diluting their authority. Nonetheless, this presents a new set of challenges for the group and the community's progress. This also means that attempts by authorities to implement occupational licensing—to raise the quality of thought in the age of post-9/11, and to control the supply of *asatizah*—negates reformist discourses, though it curbs radicalism. Furthermore, with the evolution of social media, charisma remains key in defining authority rather than content, though the two should not be considered zero-sum. More significantly, this means religious authority is not restricted to madrasah graduates or those trained in the religious sciences, especially concerning capitalism and the Islamic market.

As I have argued extensively, the social media trend does not elevate the quality of religious discourse. The reverse is seen with the community now promoting alternative Islamic medicine which frowns upon scientific knowledge, halting their move towards progress. Thus, this chapter questions the prevalent notion that local preachers are progressive and moderate while labelling external ones as regressive. Given the absence of an autonomous religious tradition in Singapore, a proper evaluation of the discourse and what constitutes moderation is needed. Though there exists the tendency to quote or cite authorities from outside and supplant it into religious debates locally, it is undeniable that religious exchange is becoming more porous, signifying that the push for local preachers does not mean Singapore is excluded from geopolitical influences.

NOTES

1 Naim (2013, p. 194) admits that "the new evangelical, Pentecostalist, and charismatic Protestant churches that have sprouted across the region in the last thirty years—much as they have in the United States, Africa, and elsewhere—are giving the Catholic church fits, and swiftly emptying its pews".
2 Behind this effort is the assumption that the *asatizah* must shoulder the promotion of moderate Islam in countering terrorism.
3 For example, typologies such as Wahhabi-Salafism and Sufism are widely applied when describing Singapore Muslims; still, they elicit different connotations when applied to other Islamic societies. Thus, broader debates in the social sciences, which apply terms such as traditionalism, progressivism and modernity must be applied to provide contexts.
4 The political elites constantly remind the community to be tolerant of other faiths, adjust to Singapore's cultural diversity, and uphold its secular ideology. Masagos Zulkifli, the Minister-in-charge of Muslim Affairs, says,

"I do not think there is anyone who wants to take the risk of creating violence or uphold an extreme viewpoint, and the Malay/Muslim community holds the same view". Masagos Zulkifli, "Masyarakat Melayu/ Islam sentiasa utama suasana harmoni, aman", *Berita Harian*, 12 December 2021. Highlighting his community's achievements, he adds, "When we hear words that were meant to create unhappiness between races, our response is intended to defend harmony and safety between different communities".

5   Since Singapore attained independence in 1965, the country has not witnessed any terrorist attacks by Muslims, unlike in neighbouring Malaysia, Indonesia, the Philippines, and Thailand. Singapore's Internal Security Department (ISD), which falls under the Ministry of Home Affairs (MHA), has been quick to detain supporters of terrorist groups Jemaah Islamiah (JI) and ISIS (Islamic State in Iraq and Syria). However, the community is not free from non-violent extremism. The community's discourse regarding the rights of religious minorities (such as Shi'a, Ahmadiah, and liberals), their attitude towards women and gender equality, and alternative viewpoints are far from progressive (Noor Aisha 2007, 2020). To be sure, these contrasting orientations resulted from the type of religious leadership of the community.

6   According to Towler (1986, p. 90), "Traditionalism as a type of religious attitude is marked by a certainty which is unquestioning. It is not only certain, it is delighted by its certainty, for the stable and secure order which it knows is something to guard and cherish. It affirms and reinforces the present structure of society, resisting every innovation".

7   By and large, Sufism emphasizes spirituality, but when asked about their views on women's leadership, they may uphold traditionalist attitudes. For instance, many *fatwa* issued by the religious councils in Southeast Asia share androcentric views about women whilst claiming to uphold Sufism. Thus, if one follows the traditionalist and progressive paradigms, one could argue that the Sufis are not always progressive. Some staunchly believe that the headscarf is mandatory for women and are intolerant of the LGBTQ+ community. Yet despite such beliefs and principles, Western governments gave Sufi masters more airtime than the Salafis-Wahhabis following 9/11, and Singapore is not an exception to this trend. Unbeknownst to many, states do partner with Sufi leaders in the battle against terrorism and have even encouraged Sufi leaders in de-radicalization movements. By contrast, the Wahhabi-Salafis are orthodox and literal in their interpretation of Islam. However, there are also diverse views among them. Some may adopt a progressive view that democracy can be a form of modern-day governance for the Muslim world. Still, the traditionalist Wahhabi-Salafis contend that only an Islamic caliphate founded during the Prophet's time is suitable. The terms "liberals" and "reformists" also require fixing. Generally, liberal Muslims uphold the view of gender equality, freedom of expression, and

the right to belief. Furthermore, they are also more tolerant towards the Shi'a and Ahmadiyyah. However, some liberals can be traditionalists too, and become obsessed with excluding the Qur'an and *Sunnah* (traditions of the Prophet); some are, ironically, equally Islamophobic (El Fadl 2022). They may also become traditionalist if they strictly deny the rights of Wahhabi-Salafis and Sufis from emphasizing rituals and reading Qur'an.

8   Anjum (2017, p. 305), for example, distinguishes three forms of reformist Islamists: the "new Islamists" as those who reduced their antipathy towards the West; the "economisation of Islamism" as those who focus on promoting developmentalist causes rather than capturing the state; and *"fiqh* of minorities" referring to Islamists who lived in the West as minorities.

9   The concept of religious leadership may vary between Sunni and Shi'a Islam. In Sunni Islam, the prophethood ends with Muhammad (d.632), and the leadership of the Islamic world was continued by his companions Abu Bakar, Umar, Uthman, and Ali. They were then succeeded by caliphs who ran governments through the hereditary monarchical system, but there was also the *ulama* class. Unlike Christians, there is no clergy concept in Islam. On the other hand, for the Shi'a, authority rests with the prophet's bloodline. The description of Sunni and Shia above risks being too general and sweeping, for as Muslims have evolved for centuries, and spread across the globe, hundreds of sects developed.

10 Islam does not distinguish between religious and secular knowledge but between revealed and acquired knowledge. Thus, Islam does not differentiate between the study of the religious sciences (Qur'an, *hadith*, jurisprudence) and the study of mathematics, sciences, geography, politics, and astronomy, among others. However, the global Islamic revivalist movement in the 1970s led to greater differentiation between religious and secular knowledge, and this separation affected the definition of an Islamic religious scholar or *ulama*. The Malay world is not excluded from this development as well.

11 However, this may not be the fault of the universities alone, as students themselves enrolled in these universities are not forthcoming in exploring the large corpus of knowledge. Moreover, as some graduates from madrasahs have been provided with the license to teach Islam under the ARS scheme, this defeats the purpose of raising the standards of Islamic education and reduces Islamic qualifications to those with pre-university levels of religious training. Conversely, there are also those who did not attend madrasah but were either enrolled in an Islamic university directly in Saudi Arabia or informal boarding schools in Yemen and have become certified *asatizah*. These alternative pathways to becoming *asatizah* raise questions about the need for madrasah education—highly subsidized by the community—for one to be recognized under the scheme.

12 In Malaysia, there is a reality contest to determine who is a preacher. The selected individual is usually more popular than a religious figure in the establishment, such as the *mufti* (chief state jurist) or official *ulama*.

REFERENCES

Alatas, Syed Hussein. 1973. *Modernisation and Social Change*. Sydney: Angus and Robertson.

Anjum, Ovamir. 2017. "Do Islamists Have an Intellectual Deficit?" In *Rethinking Political Islam*, edited by Shadi Hamid and William McCants, pp. 300–307. New York: Oxford University Press.

Azra, Azyumardi. 2004. The Origins of Islamic Reformism in Southeast Asia. Australia and Hawai'i: Allen & Unwin and University of Hawai'i Press.

Bayat, Asef. 2010. *Life as Politics: How Ordinary People Change the Middle East*. California: Stanford University Press.

El Fadl, Khaled Abou. 2022. The Prophet's Pulpit: Commentaries of the State of Islam, Vol. 1, edited by Josef Linnhoff. Dublin: Usuli Press.

Fischer, Johan and Jeremy Jammes. 2020. "Introduction: Muslim Piety as Economy: Markets, Meaning and Morality in Southeast Asia". In *Muslim Piety as Economy: Markets, Meaning and Morality in Southeast Asia*, edited by Johan Fischer and Jeremy Jammes, pp. 1–28. Oxon; New York: Routledge.

Friedman, Benjamin M. 2021. *Religion and the Rise of Capitalism*. New York: Vintage Books.

Hoesterey, James Bourk. 2016. *Rebranding Islam: Piety, Prosperity and A Self-Help Guru*. Stanford: Stanford University Press.

Lindsey, Brink and Steven M. Teles. 2017. *The Captured Economy*. New York: Oxford University Press.

Liyana, Sulaiman. 2018. "Magical Orientation of Religion among Malay/Muslims in Singapore: A Look at Modes of Healing Pertaining to Mental Illness". BA Thesis, National University of Singapore.

Mills, C. Wright. 1956. *The Power Elite*. New York: Oxford University Press.

Mizi, Wahid. 2021a. *The Art of Letting God*. Selangor: Iman Publication.

———. 2021b. *You Are Loved*. Selangor: Iman Publication.

Mohammad Hannan, Hassan and Irwan Mohd Hadi Shuhaimy. 2018. "Developing Asatizah in Singapore through the Asatizah Recognition Scheme". In *Fulfilling the Trust: 50 Years of Shaping Muslim Religious Life in Singapore*, edited by Norshahril Saat, pp. 73–88. Singapore: World Scientific Press.

Muzakki, Akh. 2008. "Islam as a Symbolic Commodity: Transmitting and Consuming Islam through Public Sermons in Indonesia". In *Religious Commodifications in Asia*, edited by Pattana Kitiarsa, pp. 205–19. London, New York: Routledge.

Naim, Moises. 2013. *The End of Power*. New York: Basic Books.
Noor Aisha Abdul Rahman. 2007. "Changing Role, Unchanging Perceptions and Institutions: Traditionalism and Its Impact on Women and Globalisation in Muslim Societies in Asia". *The Muslim World* 97: 479–507.
———. 2020. "Religious Resurgence amongst the Malays and Its Impact: The Case of Singapore". In *Alternative Voices in Muslim Southeast Asia: Discourse and Struggles*, edited by Norshshril Saat and Azhar Ibrahim, pp. 33–66. Singapore: ISEAS – Yusof Ishak Institute.
Norshahril Saat. 2018. *Tradition and Islamic Learning: Singapore Students in the Al-Azhar University*. Singapore: ISEAS – Yusof Ishak Institute.
Norshahril Saat, Azhar Ibrahim, and Noor Aisha Abdul Rahman. 2021. *Reaching for the Crescent: Aspirations of Singapore Islamic Studies Graduate and The Challenges*. Singapore: ISEAS – Yusof Ishak Institute.
"Population in Brief 2021", 2021. Singapore. https://www.population.gov.sg/files/media-centre/publications/Population-in-brief-2021.pdf.
Roy, Olivier. 2004. *Globalised Islam: The Search for a New Ummah*. New York: Columbia University Press.
Saeed, Abdullah. 2004. "The Official Ulema and Religious Legitimacy of the Modern Nation State". In *Islam and Political Legitimacy*, edited by Shahram Akbarzadeh and Abdullah Saeed, pp. 15–28. London, New York: RoutledgeCurzon.
Shaharuddin, Maaruf. 2002. "To Err is Inhuman and to Punish Divine: A Study of Religious Orientations of the Malays". Singapore.
———. 2006. "Religion and Utopian Thinking Among the Muslims in Southeast Asia". In *Local and Global Social Transformation in Southeast Asia*, edited by Riaz Hassan, pp. 315–31. Kuala Lumpur: Dewan Bahasa dan Pustaka.
———. 2022. *Elit Tradisi Dan Reformasi Di Asia Tenggara*. Petaling Jaya: SIRD.
Stolow, Jeremy. 2016. "Religion, Media, and Globalization". In *Sociology of Religion*, edited by Bryan S. Turner, pp. 544–62. West Sussex: Wiley Blackwell.
Syed Zakir, Hussain. 2012. *Keeping the Faith: Syed Isa Semait Mufti of Singapore 1972–2010*. Singapore: Straits Times Press.
Towler, Robert. 1986. *The Need for Certainty: A Sociological Study of Conventional Religion*. London; Boston; Melbourne and Henly: Routledge & Kegan Paul.
Weber, Max. 1930. *The Protestant Ethic and the Spirit of Capitalism*. 2007th ed. Routledge.
Zaman, Muhammad Qasim. 2002. *The Ulama in Contemporary Islam: Custodians of Change*. Princeton: Princeton University Press.

INDEX

A
Aadel al-Kalbani, 37
abangan, 17, 18
Abd al-Aziz ibn Baz, 37
Abdil Mughis Mudhoffir, 99
Abdul Aziz Bari, 67
Abdul Hameed Abu Sulayman, 41
Abdullah Ahmad Badawi, 45, 68
Abdullah Azzam, 39
Abu Dhabi Declaration (2019), xvi
Administration of Muslim Law Act (AMLA), 116, 121
Afghanistan, anti-Soviet war in, 23
Afra Alatas, 8
Ahmad Dahlan, 132
Ahmad Fauzi Abdul Hamid, 6
Ahmadiyyas, 20, 139
Ahmad Sonhadji Muhamad, 204, 205, 211
Akhmad Sahal, 90, 93
Aksi Bela Islam rally, 27, 90
Al-Afghani, Jamal al-Din, 132
Alam, Rudi Harisyah, 139
al-Ashaari, Abu Hassan, 51n14
al-'Awda, Salman, 37
Al-Azhar Declaration (2012), xvi
al-Baghdadi, Abu Bakr, 49n2
al-Banna, Hassan, 41
Al-Faruqi, Ismail Raji, 41, 42
al-Ghazali, Imam, 135
Ali, Denny Januar, 4
Ali-Fauzi, Ihsan, 139
Ali Hamsa, 83n3
Ali, Mukti, 19
Aljunied, Khairudin, 158–160
All Party Parliamentary Group (APPG), xiii
al-Mahdi, Imam, 49n3
al-Maturidi, Abu Mansur, 51n14
al-Muhajir, Abu Abdullah, 39, 50n7
Al-Qaeda, 38, 39, 50n9
  jihadist ideology, 34
Al Qurtuby, Sumanto, 47
al-Rasheed, Mamoon, 40
al-Wahhab, Muhammad ibn Abd, 42, 132
al-Zarqawi, Abu Musab, 45, 49n2
amar makruf dan nahi mungkar, 157, 161, 165, 166, 179
Amin Abdullah, 24
Amman Message (2004), xvi
Andina Dwifatma, 9

Anjum, Ovamir, 218n8
anti-Islamist activism, 99, 103n26
anti-Islamist counter-activism, 89–94
anti-NU establishment campaign, 137, 147
anti-NU Garis Lurus movement, 130
Anti-Sexual Harassment Bill, xiv
anti-Soviet war, in Afghanistan, 23
Apostasy Wars, 38
Arabization, x, 91
Armando, Ade, 90–92, 93, 94, 95, 96, 98, 102n12
Arya, Permadi, 90
asatizah (religious teachers), 115, 204, 205, 207, 208, 209, 211, 212, 214, 215, 216, 216n2, 218n11
Asatizah Recognition Scheme (ARS), 206, 207, 215, 218n11
Ashaarite-Maturidite traditions, 41
Asyraf Wajdi Dusuki, 45
Awwas, Irfan S., 138
Ayob Khan Mydin Pitchay, 44, 83n4
Azhar Ibrahim, 115
Azra, Azyumardi, 1–2

B
Badan Pembinaan Ideologi Pancasila, 27–28
Baghdad, European philosophy in, 20
Bahagian Hal Ehwal Agama Islam (BAHEIS), 69
Bahar bin Smith, 91
Bahasa Indonesia, 149n20
Bambang Trihatmodjo, 187
"Bangsa Malaysia", viii
Bashori, Luthfi, 136, 137, 138, 145
Basuki Tjahaja Purnama (Ahok), 26, 27, 89
Batrisya Kameel, 174, 175
bid'a (religious innovation), 135
Bielefeidt, Heiner, 69, 70, 71, 80

bin Laden, Osama, 45
black campaign, 26–27
Bon Odori festival, xv
Brunei, 2, 159–160, 162
 collectivistic culture, 177
 personalities, 177–178
 religious influencers in, 178
Bruneian IG accounts, 174–175
Bumiputeras, 66
Bunga Citra Lestari, 169–173, 177
Bunt, Gary R., 156
 #Hashtag Islam, 184
bureaucratization, 112
buzzers, 101n3

C
Caliph Abu Bakr (573–634), 38
capitalism, 112, 113, 202
 and rise of Malay middle class, 208–210
The Captured Economy (Lindsey and Teles), 206–207
Case, William, 71
Catholic Filipinos, 184
Catholicism, 143
Chowdhury, Tawfique, 44
Christianity, vii, 73, 75
 redefined religious authority in, 199
churafat (superstition), 135
Cinta Subuh (Love at Dawn), 185, 191, 195
civic pluralism, 16, 17, 19–20, 21, 25
 Muslim intellectuals roles in dissemination of, 21
civil Islam, 18, 21
Civil Islam (Hefner), 16
civil servants, 65–67
 elucidation on role of, 70
 groups of, 69
 ideals of, 78–81

Malay-Muslim, 82
  threat of extremism, 72–78
civil service, 65, 66, 69, 82
civil society organizations (CSOs), xii–xiv, xii, xiv, 98
  mutual suspicion between progressive, 97–99
Civil Society Watch (CSW), 98
coercion, 50n9
collective religious hatred, 80–81
colonial capitalism, 111–114
"Commanding Right and Forbidding Wrong in Islamic Thought" (Cook), 157
communism, 1
community-based activism, 101n4
Congress of Union of Employees in the Public and Civil Services Malaysia (CUEPACS), 81
COP26 Climate Summit, 99
Corbuzier, Deddy, 142, 143, 144
corruption, 69, 70, 81, 82
COVID-19 pandemic, 3, 72
Criminal Code, Article 156a of, 94
"cultivation of piety", 184, 185
cultural NU, 130
cyber-Islamic environment (CIE), 156
cyberspace, 88, 89, 93

D
dakwah, 22
dangdut, 185
Darol Mahmada, Nong, 90, 93, 95, 96, 98, 101n5, 102n12
Dasar Penerapan Nilai-Nilai Islam, 68
data-driven political economy, 110, 124
democratic backsliding/illiberal turn, 88

democratization, 21
  process of, 23
  of public sphere, 3
deradicalization programme, for ISIS-related detainees, 44–45
Dewan Dakwah Islam Indonesia (DDII), 18
digital anti-Islamist activism, 4
digital ethnography, 88
digital platforms, 8
Dutch colonial period, 17–18

E
e-jihad (Electronic Jihad), 156
elections
  in Jakarta, 26, 27
  in Malaysia, 4
Electronic Information and Transactions (ITE) Law
  Article 28(2) of, 94
Emma Maembong, 163, 165, 166, 167, 168, 169, 177
emotional trauma, 36
ethnic groups, 65–66, 121, 125n3
extremism, 5, 7, 43, 46
  threat of, 66, 72–78
extremist Islamist groups, 91

F
Facebook, 211, 212
fatwa, 25, 212
fear, 50n9, 78
Federal Constitution, xiv
  Article 132 of, 67
  Article 160 of, 82n1
feudalism, 111–114
Film Maker Muslim (FMM) Studios, 188, 191
fiqh (Islamic jurisprudence), 135, 203, 218n8
foreign terrorist fighters (FTFs), 44

Forex trading, 123
Front Pembela Islam (FPI), 91
functioning intellectuals
   in Muslim society, 124
   need for, 123–125

G

gender equality, 201
General Elections (GE), 4
global ISIS threat, 37–39
globalization, impact on religious discourse, 200
Global Movement of Moderates, 46
Global Terrorism Index, 43
gotong-royong, 27
Government-Linked Companies (GLCs), ix
"gradualist Islamization", 159
Greenpeace Indonesia, 99
"guided democracy", 18
GUMmies (Global Urban Muslims), 184
Guntur Romli, Mohamad, 90, 93, 96

H

Habib Syed Hassan Al-Attas, 205
hadith, 135, 156, 167, 176, 202, 203
halal consumption, 22
   patterns of, 210
halal tourism, 209–210
Hari Raya, xi
Hari Raya Aidilfitri, xiv
#Hashtag Islam (Bunt), 184
Hassan, Ahmad, 17, 18
Hatim al-'Awni, 37
Hefner, Robert, 184
   Civil Islam, 16
hijab, x, 23, 160, 161, 163, 174, 179
Hijaz Committee, 134
Himpunan Mahasiswa Islam (HMI), 19
Hinduism, 73

Hindutva, vii
Hizbut Tahrir Indonesia (HTI), 25
human rights, 70–72
Huria Kristen Batak Protestan (HKBP) community, 139
Hutahaean, Ferdinand, 102n18

I

Ibn Taymiyyah, 39, 41
Ibrahim, Anwar, 40, 42
ICERD. *See* International Convention on Elimination of All Forms of Racial Discrimination (ICERD)
IDEAS. *See* Institute for Democracy and Economic Affairs (IDEAS)
Idrus Ramli, Muhammad, 136, 137, 138
"inclusive Islamic theology", 20
Indonesia
   commercial television in mainstreaming Islam in, 183
   inter-faith issues/Islamist threats in, 21
   Islamic organizations in, 131
   Islamic resurgence in, 184
   Islam in, 20, 87, 131
   liberal Islamic actors in, 88
   political liberalization, 89
   social polarization in, 4
Indonesian IG accounts, 169–173
Indonesian Islam, recent trends in, 25–28
Indonesian media
   Islamic representation in, 185–188
Indonesian Muslims, 21, 183
   commitment towards moderate Islam, 28
   in neoliberal post-New Order Indonesia, 22
information capitalism, 110
Instagram (IG), 211, 212
   Bruneian IG accounts, 174–175

data obtained from accounts, 162–163
global lifestyle in Islamic manner on, 184
Indonesian IG accounts, 169–173
Malaysian IG accounts, 163–169
Muslim female personalities, 161–162
Institute for Democracy and Economic Affairs (IDEAS), xii
Institute of Policy Studies, 121
Intan Najuwa, 164, 165, 168, 169
International Convention on Elimination of All Forms of Racial Discrimination (ICERD), ix
International Institute of Islamic Thought (IIIT), 41
International Islamic University of Malaysia (IIUM), xii, 41, 42
Internet, 65, 156
　advancement of, 3
　double-edged sword for Islam, 157
　emergence of, 186
　NU establishment through, 131
　reach of, 178
　and social media, 5–6
　user-generated content on, 189–190
Internet-based schism, 129, 131
Iranian Revolution, ix, 160
Islam, vii, viii, 65, 198, 218n10
　as an official religion, 73
　apocalyptic traditions, 49n3
　and civic pluralism, 16
　conservative interpretations of, 91
　converting indigenous children to, 75
　digitization of, 156
　discourses on, 115
　in Indonesia, 15, 20, 87, 131
　interpretation of, 217n7

intersection of social problems and, 120
Malay civilization with, x
in Malaysia, viii
with modernity, 48
public and social dimension of, 124
representations of, 185
and secularism, 158
social dimension of, 111
social problems unaddressed under social dimension of, 122–123
sounds and images about, 155
source of moral teachings, 19
in Southeast Asia, 9, 158
teach and preach about, 206, 209
transmission of, 3–6
Islam Berkemajuan (Progressive Islam), 28
Islam Hadhari, 68
Islamic bureaucracy, 42
Islamic civilization, 40
Islamic communities, 186
Islamic Development Bank (IDB), 42
Islamic "Golden Age", 122, 123
Islamic ideology, 34
Islamic law, 23
Islamic organizations, Internet-based schism within, 131
Islamic populist campaigns, 27
Islamic reformist movement, 132
Islamic Religious Council of Singapore (MUIS), 8, 111, 116–118, 123, 124, 205
Islamic resurgence, 184
Islamic soap operas, 186, 187
Islamic State of Iraq and Syria (ISIS), 6, 35, 49n2, 49n3
　appropriation of violent extremism, 35–37
　global threat, 37–39
　violent ideology, 35

Islamic studies, 90
Islamic tour packages, 210
Islamic values and beliefs, resurgence of, 159
Islamic web series, 188–191, 193, 194, 195
Islamism, 17, 24, 49n4, 87
   intrusion of, 25
   liberal Islamic activists against, 88
   rise of, 89
   shift from politics, 22
Islamist activists, 100
   for alleged blasphemy, 92
   lacklustre response, 94–97
   moderate and extremist identities, 39–45
Islamist groups, 17, 20, 22, 23, 25
   momentum for, 21
Islamist political campaigns, 28
Islamization, ix–x, 45
   of digital world, 156
   of knowledge scheme, 42
   of public education, 47
"Islamization of Knowledge", ix
Islam Nusantara (Archipelagic Islam), 28
Islam Wasatiyyah, 68

J

Jabatan Kemajuan Islam Malaysia (JAKIM), ix, 69
Jabatan Pendaftaran Negara (JPN), 72, 73
Jakarta gubernatorial election, 26, 27
Jamaluddin Al-Afghani, 37
Jaringan Islam Liberal (JIL), 24, 88, 90, 91, 94, 95, 101n4, 101n5
Jemaah Islamiah (JI), 200
jihadist Muslims, 25
jihadists, 49n4

Jokowi. *See* Widodo, Joko
"Jokowi Phenomenon", 26

K

kadrun, 92, 102n10
Keluarga Film Maker Muslim (KFMM), 188
Keluarga Malaysia, 68
Ketua Setiausaha Negara, 67
khutbah, xv
Komaruddin Hidayat, 6
Komisi Pemberantasan Korupsi (KPK), 97
Komunitas Katolik Garis Lucu, 142, 143, 144
Kuntadhi, Eko, 90, 93, 103n26

L

Laskar Jihad, 23
liberal Islamic activism, 88, 89, 96
licensing, regulating authority through, 206–208
Lindsey, Brink
   The Captured Economy, 206–207
Liyana Musfirah, 212, 213
Liyana Yus, 174

M

Madjid, Nurcholish, 16, 20, 21
Mahathir Mohamad, 42, 45, 51n11, 68
Mahomedan Marriage ordinance, 112–113
Maimoen, Muhammad Najih, 136, 137, 138
Majelis Ulama Indonesia (MUI), 24–25, 91
Majlis Agama Islam, 69
Malay identity, ix–x
Malay-Muslims, 66, 82
   civil servants, 72, 82
   parties, xiv
   psyche, 46

"Malay Problem", 120
Malaysia
   ambivalence between moderate and extremist Islamist identities in, 39–45
   anatomy of system, 67–70
   elections in, 4
   Internet users in, 3
   Islam in, viii
   religious transformation, consequences of, xiii
   role of public administrators, 65
   teachers in, 75
Malaysian branch of Al-Madinah International University (MEDIU), 44
Malaysian domestic politics, 44
Malaysian IG accounts, 163–169
Malaysian Islam, xiii, xiv, xvi, 42
mandi safar, xi
Marrakesh Declaration (2016), xvi
Marxist-Leninist ideology, 184
Masagos Zulkifli, 217n4
Maulidur Rasul, xv
mediatized piety, 191–194
Melayu Islam Beraja (Malay Islamic Monarchy, MIB), 159
middle-class Muslims, 208–210
Mizi Wahid, 211–213
   You Are Loved, 211
moderate Islam, 158
moderate religious trendsetters, 203
moderation, 41
monarchy, xiv–xvi
"Monas Incident", 96
Muath al-Kasasbeh, 38
Muhammad Abduh, 37, 132
Muhammad ibn Salih al-Uthaymeen, 37
Muhammadiyah Garis Lucu, 143
Muhammadiyah organization, 5, 15, 24, 25, 132, 147

multicultural demography, 2
Muslim female personalities, 161–162
   Bruneian IG accounts, 174–175
   Indonesian IG accounts, 169–173
   Malaysian IG accounts, 163–169
Muslim intellectuals, 18, 20, 194
   emergence of, 19
   in New Order regime, 15
   role of, 16
   roles in dissemination of civic pluralism, 21
Muslim mass organizations, 15, 24, 25, 28
Muslim-minority communities, vii
Muslims, 2
   community, 115, 120
   extremism, contemporary phenomenon of, 39
   identity, 183
   long-term advancement of, ix
   preachers in new media age, 210–215
   religious organizations, 111
   terrorists, 23
   in Thailand and the Philippines, 2
   traditionalist organization, 134
   vigilante groups, 24
Muslim.SG, 116, 117, 119, 122, 123, 124
Muslim women, multi-million-dollar industry for, 160

N

Nahdlatul Ulama (NU), 5, 15, 25, 28, 89, 129, 130
   social, political, and religious ideas, 132–136
Najib Razak, 45, 46, 68
Nasiruddin al-Albani, 37
National Alliance for Freedom of Religion and Belief (AKKBB), 96

National Council of Islamic Religious Affairs, xv
National Culture Policy, viii
National Registration Department, 73
Natsir, Muhammad, 17, 18
Negara, Rukun, viii
Negeri Sembilan, xv
neo-liberal capitalism, 1
   inequalities of, 110
neo-liberal ideology, 8, 111, 113
neoliberalism, 111–114
New Order era, 23, 28, 158, 186, 194
non-governmental organizations (NGOs), 8, 21, 93, 98, 110, 205
non-Muslim minorities, 40
non-Muslim religious traditions, 42
non-Muslims, 20, 46–47, 72
non-violent extremism, 80, 81, 82
Novel Bamukmin, 94, 95
NU Garis Lucu (NU Funny Brigade), 132, 144–147
   Instagram post by, 139–140
   social media and Internet posts by, 131
   sustaining hegemony of religious moderation, 138–144
   Twitter posts by, 140–141
NU Garis Lurus (NU Straight Brigade), 129, 130, 132, 144–147
   camp, 8
   challenging NU establishment's hegemony, 136–138
   social media and Internet posts by, 131
Nurcholish Madjid, 19

O

occupational licensing, 199, 200, 206–207, 210, 215–216
Old Order era, 17–18
online platforms, 8

Orang Asli, 73–74
Organization of Islamic Cooperation (OIC), 68
The Origins of Islamic Reformism in Southeast Asia, 2

P

Pakatan Harapan (PH), 72, 77
palace buzzers, 95, 101n3
Palestine-Israel conflict, 208
Pancasila, 18, 20, 25
Papuan Armed Criminal Group (KKB), 98
Parliamentary Select Committees, xiii
Partai Demokrasi Indonesia Perjuangan (PDI-P), 93
Partai Keadilan Sejahtera (PKS), 91
Partai Nasional Indonesia (PNI), 17–18
Parti Islam Se-Malaysia (PAS), ix
Parti Warisan Sabah (Warisan), 72
Pegawai Tadbir dan Diplomatik, 67
perda syariah (Islamic law), 23
Pergerakan Indonesia Untuk Semua (PIS), 93, 96
Persis, 17, 18
Philippines, Muslims in, 2
pluralism, 41
pluralist Islam, 25
pluralist-Islamist contestation, 17, 18
pluralists, 15
Policy on the Inculcation of Islamic Values, 75
political economy, 110
political elites, 216n4
political financing reform, xiii
political identity, 70, 71
political Islam, ix
political liberalization, 89
post-9/11 discourse, 201
post-New Order era, 16, 21–25

The Power Elite, 203
Prabowo Subianto, 26
preachers,
  in Malaysia, x
  in new media age, 210–215
  traditionalist Muslim, 132, 133
presidential election (2014),
  Indonesia, 26–27
private televisions (TV), emergence
  of, 186–187
progressivism, 200, 202
Prophet Muhammad, 34, 40, 134,
  202
proselytization, vii
pro-Widodo social media influencers,
  90
psychological feudalism, 112
public policy, xii, xiii, vii, 65
public service, 67
public sphere, 3, 4, 15, 144–147
punitive legislation, x
"purification of Islamic identity",
  194

Q
Qur'an, 3, 27, 39, 40, 92, 119, 135, 146,
  167, 176, 202, 209, 218n7
interpretations of, 156
Qur'anic exegesis, 204, 205, 211

R
Rabat Plan of Action 2013, 80, 81
Rabitat al-'Alam al-Islami, 37
racism, 72, 81
radicalism, 9, 69
radical Muslim group, 23
Rahman, Fazlur, 19
Rajawali Citra Televisi Indonesia
  (RCTI), 186–187
Raline Shah, 169, 172
Rashid Rida, 37

reformasi era, 22–25, 28
religious affairs, state's grip on, 87
religious authority, 206–208, 213,
  215
religious conflicts, 139
religious conservatism, 88
religious discourse, globalization
  impact on, 200
religious elites, 198, 199, 214
  regulating authority through
    licensing and limitations,
    206–208
  in Singapore, 203–205
religious extremism, 178
religious identity, exploitation of, 25
religious influencers, 210
religious knowledge, fundamentals
  of, 51n12
religious leadership, concept of,
  218n9
religious minorities, 71, 72, 78, 80,
  81, 82
  allegations from, 73
  negative experiences of, 70
religious observance, evolution of,
  vii
religious organizations, 110
  in Singapore, 111
  surveillance capitalism and,
    116–120
religious orientations, 109, 110, 111,
  201
  capitalism impact on, 113
  in Singapore, 114
religious teachers, 213
religious tolerance, 46
religious traditionalism, 114
renewal movement, 20
Resilient, Inclusive, Contributive,
  Adaptive and Progressive
  (RICAP), 117

Rizieq Shihab, 91
Rohingya crisis, 208

S
Saddam Hussain, 49n2
Safar al-Hawali, 37
Said Agil Siradj, 129, 130, 138
Salafi activism, 49n1
Salafi-centric theology, 41, 42
Salafi Islamic movement, 91
Salafi-Jihadi ideology, 6
Salafism, 5, 23, 24, 34, 35, 36
   to Salafi-jihadism to terrorism, 45–48
   Wahhabi co-optation of, 37
Salafization, 42, 48
SalamSG TV, 117
Saleh al-Fawzan, 37, 38
Sarekat Islam, 133
Saudi Arabia, 37, 134
Sayyid Qutb, 45
sectarianism, 22, 69
secularism, 158, 159
secularism, pluralism, and liberalism (SEPILIS), 129
secular state, 17
self-development, 191
self-identify, 121–122
September 2001 terrorist attacks, 200
Shi'a Muslims, 20, 71
Shihab, Habib Rizieq, 24
Shihab, Husin Alwi, 99, 103n25
Shi'ites, 36, 38, 39
Singapore
   absence of autonomous religious tradition in, 216
   colonial capitalism, 111–114
   Internal Security Department, 217n5
   Internet users in, 3
   religious elites in, 203–205

religious market, 210
September 2001 terrorist attacks, 200
Singapore Islamic Scholars and Religious Teachers Association (PERGAS), 8, 111, 118–120, 123, 124, 205
Singapore Muslim Identity (SMI) values, 117
Singapore Muslims, 114, 198, 200
Siregar, Denny, 89–90, 93, 94, 97
Sisterlillah Community, 188
Skam, 190
social media, x, 4, 8, 65, 96, 115
   Internet and, 5–6
   NU Garis Lucu, 140–143
   NU Garis Lurus, 131
   outreach of, 211–212
   pervasive influence of, 180
   popularity of, 26
   prevalence of, 214
   proliferation of, 28, 130
   reach of, 178
   religious discourse, 216
   religious elites in Singapore, 203–205
   role of, 156
   significance of, 185
   strategic use of, 26
   technological and interactive capabilities of, 184
   use in political mobilizations, 25
   women on, 176
social media activists, 91
social media campaigns, 88, 92
social media community, 129–130
social media influencers (SMIs), 157
social problems, 120–123
socio-cultural Islamism, 25
Southeast Asia, vii
   complexity of, 5

Islam in, 9, 158
maritime, 1, 2, 9, 155
Southeast Asia Regional Centre for Counter-Terrorism (SEARCCT), 43
spiritual anxiety, 183
spirituality, 205, 210–212, 214, 217n7
structural NU, 130
Sufism, 42, 202, 216n3, 217n7
Suharto (President), 6, 158, 186, 187
Sukarno (President), 17, 18
Sultan Hassanal Bolkiah, 159
Sunnah, 218n7
Sunni Arabs, 36
Sunni Muslim, ix, 38, 49n2, 77
surveillance capitalism, 110, 114
   dataization and, 124
   and religious organizations, 116–120
Surya Citra Televisi Indonesia (SCTV), 186–187
Susilo Bambang Yudhoyono, 27
Syafii Maarif, 16, 24
syariah, 138
Syariah Courts (Criminal Jurisdiction) Act 1965, x
Syed Abdillah Aljufri, 205, 211
Syed Isa Semait, 204–205
symbolism-ritualism, 192

T

takfir, 38, 49n5
takhayul (superstition), 135
Taliban, 97, 103n24
tariqah, 204
tasamuh (tolerance), 135
tazkirahs, x
Teles, Steven M.
   The Captured Economy, 206–207
Televisi Republik Indonesia (TVRI), 186

terrorism, 5, 9, 43, 45–48, 139
Thailand, Muslims in, 2
TikTok, 188
traditionalism, 8, 199, 200, 201–202, 217n6
   as dominant religious orientation, 114–116
traditionalist Muslim preachers, 132, 133
traditionalists, 133, 203
transnational Islamic movements, 15
Transparency International Indonesia (TII), 98
Tunku Abdul Rahman, xii
Twitter, 211, 212

U

ulama (religious scholars), 3, 133, 134, 135, 203, 204, 206, 219n12
Ulil Abshar Abdalla, 96
umma, 208
United Malays National Organisation (UMNO), ix, 46
United Nations (UN) Refugee Convention, xii
United States Agency for International Development (USAID), 95
Universitas Islam Internasional Indonesia (UIII), 28
urban Muslims, 5, 188, 189, 194
user comments, analysing of, 191–194
user-generated content (UGC), 189–190
usra, 51n13
usul al-fiqh (sources of Islamic jurisprudence), 135

V

vanguard activists, 101n4
vigilante groups, 24

violence, 35–37, 76, 201, 217n4
violent jihad, 4

W
Wahhabi-Salafism, 42, 44, 45, 46, 47, 216n3
Wahhabism, 5
Wahid, Abdurrahman, 16, 20
wasathiyah Islam (Middle Way Islam), 28
wasatiyyah, 39, 40
Widodo, Joko, 4, 8, 26, 27, 28, 29, 87, 88, 89, 90, 92, 94, 96, 97, 146
World Assembly of Muslim Youth (WAMY), 37

World Bank, 3
World Islam Congress, 133
world wide web (www) domain, 7

Y
Yaqut Cholil Qoumas, 146
You Are Loved (Mizi), 211
youth organizations, 18
YouTube, 184, 188, 189
YouTube Partner Program, 95

Z
Zahid Zin, 211, 213

www.ingramcontent.com/pod-product-compliance
Lightning Source LLC
Chambersburg PA
CBHW072144290426
44111CB00012B/1971